SEISMIC HAZARD AND

RISK ANALYSIS

ORIGINAL MONOGRAPH SERIES
Engineering Monographs on Earthquake Criteria,
Structural Design, and Strong Motion Records
Coordinating Editor: Mihran S. Agbabian

MNO-1   *Reading and Interpreting Strong Motion Accelerograms,* by Donald E. Hudson, 1979

MNO-2   *Dynamics of Structures, A Primer,* by Anil K. Chopra, 1982

MNO-3   *Earthquake Spectra and Design,* by Nathan M. Newmark and William J. Hall, 1982

MNO-4   *Earthquake Design Criteria,* by George W. Housner and Paul C. Jennings, 1982

MNO-5   *Ground Motions and Soil Liquefaction During Earthquakes,* by H. Bolton Seed and I. M. Idriss, 1983

MNO-6   *Seismic Design Codes and Procedures,* by Glen V. Berg, 1983 (out of print)

MNO-7   *An Introduction to the Seismicity of the United States,* by S. T. Algermissen, 1983

SECOND MONOGRAPH SERIES
Engineering Monographs on Miscellaneous Earthquake
Engineering Topics

MNO-8   *Seismic Design with Supplemental Energy Dissipation Devices,* by Robert D. Hanson and Tsu T. Soong, 2001

MNO-9   *Fundamentals of Seismic Protection for Bridges,* by Mark Yashinsky and M. J. Karshenas, 2003

MNO-10 *Seismic Hazard and Risk Analysis,* by Robin K. McGuire, 2004

SEISMIC HAZARD AND
RISK ANALYSIS

by

ROBIN K. McGUIRE

Risk Engineering, Inc.
Boulder, Colorado

This monograph was sponsored by the
Earthquake Engineering Research Institute
with support from the Federal Emergency Management Agency

EARTHQUAKE ENGINEERING RESEARCH INSTITUTE
MNO-10

The publication of this book was supported by the Federal Emergency Management Agency under grant #EMW-2001-CA-0237.

This is the third volume of a second monograph series published by EERI entitled "Engineering Monographs on Miscellaneous Earthquake Engineering Topics."

EERI is a nonprofit corporation. The objective of EERI is to reduce earthquake risk by advancing the science and practice of earthquake engineering; by improving the understanding of the impact of earthquakes on the physical, social, economic, political, and cultural environment; and by advocating comprehensive and realistic measures for reducing the harmful effects of earthquakes. Any opinions, findings, conclusions, or recommendations expressed herein are the author's and do not necessarily reflect the views of the Federal Emergency Management Agency or EERI.

Copies of this publication may be ordered from EERI, 499 14th Street, Suite 320, Oakland, California 94612-1934; tel: (510) 451-0905; fax: (510) 451-5411; e-mail: eeri@eeri.org; web site: http://www.eeri.org. Printed in the United States of America.

ISBN #0-943198-01-1
EERI Publication No. MNO-10
Technical Editor: Douglas Becker
Production Coordinator: Eloise Gilland
Layout and Production: Laura Moger

FOREWORD

The original seven EERI monographs were published from 1979 to 1983 and grew out of a seminar on earthquake engineering organized by EERI and presented in several cities. The monographs covered the basic aspects of earthquake engineering in some detail, including seismicity, strong-motion records, earthquake spectra, liquefaction, dynamics, design criteria, and codes. The themes were fundamental and focused, and the content was thorough and generally noncontroversial. These monographs filled a gap in available documents and were highly acclaimed.

Much has changed over the last 20 years. The amount of documentation covering earthquake engineering issues has exploded with the availability of research reports, conference proceedings, journal articles, and textbooks. Narrow, well defined, and basic subject areas that need separate documentation in the monograph style are now harder to identify. However, because of continued interest in the original series and inquiries to the EERI office, the demand for information presented in this format remains high.

EERI intends to capture the essence of the format by publishing, from time to time, additional monographs covering a wide variety of subjects. The new monographs will still be expositions of narrowly focused aspects of earthquake engineering prepared by especially qualified experts. However, the monographs may provide background and insight on a subject that will be of particular value to readers from different specialties or disciplines than the monograph authors. For a given subject, the intended audience may include design professionals, researchers, social scientists, or policy makers. The new monographs are not intended to be design guides or detailed and highly technical state-of-the-art papers. The contents will therefore tend to be basic and conceptual, and in general they will not include material that may quickly become outdated. Rather than creating a prioritized list of subjects and rigid publishing schedules, EERI approves monograph subjects individually as the opportunities arise.

The present monograph on seismic hazard and risk analysis is the third of the new series. Technical review was provided for EERI by Thalia Anagnos, Walter Arabasz, and William T. Holmes.

WILLIAM T. HOLMES
CHAIR, MONOGRAPH COMMITTEE
February 2004

PREFACE

This monograph is intended as a general introduction to methods of seismic hazard and risk analysis. Perhaps you are studying the earth sciences or earthquake engineering and wish to study how your field can contribute to reducing earthquake losses. Perhaps you have been asked to provide input into a probabilistic study of a site or facility, and you wish to understand how your input will influence the results. Perhaps you are reviewing a probabilistic study of seismic hazards or risks, and you wish some additional background on what constitutes a complete study. Or perhaps you are undertaking a study of seismic hazard and risk yourself, and you wish to build on experience from previous studies. I have tried to show examples and give guidance for all these potential uses.

I assume that you know the elements of probability theory and are comfortable with probability density functions, cumulative distribution functions, and conditional distributions. Otherwise, there are many standard texts available, but I would recommend using one that is written for engineers, not mathematicians; an example is Benjamin and Cornell's *Probability, Statistics, and Decision for Civil Engineers* (1970). In any case, the probability theory in this monograph is not very complex, and you can skip the details without any loss of general understanding. I assume also that you are familiar with seismology, magnitude definitions (and the difference between earthquake magnitude and intensity), and representations of strong ground motion (in particular, the response spectrum). For further background in these areas, Charles Richter's classic *Elementary Seismology* (1958) and Bruce Bolt's *Earthquakes* (1993) are good references for seismological concepts, and EERI publications—particularly, recent volumes of *Earthquake Spectra*—provide good material on strong ground motion and structural response.

Throughout this monograph, I give practical advice on what is more important in certain applications and on what is less important. Inevitably, there will be exceptions to this advice, so be sure to confirm, with your own experience, any rules of thumb that you read here.

R. K. McGuire,
Boulder, Colorado
February 2004

ACKNOWLEDGMENTS

I owe a debt of gratitude to Thalia Anagnos, Walter Arabasz, Julian Bommer, and Bill Holmes for reviewing various drafts of this monograph through its long gestation. Jim Dewey reviewed parts of Section 3; Norm Abrahamson, Dave Boore, Ken Campbell, and Gabriel Toro reviewed parts of Section 4; and Charlie Kircher and Hope Seligson reviewed parts of Section 6, for which I am appreciative. Katherine Morgan and Susan Cabaniss shepherded the manuscript through its many stages and reviews, with good humor and grace. The inevitable errors are, of course, my own (no worthwhile venture has negligible risk).

DEDICATION

To the local Dakota tribe.

TABLE OF CONTENTS

Foreword v
Preface vii
Acknowledgments ix
Symbols xiii
1 Introduction 1
2 Methodology 5
   2.1 Overview 5
   2.2 Definitions 6
   2.3 PSHA for a Specific Site 11
   2.4 Translating Hazard into Risk 17
   2.5 Seismic Risk Analysis for a Group of Sites 20
3 Seismicity and Properties of Earthquake Sources 25
   3.1 Seismic Sources 25
   3.2 Earthquake Magnitude and Magnitude Scales 32
   3.3 Magnitude Distributions 35
   3.4 Stress Drop and Seismic Moment 56
   3.5 Earthquake Occurrences in Time 63
   3.6 Fault Rupture Characteristics 64
   3.7 Intensity 65
4 Estimating Earthquake Ground Motion 71
   4.1 Importance of Earthquake Shaking 71
   4.2 Empirical Ground Motion Equations 74
   4.3 Stochastic Methods of Estimating Ground Motion 91
   4.4 Ground Motion Uncertainties 98
5 Seismic Hazard Analysis 105
   5.1 Introduction 105
   5.2 Basic Seismic Hazard Calculations 106
   5.3 Anatomy of Fault Hazard 108
   5.4 Anatomy of Hazard from Area Sources 125

5.5 Logic Trees 135
5.6 Effect of Local Site Conditions 137
5.7 Observations 141
6 Estimating Seismic Risk 143
6.1 Introduction 143
6.2 Empirical Methods of Damage Estimation 145
6.3 Analytical Methods of Damage Estimation 153
6.4 Comparisons of Damage Estimates 161
6.5 Integrating Seismic Hazard to Seismic Risk 163
6.6 Other Losses 172
6.7 Summary of Seismic Risk 176
6.8 Final Thoughts 177
References 179
Appendix A: Derivation of β and Rate for the
Exponential Magnitude Distribution for
Data with Unequal Periods of Completeness 189
Appendix B: Alternative Magnitude Distributions 193
Appendix C: MMI Scale of 1931 197
Appendix D: Stochastic Methods of Estimating
Ground Motion 203
Appendix E: Beta Distribution Plots 213
Appendix F: Derivation of Risk Equation 219

SYMBOLS

This monograph covers a number of topics in seismology and earthquake engineering, and standard symbols in such fields often overlap. For example, μ is the standard symbol for "shear rigidity of the earth's crust" in seismology, but it means "ductility ratio" in earthquake engineering. Rather than creating a set of unique symbols, this monograph uses the following standard symbols in the hope that their context will make their meaning clear.

A, a	amplitude of ground motion
a^*	reference design amplitude
a, b	parameters of the exponential magnitude distribution
a, b, c	parameters of nonlinear structural model
$a'(f), a(\omega)$	Fourier amplitude of acceleration for frequency of f or ω
$a'_{gm}(f)$	Fourier amplitude of ground acceleration
$a'_s(f)$	Fourier amplitude of acceleration at the source
a_T	total area of fault slip
A_R	change in ground motion for factor of 10 decrease in annual frequency
$\overline{AF}_{rp}$	mean soil amplification for return period rp
$b_0, b_1, b_2...$	constants in ground motion equation
$\overline{C}, \overline{c}$	vector of earthquake characteristics
$c_0, c_1, c_2...$	constants in ground motion equation
$\hat{c}$	median structural capacity
c, d, γ	parameters of the magnitude–seismic moment relation

$c(f)$ — soil, near-surface, and crustal amplification

d — shortest distance to surface projection of rupture

D — depth to basement rock

D, d — damage

$d_0, d_1, d_2...$ — parameters of logistic regression for damage

ds — damage state

E — energy released during fault slip

$E[.]$ — expected value of [.]

$e_1, e_2, e_3...$ — earthquake events

f — probability density function

f — variable indicating fault type

F — cumulative distribution function

f, f_n — frequency (Hz)

f_{cent} — central frequency of oscillator

f_s — factor of safety

G — complementary cumulative distribution function

$g_a(f), g_a(\omega)$ — power spectral density function of ground acceleration

h — source depth

$h_x(\omega)$ — transfer function for single-degree-of-freedom oscillator

I_e — epicentral intensity

I_s — site intensity

k, k', k'' — constants in magnitude distribution

K_{AF} — negative logarithmic slope of soil amplification versus rock amplitude

K_H — negative logarithmic slope of hazard curve

l	earthquake location
$l(.)$	likelihood function for (.)
M, m	earthquake magnitude (see Table 2)
$\overline{m}$	mean magnitude
M_o	seismic moment
$\dot{M}_o$	rate of seismic moment release
MMI, mmi	Modified Mercalli intensity
n	number of half-cycles of response
$n(m)$	number of earthquakes of magnitude m or greater per unit of time
$n_p(m)$	number of earthquakes in interval centered on magnitude m, per unit of time
$P[.]$	probability of event defined as [.]
p_f	peak factor, ratio of peak to rms
P_F	probability of failure
$p(f)$	high-frequency filter
PGA	peak ground acceleration
$q(f)$	attenuation of ground motion in travel path
R, r	source-to-site distance
rp	return period
$r_{\theta\phi}$	radiation pattern effect
R_y	yield strength reduction factor
s	duration of strong motion
s	variable indicating soil type
$\overline{s}$	vector of source properties
$\dot{s}$	average rate of slip on fault
SA_u	spectral acceleration at ultimate point

SA_y spectral acceleration at yield point

$\hat{sd}_{ds}$ median spectral displacement for damage state ds

SD_u spectral displacement at ultimate point

SD_y spectral displacement at yield point

T structural period, sec.

t, t' exposure time

U_R aleatory uncertainty

U_K epistemic uncertainty

v_s shear wave velocity

v_a reference shear wave velocity

x_p number of standard deviations of structural capacity corresponding to HCLPF

Y_i binary variable (i.e., 0 or 1) in logistic regression for damage

z_i binary variable (i.e., 0 or 1) in ground motion equation

β parameter of the exponential magnitude distribution

β parameter of the beta damage distribution

β_c logarithmic standard deviation of structural capacity

β_{ds} logarithmic standard deviation of spectral displacement for damage state ds

Γ gamma function

γ parameter of the magnitude-seismic moment relation

$\gamma(a)$ annual frequency of exceedance for amplitude a

$\gamma'(a)$ annual frequency of occurrence for amplitude a

Δm magnitude interval

$\Delta\sigma$	stress drop
ε	logarithmic ground motion deviation
ε_C	complementary cumulative definition of logarithmic ground motion deviation
ε_D	density definition of logarithmic ground motion deviation
κ	attenuation of ground motion in near-surface rock
λ_k	moment k of spectral density function
μ	ductility ratio
μ	shear rigidity of the earth's crust
ν	rate of earthquake occurrence
$\nu_{m_{\min}}$	rate of earthquake occurrence above magnitude $m_{\min}$
ξ	damping
ρ	density of the earth's crust
σ	standard deviation
σ_s	logarithmic standard deviation of soil amplification
σ_x	rms response of oscillator
ω	circular frequency

SEISMIC HAZARD AND RISK ANALYSIS

by

ROBIN K. McGUIRE

Risk Engineering, Inc.

Earthquakes which are normally recurring phenomena of the earth's crust have in the past caused considerable loss of property and life, and much of the distress and destruction has been due to lack of knowledge of earthquakes and their peculiar mode of action and of proper precautions against injury.

Seismological Society of America, 1910

1 INTRODUCTION

In 1910, the Seismological Society of America identified the three parts of the earthquake problem that merit study: the event itself (when, where, and how earthquakes occur), the associated ground motions, and the effect on structures. These are still the fundamental elements in evaluating earthquake risk. Reducing this risk requires knowledge, planning, and resources: earthquakes are the only remaining type of great, naturally occurring catastrophe that cannot be predicted. Resources for earthquake safety compete with resources for reducing risks from other hazards, and decisions on reducing earthquake risk are made in the context of the size and likelihood of that risk. Hence, seismic risk analysis is important.

A case can be made that all decisions on risk are made in a probabilistic context, balancing the costs of risk reduction with the probability of the event and its consequences. When the annual probability of danger is below 10^{-5} per year (as it is for seismic damage in many parts of the world), it is often considered minuscule in comparison with other dangers and can be ignored. As an example, the average risk of individual fatality from extreme weather phenomena for people in the central and eastern United States is about 5×10^{-6} per year[1], and those people continue to live in flood- and wind-prone areas.

On the other hand, when the annual probability of danger exceeds 10^{-2} (the annual probability of death in developed countries for a typical citizen), it is considered too high, and efforts are made to reduce it. But in the annual probability range of 10^{-2} to 10^{-5} (the annual probability range of significant earthquake-induced damage to single facilities in any highly seismic region of the world), a careful, quantitative analysis is needed to avoid putting too large or too small a percentage of risk reduction resources into reducing earthquake dangers, as compared with reducing other types of possible dangers.

Two other factors also indicate that a formal risk assessment is appropriate for earthquakes: the potential losses are typically substantial, and multiple disciplines are involved. Potentially large losses justify the significant effort involved in a seismic risk assessment, and a formal risk assessment allows the disciplines of seismology, geology, strong-motion geophysics, and earthquake engineering to communicate through a common language of best estimates and uncertainties. Without this language, key parameters tend to be passed from one discipline to the next without regard for how realistic or probable they are.

Since the seminal paper by Allin Cornell (1968), "Engineering seismic risk analysis," great progress has been made in the acceptance and use of probability methods in earthquake problems. Professionals no longer say, "We don't have enough data for a probability analysis," or "We need to gather a few more years' worth of data before we can make good assumptions." Likewise, professionals no longer hear the criticism, "Probability methods are fatally flawed because they can never predict the next earthquake." Instead, earth scientists at scientific meetings now debate the validity of alternative models for calculating near-term (30-year) probabilities of large earthquakes on the San Andreas Fault in California. This is outstanding progress. The earth continues to go bump in the

---

[1] From 1981 to 2000, approximately 20,000 deaths were attributed to hurricanes, tornados, heat waves, and flooding in a population averaging about 200 million, according to the Statistical Abstract of the United States, 2000.

night, seismic risk mitigation decisions are made daily, and a well-informed, if approximate, analysis of seismic hazards and risks truly benefits the decision process. In fact, all seismic hazard and risk applications are approximate, in the sense that seismology, ground motion, and engineering models will continue to evolve and improve. Professionals must simply be comfortable with the concept of a "good decision with a possibly bad outcome," just as motorists are every time they drive through a busy intersection when the traffic light turns green.

Many disciplines contribute to seismic risk studies, and yet there is no good compilation of how the details of geology, seismology, strong-motion geophysics, and earthquake engineering apply to the evaluation of seismic risk. Several sources that describe probabilistic seismic hazard analysis (PSHA) are worth reading. McGuire and Arabasz (1990) introduce the jargon and describe how the elements fit together. Reiter (1990) describes PSHA and its deterministic counterpart, raising many relevant issues from a regulatory perspective. Kramer (1996) includes a concise description of PSHA, along with many good references. A nonquantitative summary of PSHA is included in Yeats, Sieh, and Allen (1997), from a geological point of view. Hanks and Cornell (1999) provide an entertaining summary of issues related to the history and misinterpretation of PSHA. Thenhaus and Campbell (2003) present a good overview and examples of PSHA. Khater, Scawthorn, and Johnson (2003) identify the major elements of loss estimation in a qualitative way. But nowhere is the connection between PSHA and seismic risk fully described in a quantitative format. For example, engineers cannot just choose the 100-year ground motion, analyze a structure for that ground motion, and see whether the structure is safe. This monograph is intended as a first step in connecting seismic hazard and seismic risk. Without this connection, seismic hazard studies would be merely an interesting avocation.

In the presentation of cross-disciplinary ideas, some of the mathematical notation becomes confusing, but that cannot be helped. For example, in probability applications it is standard to use an upper-case letter to designate a random variable and a lowercase letter to designate a particular value of that random variable. Where possible, the present monograph follows this convention, but in seismology, certain nomenclature is standard: $\mathbf{M}$ is moment magnitude, M_o is seismic moment, and so on. So it is neither possible nor desirable to be dogmatic about notation.

3

The remainder of this monograph is organized as follows. Section 2 defines key terms and presents an overview of probabilistic seismic hazard and risk computations to show how all the elements fit together. Then Sections 3 through 6 examine the elements in more detail—how to describe earthquake source characteristics, estimate seismic ground shaking, perform seismic hazard analyses, and estimate seismic risk.

In estimating the hazard, both as to frequency and violence in the United States and Canada, we have to rely chiefly upon a compilation of the history of quakes ...although the underlying geologic conditions also give valuable evidence upon earthquake probability.

John R. Freeman, 1932

2 METHODOLOGY

2.1 Overview

Decisions to mitigate seismic risk require a logical and consistent approach to evaluating the effects of future earthquakes (and the uncertainty about those effects) on people and structures. To achieve this logic and consistency, it helps to view the methodology as consisting of four steps, as shown in Figure 1. First is the PSHA, which gives a probabilistic description (a frequency of exceedance) of earthquake characteristics such as ground motion amplitudes and fault displacement. Second is the estimation of earthquake damage to artificial and perhaps natural structures. An example is the analysis of the response of, or damage to, mechanical equipment in a power plant during earthquake ground motions; another example is the estimation of the probabilities of rockfalls or slides occurring at various levels of ground motion for a rock outcrop above a mountain highway. Third is the translation of the seismic hazards into seismic risks (frequencies of damage or loss) by using the selected damage or loss functions. Fourth is the formal or informal analysis of earthquake mitigation decisions, wherein the options, uncertainties, costs, decision criteria, and risk aversion of the decision maker are incorporated into the decision process. The ultimate goal of both seismic hazard and seismic risk analysis is to develop the elements that can be used to make rational deci-

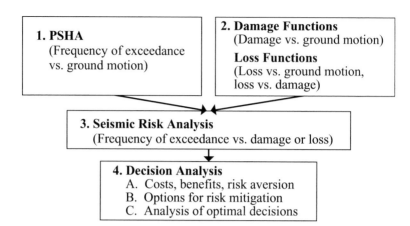

Figure 1. Steps in the mitigation of earthquake risk.

sions on seismic safety. The decision process should incorporate uncertainties in the earthquake process and ground-motion characteristics, uncertainties in the effects of earthquakes on people and structures, costs of seismic safety and potential losses, and aversion to risk.

This section summarizes the PSHA, damage and loss functions, and risk analysis. Subsequent sections describe the detailed assumptions that go into such an analysis. It should be remembered, as Figure 1 emphasizes, that PSHA and risk analysis are inputs into a larger decision-making process, not ends in themselves. The formal process of decision making to reduce seismic risk is not examined here; that topic deserves special study in its own right.

2.2 Definitions

Definitions are especially important for seismic risk applications, in which technical terms have been used with varied meanings, both loose and strict, over the years. Below are some of the more critical definitions that this monograph adopts:

- **Earthquake:** the entire phenomenon of fault rupture releasing stored strain in the earth's crust and propagating energy from the source in the form of vibratory waves in all directions. This is analogous to the term "hurricane" referring to atmospheric pressure fields over the ocean creating a pattern of strong winds that often move to landfall and inland, with wind speeds decreasing with distance from the storm track.

6

Specific reference is made to the earthquake source or the earthquake ground motion, as appropriate, just as references are made to a hurricane's barometric pressure differential or wind speed. In this context, the ground motion is an earthquake property or characteristic, not an effect. Comments such as "An earthquake occurred in Northridge" serve as shorthand, meaning that Northridge was the center of damage; this is like saying "A hurricane struck Miami."

- **Seismic hazard:** a property of an earthquake that can cause damage and loss. Examples are a ground motion amplitude in a certain range, a tsunami-induced wave reaching a certain elevation in a harbor, or a fault displacement larger than a specified amount on a known fault. A PSHA determines the *frequency* (the number of events per unit of time) with which a seismic hazard will occur. Typically, the seismic hazard is calculated as a frequency that a ground motion amplitude is *greater* than a specified value. It is common to use "seismic hazard" and "frequency" interchangeably—as in saying of a frequency plot, "This curve shows the seismic hazard at site A."

- **Earthquake damage:** a destructive physical effect on a natural or artificial structure. Examples are the effects of seismic shaking on a building (e.g., broken windows, spalled concrete on columns, or broken equipment and piping).

- **Seismic hazard curve:** a graphical curve depicting the frequency (the number of events per unit of time—usually per year) with which selected values of a seismic hazard such as ground motion amplitude are expected to occur (or, more typically, are expected to be exceeded).

- **Damage function:** a relationship between levels of damage and the corresponding levels of shaking. For example, with this function, the damage to a structure for a given ground motion input can be estimated. Damage functions can be derived either empirically or analytically.

- **Loss function:** a relationship between monetary or human loss (for example, the number of casualties) and earthquake damage or levels of ground shaking. Loss may be estimated directly from ground motion amplitudes, either in monetary units or as a fraction of building value, or the levels of damage can be estimated first, and then the loss from the estimated damage can be calculated.

- **Seismic risk:** the probability that some humans will incur loss or that their built environment will be damaged. These probabilities usually represent a level of loss or damage that is equaled or exceeded over some time period. The loss or damage must be quantified; it might be a monetary loss in a defined range, the number of casualties in a region, or the cost to repair a facility as a percentage of replacement cost. Seismic risk is calculated with a set of earthquakes, the associated loss or damage, and the associated probability of occurrence or exceedance.
- **Aleatory (or random) uncertainty U_R:** the probabilistic uncertainty that is inherent in a random phenomenon and cannot be reduced by acquiring additional data or information. In the past, this type of uncertainty has been called randomness, or inherent variability.
- **Epistemic (or knowledge) uncertainty U_K:** the uncertainty that results from lack of knowledge about some model or parameter. This type of uncertainty *can* be reduced, at least conceptually, by additional data or improved information. In the past, U_K has also been called statistical or professional uncertainty, or simply uncertainty.
- **Uncertainty:** a general term for both U_R and U_K.
- **Recurrence interval:** the mean (average) time between occurrences of a given type of earthquake—for example, an earthquake of a specified magnitude—on a fault or in a region.
- **Return period:** the mean (average) time between occurrences of a seismic hazard—for example, a certain ground motion at a site, or a certain level of damage or loss.
- **Deaggregation:** statistical decomposition of a hazard to show the relative contributions by magnitude, distance, and ground motion deviations. Further explanation of this term is in Chapter 5. The term "deaggregation" is preferred over "disaggregation," for consistency with other earthquake science terms such as "deamplification" and "deconvolution."

The following discussion explains why some of these definitions have been adopted for this monograph. Seismic hazard is quantified by a *frequency*, rather than a probability, for two reasons. First, frequencies from multiple sources are additive, even if the result exceeds unity. Thus, defining a hazard by using frequency is simpler. Second, frequencies of occurrence can be compared with other hazards and with design decisions on a frequency basis. This avoids illogical arguments based on arbitrarily dividing the exposure time into smaller and smaller units, so as to obtain a lower probability of occurrence during a given exposure time, such as a short construction period (e.g., three months). Making decisions based on frequency achieves a consistent level of seismic safety for all structures, regardless of their proposed lifetimes. A "seismic hazard curve" expresses the frequency of occurrence as a function of an earthquake hazard, such as ground motion amplitude. "Frequency of occurrence" can be expanded to be the frequency with which a ground motion amplitude greater than a given value will occur; this is called "frequency of exceedance."

There is a distinction between damage and loss: damage refers to physical effects, such as the effect on structures. Loss is the associated monetary or social consequence. Damage to structures may be expressed in categories, such as these:

- No damage
- Slight (damage to architectural features)
- Minor (damage to structural features that can be repaired easily)
- Moderate (damage to structural features that can be repaired with significant effort)
- Major (damage that is not worth repairing)
- Total (collapse)

Structural engineers can estimate damage, but estimating loss may involve considering additional factors like inflated costs of labor and materials after a major earthquake (which is called "demand surge") or insurance deductibles. The destruction of a building's contents and the interruption of business are additional losses that might occur. Buildings suffer damage during an earthquake, but the owner (or perhaps the insurer) incurs the loss. Confusion occurs between these terms because both are often quantified as a percentage of the replacement value of the structure.

The term "exposure time" has generated some confusion. It is used, for example, in defining the ground motion with a 2,475-year return period as the motion "that will be exceeded with a 2% probability during an exposure time of 50 years," with 50 years being the nominal lifetime of major civil structures. This does not mean that someone who wants to build a warehouse with an expected lifetime of 10 years can design it on the basis of a 2% probability-of-exceedance level in

10 years. The reason is that the 2%-in-50-years criterion (which is calibrated to a great deal of engineering judgment and experience) really means a frequency of 1/2,475 per year, and the design of a structure should be based on that criterion. It would be false logic to design a warehouse for the 2%-in-10-years ground motion, then demolish it in 10 years and build a replacement whose design is based on the same seismic criterion. This logical fallacy can be further illustrated by extending the concept to even shorter periods, such as designing a temporary warehouse on the basis of the 2%-in-6-months ground motion, which would be very low, and then replacing the temporary warehouse every 6 months. When an earthquake eventually occurs, the warehouse in place at that time will collapse, perhaps with casualties, and public safety will not have been protected.

A 10% probability of exceedance in 50 years corresponds to a 475-year return period, and the question sometimes arises, "What is special about the 475-year return period?" This period is derived by assuming a Poisson process for ground motion occurrences, wherein the probability of an event, P, is related to the annual frequency of exceedance of the ground motion γ and the exposure time t through

$$P = 1 - \exp(-\gamma t) \qquad (1)$$

Rearranging this gives

$$\gamma = -[\ln(1 - P)]/t \qquad (2)$$

Substituting a probability $P = 0.1$ and an exposure time $t = 50$ years gives $\gamma = 0.002107$ per year, which is 1/475 years.

The same result can be obtained from the binomial distribution, which represents the Poisson process in discrete form. If it is assumed only that exceedances of ground motion in successive years are independent and that the probability of nonexceedance in any year is 1-γ, then a 90% probability of *nonexceedance* in $t = 50$ years is expressed as

$$
\begin{aligned}
P[nonexceedance\ in\ t\ years] &= P\,[nonexceedance\ in\ year\ 1]\\
&\quad \times\ P\,[nonexceedance\ in\ year\ 2]\\
&\quad \bullet\bullet\bullet\\
&= (P\,[nonexceedance\ in\ any\ year])^t\\
&= (1\text{-}\gamma)^t\\
&= 0.9 \qquad (3)
\end{aligned}
$$

which gives $\gamma = 0.002105$ per year for $t = 50$ years, which again is

Table 1. Examples of uncertainties in seismic hazard analysis.

Aleatory Uncertainties U_R
- Future earthquake locations
- Future earthquake source properties (e.g., magnitudes)
- Ground motion at a site given the median value of motion
- Details of the fault rupture process (e.g., direction of rupture)

Epistemic Uncertainties U_K
- Geometry of seismotectonic and seismogenic zones
- Distributions describing source parameters (e.g., rate, b value, maximum magnitude)
- Median value of ground motion given the source properties
- Limits on ground shaking

1/475 years. The slight difference from the Poisson result arises because of the discrete representation of time with the binomial distribution. So the 475-year return period is derived from a 10% probability of exceedance in 50 years under very simple assumptions about ground motion occurrences.

Many words have been used to differentiate U_R from U_K. The currently popular terms "aleatory uncertainty" and "epistemic uncertainty" offer the advantage of explicitness at the price of length and unfamiliarity. This monograph uses U_R, U_K, and the general term "uncertainty" in the hope that their meanings will be clear and their usage concise. Examples of U_R and U_K uncertainties are in Table 1. Note that, although U_R uncertainties conceptually represent uncertainties within current models that cannot be reduced by better data, this does not preclude research on how to build better models to understand earthquakes. In fact, with time there is a migration of uncertainty from U_R to U_K. The important point is to specify which uncertainties are included in each category in a particular study.

2.3 PSHA for a Specific Site

A PSHA for a specific site consists of determining the frequency with which an earthquake characteristic (e.g., peak acceleration) takes on a defined range of values (e.g., > 0.5 g) during some fixed time t in the future (e.g., 50 years). Here the earthquake characteristic is quantified by the variable C, and the range of values is typically defined as an exceedance of a specific value c. Characteristic C may be the peak acceleration of the earthquake ground motion at the site, a level of Modified Mercalli Intensity (MMI), the duration of seismic shaking, or the displacement caused by a fault beneath a facility's foundation; the methodology is general enough to encompass these applications. Next, the mathematical basis for seismic hazard calculations is derived so that all inherent assumptions can be stated explicitly.

Figure 2 schematically shows the procedure for conducting a PSHA. This figure illustrates the specific hazard of ground motion, but it could be redrawn in like fashion for any other earthquake hazard. Step A divides the earthquake threat into sources (these may be identified faults or geographical areas) that produce earthquakes and earthquake characteristics. It is assumed that earthquakes act independently—that is, the occurrence of an event at one source does not affect the occurrence of events at other sources. This assumption of independence is common, but it may be relaxed, as discussed below. The seismic hazard at the site for earthquake characteristic C is defined as the frequency γ with which a specific value c is exceeded during time t.

This total frequency γ is made up of contributions from each independent source j, where the frequency of exceedance of a specified value of c from each source is calculated as

$$\gamma_j(C \text{ exceeds } c) = \gamma_j(C > c)$$
$$= \nu_j \iint P_j[C > c \mid \bar{s} \text{ at } l] P[\bar{s} \text{ at } l] d\bar{s} \, dl \quad (4)$$

where

γ_j = the frequency with which c is exceeded from earthquakes at source j

$\bar{s}$ = a vector of source properties

ν_j = the rate of occurrence of earthquakes of interest at source j

$P_j[C > c \mid \bar{s} \text{ at } l]$ = the probability that c is exceeded at the site, conditional on an earthquake at source j, with properties $\bar{s}$ at location l (the vertical line means "given that")

$P[\bar{s} \text{ at } l]$ = the probability that an earthquake with source properties $\bar{s}$ occurs at location l

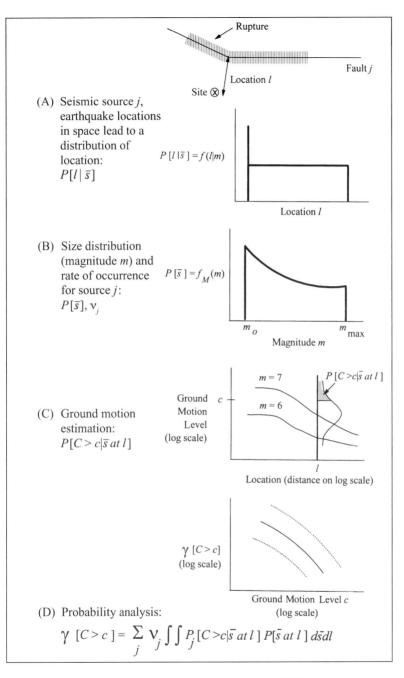

(A) Seismic source j, earthquake locations in space lead to a distribution of location: $P[l \mid \bar{s}]$

$P[l \mid \bar{s}] = f(l \mid m)$

(B) Size distribution (magnitude m) and rate of occurrence for source j: $P[\bar{s}], \nu_j$

$P[\bar{s}] = f_M(m)$

(C) Ground motion estimation: $P[C > c \mid \bar{s} \; at \; l]$

(D) Probability analysis:

$$\gamma \, [C > c] = \sum_j \nu_j \int \int P_j [C > c \mid \bar{s} \; at \; l] \, P[\bar{s} \; at \; l] \, d\bar{s} dl$$

Figure 2. The steps in performing a PSHA.

13

In the example shown in Figure 2, $P[\bar{s}\,at\,l]$ is evaluated as $P[l|\bar{s}\,]P[\bar{s}\,]$. $P[l|\bar{s}\,]$ is shown in step A as a probability density function $f(l/m)$ that is conditional on magnitude (a source property) and uses distance from the rupture to the site to quantify earthquake location. $P[\bar{s}\,]$ is shown in step B as the probability density function $f_M(m)$, which uses magnitude to parameterize the earthquake source. Thus $P[\bar{s}\,at\,l]$ in equation 4 is evaluated as $f(l|m)f_M(m)$.

The ground motion equation or its equivalent is used to calculate $P_j[C > c|\bar{s}\,at\,l]$ in step C. Given the earthquake location l, parameterized with the distance r between the site and the closest point of rupture, and given the source properties $\bar{s}$, the distribution of ground motion, fault displacement, or other characteristic C can be calculated. From this distribution comes the required probability, $P_j[C > c|\bar{s}\,at\,l]$.

The rate of earthquake occurrences v_j requires a careful definition of the events that will be considered. For many analyses, v_j is just the rate of earthquake occurrence above some minimum magnitude m_{min}. Magnitude m_{min} may be selected on the basis of magnitudes that will damage structures, and it may differ from the magnitudes used to estimate v_j from instrumentally recorded earthquakes. For fault displacement hazard, v_j may be defined as the rate of thrust- or oblique-slip earthquakes producing a displacement at the surface.

The total seismic hazard at the site is calculated as

$$\gamma[C > c] = \sum_j \gamma_j[C > c] \qquad (5)$$

Here γ is the total frequency with which C exceeds c, and it equals the sum of contributions from all sources. Note that, if c is set to 0, then

$$\gamma[C > 0] = \sum_j v_j \qquad (6)$$

That is, the total rate of exceedance of zero is just the sum of rates of earthquake occurrences on all sources. This calculation assumes that all earthquakes on modeled sources will have some nonzero effect C at the site, albeit perhaps in the microtremor category. Equation 6 provides one useful check for computer calculations that can be performed by hand.

14

All the uncertainties discussed so far, in the form of probabilities in the integrand of equation 4, are U_R uncertainties. That is, they represent intrinsic, random variations that cannot be reduced by additional data or current theories. The seismic hazard analysis integrates over these uncertainties, and the vertical axis of a seismic hazard curve (such as the curve in step D of Figure 2) represents them.

U_K uncertainties are treated by representing the inputs to the analysis (steps A–C in Figure 2) using alternative values, calculating an alternative value of γ, and deriving an alternative hazard curve. The dashed lines in step D represent these alternative calculations. If weights are assigned to the alternative inputs, or if they are selected via simulation with intrinsic weights, then the alternative hazard results can be interpreted quantitatively. Then it is possible to make statements such as "I am 85% confident that the annual frequency of exceedance of 0.2 g peak ground acceleration (PGA) is less than 10^{-2}." This statement would follow from the 0.85 fractile seismic hazard result (or curve).

Much has been said over the years about the lack of understanding of earthquake processes and the implication that professionals simply do not know enough to perform a meaningful seismic hazard analysis. On the contrary, a modern seismic hazard analysis can account for U_K uncertainties and yield meaningful results for decision making. Picking arbitrary deterministic design values in the face of such uncertainties will lead to nonoptimal decisions and a waste of resources.

Often the *mean* seismic hazard result (the mean with respect to U_K uncertainties) is used as a single measure of seismic hazard for decision making. It is important to understand that the mean seismic hazard *cannot* in general be calculated by using mean values of the input parameters, because of the nonlinear nature of the calculation in equation 4 (there are some parameters for which the use of the mean value gives exact or approximate mean seismic hazards, such as the rate v_j). The full distribution of source parameters, earthquake locations, and ground motion equations generally must be used to calculate the distribution of hazard, from which the mean value can be determined.

Several implications of this mathematical calculation of seismic hazard are important. Seismic hazard calculations depend only on the *rate* of occurrence of earthquakes at each source, not on the probability distribution of events in time. Specifically, seismic hazard calculations do not require the assumption that earthquakes occur independently in time as a Poisson process. If a memory model is used, or a long- or intermediate-term earthquake prediction is available, then this information can be used to calculate the rate of occurrence of earthquakes for the time period of interest. For example, a seismologist or geologist might want to estimate the rate of occurrence of a specific-magnitude earthquake on a fault (often called a "characteristic" earthquake because the fault has the characteristic of producing only large events of that single magnitude). If the calculated probability of occurrence of that characteristic earthquake on the fault is 0.1 in 30 years, then the rate of occurrence of that earthquake on the fault is 0.0033 per year for the next 30 years (in this case, the annual rate is estimated as the annual probability).

The source $\bar{s}$ vector may comprise many parameters: magnitude, seismic moment, stress drop, rupture direction and velocity, and so on. It is necessary and appropriate to specify only sufficient source parameters to estimate characteristic C and its uncertainty U_R. There is a tradeoff between the accuracy gained by using additional parameters to estimate C and the additional calculations required to integrate over those parameters. As discussed in Section 4.2, in some cases there may be no advantage at all to including some parameters such as fault rupture direction, even though they allow a more accurate estimation of C.

Earthquake characteristic C may be PGA, peak ground velocity, spectral acceleration, MMI, strong-motion duration, fault displacement, or any other useful measure for predicting structural response, damage, or other effect. Performing seismic hazard analyses for more than one parameter (more than one definition of C) requires caution in formulating the solution, because of the correlation of variables. Multivariate seismic hazard analysis is not discussed further here; however, Bazzurro and Cornell (2002) offer a useful discussion of this topic.

Some special applications deserve comment. If a particular fault is thought to have a "characteristic earthquake" that occurs at regular intervals, then this model can be handled in the format of equation 4. $P[\bar{s}]$ will be a narrow distribution, and in the limit only one set of source parameters—those of the characteristic event—are allowed, with a probability of 1. $P[l]$ may be very narrow as well, if the location of the future event is well known. The rate ν_j will be the rate of occurrence of the characteristic event over the time period of interest. This rate will vary as a function of absolute time, being higher over periods when the characteristic earthquake is expected and lower

16

over other periods. Thus the seismic hazard for a characteristic event is no more complex to compute than hazards for other descriptions of seismicity.

An earthquake prediction expressed as the probability of occurrence of a future event can also be handled mathematically. The seismic sources must represent fault segments or areas within which the earthquake predictions are homogeneous (that is, uniform in space). The application is then similar to the one that was just described for characteristic earthquakes, with v_j calculated from the probability of the event when given the observation of (or lack of) precursors.

These applications of characteristic earthquakes and earthquake prediction capability illustrate that PSHA can and should be used to refine the perception of hazards from earthquakes, as technology advances. There will not be a step-function change in seismic hazard methodology, proceeding from gross probabilistic models to detailed deterministic calculations. However, analysts will become more able to forecast future earthquake occurrences and effects, resulting in more refined estimates as they develop and adopt new theories about earthquake forecasts and ground motion estimation.

2.4 Translating Hazard into Risk

Earthquake damage is associated with direct consequences (damage to property or loss of function) and indirect consequences (such as loss of productivity or jobs). The most direct way to make probabilistic estimates of earthquake damage D is to express D as a function of earthquake source parameters $\bar{s}$ and location l:

$$P[damage\ exceeds\ d\ |\ earthquake] = P[D > d\ |\ \bar{s}\ at\ l] \quad (7)$$

Then the probability of damage exceeding d given $\bar{s}$ at l can be substituted for the probability of an earthquake characteristic exceeding c given $\bar{s}$ at l in equation 4, and the PSHA procedures can be used to directly estimate earthquake damage.

In practice, this direct procedure is almost never used. Most earthquake damage is caused by or related to ground shaking, so the conventional procedure is to estimate damage as a function of various ground motion amplitudes:

$$P[D > d] \cong \int P[D > d\ |\ c]\gamma'(c)dc \quad (8)$$

17

where $\gamma'(c)$ is the frequency *of occurrence* of characteristic c. This is obtained from equation 5 by differentiation, much as a density function for a random variable can be obtained from the complementary cumulative distribution function:

$$\gamma'(c) = -\frac{d\gamma[C > c]}{dc} \qquad (9)$$

There is a practical reason for this separation of analyses for ground motion characteristics and damage: a single earthquake provides many data for estimating $P[D > d|c]$. For example, damage can be estimated as a percentage of replacement value for highrise reinforced-concrete structures as a function of peak ground acceleration, over a wide range of acceleration, for one well-instrumented major earthquake in an urban area. However, if equation 7 is used, then that same earthquake provides data for estimating damage only as a function of source-to-site location l and not as a function of source properties $\bar{s}$. A large number of earthquakes would have to be studied to obtain enough data to evaluate $P[D > d|\bar{s} \, at \, l]$ in equation 7 over a wide range of values $\bar{s}$ and l. Therefore, it is more practical to calculate seismic risk by first conducting a PSHA and then translating hazards into damage with equation 8.

Note that, unlike seismic hazard, seismic risk is quantified by a probability, not a frequency. This follows convention in the risk analysis field, and it results in the approximation in equation 8, rather than an equality.

Figure 3 shows examples of published empirical relationships between property damage and ground motion (after Kircher et al. 1997). In this figure, earthquake characteristic c is represented on the horizontal axis as MMI level, and damage d is represented by the repair cost as a percentage of property value. A similar comparison could be made by using instrumental measures of ground motion, such as peak acceleration. Often, there is a power law relationship between damage and instrumental measures, and there is always a large amount of uncertainty in any relationship.

For this type of correlation, several approaches might be used to estimate the probabilities that damage levels will be exceeded. The most direct is to assume a one-to-one relationship between D and c, ignoring the variations in Figure 3. Probabilities of ground motion characteristics could then be translated directly into probabilities of damage by using a monotonic relationship, such as one of those il-

18

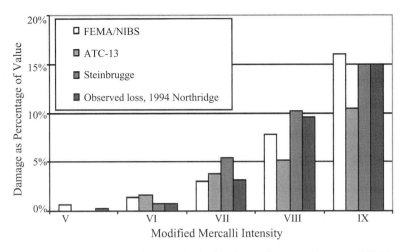

Figure 3. Loss estimates (including loss of contents) versus MMI for wood-frame structures, together with observed loss from the 1994 Northridge earthquake (after Kircher et al, 1997).

lustrated in Figure 3. Ignoring these uncertainties would underestimate the probabilities of damage, however.

As an alternative, uncertainties in D when c is given can be considered to be independent of earthquake source properties $\bar{s}$ and l. That is,

$$P[damage > d \mid ground\ motion\ characteristics\ at\ the\ site]$$
$$= P[D > d \mid c]$$
$$= P[D > d \mid c\ from\ \bar{s}\ at\ l] \quad (10)$$

This implies that knowledge of c is all that is required to predict damage, and equation 8 can be applied with multiple techniques (e.g., Figure 3) that are used to estimate $P[D > d|c]$. This approximation is useful as long as the right characteristic is chosen to estimate damage. For example, a long-period measure of ground motion should probably be used to predict damage to the main span of the Golden Gate Bridge, not PGA, because long suspension bridges respond to long-period energy in ground motion, and PGA is related to high-frequency energy.

Sophisticated analytical methods are now being developed and applied to estimate detailed characteristics of ground motion during earthquakes and to estimate how such motion will damage structures. These efforts are encouraging, and Section 6 presents examples of them. Such methods will achieve credibility as they are shown to predict damage before a specific earthquake more accurately than empirical methods do.

To estimate losses from damage, the damage descriptors must be translated into monetary loss or other quantitative units such as the number of people requiring hospitalization. This separate step may be straightforward if damage is expressed as a percentage of the structure's replacement value. The loss estimate may be more complex if it involves interruption of business during repairs, loss of market share, insurance deductibles, costs of bringing older structures up to current building codes, and so on. It is wise to consider this last step deliberately so that the estimates of loss consider all factors that are relevant to the decision process.

2.5 Seismic Risk Analysis for a Group of Sites

A more sophisticated hazard analysis is required to perform a seismic risk analysis for a group of dispersed sites or for a facility that extends over a large area (such as a "lifeline" facility). This is called for in estimating the risk of future earthquake damage in a region or in determining the risk of failure of a multiple-route pipeline system supplying water to a city.

Risk analysis for widely dispersed but interrelated facilities can be performed by treating the facilities as a set of multiple sites. This is a good approximation for virtually all applications: total damage estimates for urban areas in a state, loss of functionality of a highway system with multiple routes and bridges susceptible to seismic damage, percent failure of offshore oil-producing facilities during an earthquake, and so on. The analysis proceeds via the following steps.

First, select sites. These could be the centers of population for total damage estimates or points of vulnerability (such as bridges, towers, fault crossings, or switchyards) for extended lifeline facilities.

Second, define "failure." As an example, a widely extended facility might fail if earthquake damage $D_1 > d_1$ at site 1 and $D_2 > d_2$ at site 2 occurs, or damage $D_3 > d_3$ at site 3 occurs. For total loss estimates in a region, failure might be defined as the sum of losses at all sites exceeding a prescribed value.

20

Third, express failure in Boolean algebra. For the extended facility described above, failure is defined as

$$failure = (D_1 > d_1 \cap D_2 > d_2) \cup (D_3 > d_3) \qquad (11)$$

For total monetary loss estimates, failure might be defined as a mathematical expression:

$$\sum_i (D_i) > \$10 \; billion \qquad (12)$$

where D_i is the monetary loss at site i from a specific earthquake.

Fourth, develop damage or loss functions. These functions predict earthquake damage or loss to facilities at each site as a function of earthquake characteristics (such as ground shaking, fault displacement, or permanent ground displacement caused by liquefaction). Equations must also be adopted to predict the earthquake characteristics. For example, for damage caused by ground shaking, ground motion equations are needed that predict the mean ground motion and its uncertainty U_R from site to site as well as the correlation in ground motion from site to site.

Fifth, develop a method for calculating the probability of failure (defined in the third step) given a vector of earthquake characteristics $\bar{c}$ for all sites. Any correlation of damage D (such as damage caused by common strengths of materials) should be included in this failure probability calculation.

Sixth, calculate the probability of failure P_j from earthquakes on source j as

$$P_j[failure] \simeq \nu_j \iint P[failure|\bar{c}]P[\bar{c}|\bar{s} \; at \; l]P[\bar{s}]P[l]d\bar{s}dl \quad (13)$$

$$P[failure] \simeq \sum_j P_j[failure] \qquad (14)$$

where the variables are as previously defined for equation 4. The calculation for total probability of failure is similar to equation 5.

The above steps have deliberately emphasized estimating the earthquake damage and failures (the second and third steps) before predicting the earthquake characteristics (the fourth step). It is important to first concentrate on modeling the engineering system in the best possible way and then decide on the appropriate earthquake characteristics to support that model, not vice versa.

It is worth noting that the probability of failure for systems comprising dispersed sites cannot be calculated from seismic hazard maps, except for trivially simple cases. The reason is that a seismic hazard map summarizes results calculated separately for each point on a grid, via equation 4. There is no information on $P[\overline{C}|\overline{s}\ at\ l]$ as required by equation 13, so the risk to a dispersed facility cannot be determined. This is true even if a deterministic ground motion equation and loss function are adopted. Several potentially important studies have misunderstood this point, and thus their results are meaningless.

In principle, equation 13 is straightforward. In practice though, it may be difficult to apply unless one or more simplifying assumptions are used. The first complication is in evaluating the probability of failure for a given earthquake. Earthquake characteristics at separate sites are neither perfectly dependent nor perfectly independent. Given an expected characteristic at each site (conditional upon the earthquake), deviations from the expected values are correlated from site to site because of common source parameters during any single earthquake, and, depending on the sites, perhaps a common propagation path and surficial geology. The exact or even the approximate calculation of these multiple correlations is a formidable task that can usually be accomplished only with Monte Carlo simulation.

A second difficulty is that the earthquake resistance of engineered facilities is usually correlated at different sites because of similar design and construction techniques. For a region or a dispersed facility represented by more than a few sites, the calculation of probabilities of failure for partially correlated resistances is a substantial numerical task. For correlated lognormally distributed variables (a common model), the number of multiple numerical integrations required is, in the general case, equal to the number of sites. This requirement is just for calculating the probability of failure for a given set of earthquake characteristics; these multiple numerical integrations must be performed for all sets of characteristics, all source properties, and all earthquake locations.

The most common method for avoiding these complications is to assume that both earthquake characteristics and damage are deterministic (that is, to assume that the ground motion equation and the loss function have no U_R component). In this case, a straightforward calculation determines whether there is system failure for a specific earthquake. $P[\overline{C}|\bar{s}\ at\ l]$ in equation 13 indicates, for example, the median predicted ground motions at each site, and $P[failure|\overline{C}]$ is 0 or 1 according to the failure criterion (the third step) and whether certain critical amplitudes have been exceeded at critical sites according to the failure definition. Assuming deterministic characteristics and effects will generally affect the risk assessment by underestimating the probability of failure over all earthquakes, just as assuming a deterministic ground motion equation will underestimate the seismic hazard. This simplified method should be avoided.

Methods of calculating earthquake damage and loss that are based on a geographic information system (GIS) have become popular for applications in a region. With these methods, large databases of building inventories, soil conditions, and faults can be combined to estimate and display damage and loss over a region, either for scenario earthquakes or after an actual event, for emergency response purposes. The mathematical methods used in GIS applications for individual earthquakes follow the methods described here, and an understanding of these methods is important to understanding the applicability and limitations of GIS-based results. Expanding a GIS application from scenario earthquakes to include multiple random events and risk analysis is also possible, but it will be more efficient with software specifically designed for that purpose.

The assessment of seismic risk for multiple sites is not discussed further in this monograph. Analyses depend to a large extent on the specific application being pursued. All applications, however, can be cast in the mathematical framework outlined above. The effect of correlating earthquake characteristics and damage among sites can generally be bounded by analyzing extremes (perfect correlation or zero correlation); the range of failure frequency expressed by these extremes depends on the particular application and on the definition of failure.

Every earthquake contains a surprise.

Clarence Allen, 1952

3 SEISMICITY AND PROPERTIES OF EARTHQUAKE SOURCES

Understanding earthquake hazard and risk requires knowledge about where earthquakes will originate, what characteristics the energy release and ground motion will have, and what the effects will be on humans and structures. For a historical earthquake, these aspects can be studied to a greater or lesser extent, depending on the data available and the time elapsed since the event. Also, fundamental physical relationships can be used to derive estimates of earthquake source properties and ground motion characteristics to provide guidance where data are sparse. Earthquake hazard and risk analysis is concerned with damage and loss from *future* events, and the key to a good analysis is to make credible estimates and express uncertainties about the source properties and effects of *future* earthquakes.

3.1 Seismic Sources

The first step in analyzing historical seismicity and making projections about future seismicity is to define seismic sources. There are two general types:

- **Area sources** are areas within which future seismicity is assumed to have distributions of source properties and locations of energy release that do not vary in time and space. In the simplest case, historical seismicity alone is used to define the geometry of area sources.
- **Fault sources** are faults or zones for which the tectonic features causing earthquakes have been identified. These are

usually individual faults, but they may be zones comprising multiple faults or regions of faulting if surface evidence of these faults is lacking but the faults are suspected from seismicity patterns, tectonic interpretations of crustal stress and strain, and other evidence. Regions of blind thrust earthquakes are a good example of the latter.

Using uniform distributions in time and space to describe the properties of area sources implies only that present knowledge about earthquake occurrences requires such an interpretation. If an area source is needed with a source property distribution that is different in one part of the zone from another, then two area sources could be used to represent earthquake occurrences. None of this is to say that future earthquakes will demonstrate uniformity of occurrence within each source over a finite time; indeed, they will not do so over the short term, and they may not do so over the long term. The point is that area sources represent the present *understanding* of future seismicity and its characteristics.

One study of seismic hazard (EPRI 1986) relaxed the assumption of uniform seismicity rates within area sources and used historical seismicity to determine these rates. In this application, large area sources were divided into discrete geographical 1° cells, and seismicity rates were estimated from maximum likelihood techniques for each cell. Other parameters (the maximum magnitude distribution and the probability of activity) were uniform across the source, however. This application should be viewed as a special case of an area source, and such special applications should be encouraged where they are useful to the analyst in characterizing future seismicity. In other words, the definitions of seismic sources should be flexible enough to reflect the best seismological interpretations.

A "background source" is a special case of an area source that represents all seismicity that is not explained by other sources. Therefore, background sources conceptually are "none-of-the-above" sources, representing seismicity when other sources are not active. For background sources, it is common to vary the seismicity rate (and often the b value; see equation 15) in space, calibrating values via historical seismicity. The U.S. national seismic hazard maps (USGS 2001) use this form of a background source.

Fault sources do not necessarily have uniform distributions of earthquake frequencies and locations, as emphasized by recent studies. Faults such as the San Andreas are often divided into segments in which rupture occurrences are preferentially restricted in each segment separately, although multiple segments may rupture in larger earthquakes.

Data and interpretations for defining the boundaries of area sources may be related to any or all of the following:

- Preinstrumental macroseismicity
- Instrumental macroseismicity and microseismicity
- Regional crustal geology
- Tectonic style of crustal deformation (e.g., extensional or thrust regimes)
- Local geology, including observed or inferred intrusive bodies
- Measured or inferred states of crustal stress
- Measured or inferred rates of crustal strain, both horizontal and vertical
- Inferred zones of weakness associated with crustal features (e.g., rifts)

Fault sources may be identified or inferred on the basis of the above general types of information plus additional specific data from the following:

- Field mapping of fault exposures
- Geophysical surveys
- Aerial photos and satellite imagery
- Special seismicity studies (high-accuracy seismograph networks, focal mechanism studies)
- Modeling of active tectonic mechanisms or processes

Traditionally, historical seismicity (both preinstrumental and instrumental) has been used as the first indicator of which areas should be further examined to develop a correlation between seismicity and crustal structure or any other observable property of the earth. This practice follows the simple notion that two factors are required to cause an earthquake: (1) a zone of weakness (i.e., a fault) suitably oriented to slip under the crustal stress state and (2) a local shear stress high enough to trigger the frictional slip. Historical earthquakes tell where these conditions have been fulfilled in the past and where they might be fulfilled in the future.

The above two requirements for earthquake occurrence should be kept in mind when area sources are being determined. Two adjacent areas may exhibit similar crustal geology, but if their stress regimes are dissimilar, then the two areas should not be treated as a single area source. Sufficient conditions for earthquake occurrences in one region may be insufficient in another if the state of crustal stress (along with the causative mechanism) are different. Finally, to accurately assess earthquake hazards and risk, determining where earthquakes probably will *not* occur (or where seismicity will be low) is often as important as determining where they probably *will* occur (or where seismicity will be high).

The procedure for defining earthquake sources, both areas and faults, is best considered and treated as an application of physical principles with substantial doses of scientific judgment. The most reliable and useful calculation of seismic hazard generally begins with the drawing of several sets of sources, each representing a different interpretation of the factors listed above. Then the hazard is calculated for each interpretation, and subjective weighting is applied to combine the results. The methods for defining seismic sources might range from the simple to the complex. As a first cut, assume that future events will occur in the location of past events and draw sources around concentrations of historical seismicity. The logic is simple and has the implicit, attractive assumption that historical earthquakes indicate regions where crustal strain energy has been sufficiently high to cause earthquakes and where faults have been available to release that energy. At the other extreme, a tectonophysicist could construct a physical system that defines the tectonic processes causing crustal stress, that identifies crustal structures oriented in the right way to relieve that stress, and that draws several sets of sources consistent with several interpretations of these processes, stresses, and structures.

With multiple interpretations of seismic sources, how can they be folded into a quantitative analysis with some measure of consistency? The answer lies in assessing the *subjective credibility* of the sources—that is, how accurately each set of sources represents the occurrence of earthquakes. The term "subjective credibility" is used to emphasize the intent to evaluate how scientifically credible each set of sources is, on the basis of empirical data, theory, analogies with other regions, or any other defensible method. The assessments are necessarily subjective because professionals can and should use the best judgment and experience in making them. These credibilities are treated like *probabilities*—for example, they must sum to unity. But, as some critics have pointed out, the chance that *any* source interpretation is correct is close to zero, because knowledge and understanding of earthquakes are constantly growing; it will be possible to make completely different (and improved) interpretations five years from now. Therefore, subjective credibilities are assessed today, with the goal of contributing to informed decision-making.

It is easiest to evaluate subjective credibilities by beginning with the credibility of different methods of drawing seismic sources, such as these:

- Historical seismicity
- Crustal geology
- Tectonic processes
- Uniform hazard (the "know-nothing" hypothesis)

The latter method implies that earthquakes are equally likely at any location. This assumption is discussed further in this section. For example, scientists or engineers may believe that they can identify possible tectonic processes in an area (for example, east-west compression that is relieved by north-south-striking thrust faults) with 50% confidence. This implies that (1) with data on crustal stress, strain, geology, and seismicity from many regions of the world, it would be possible to list (and draw area sources for) the tectonic processes thought to be active in that region; and (2) the list for each region would include the true tectonic process for that region about 50% of the time. Accordingly, a total credibility of 0.5 would be assigned to area sources developed through consideration of tectonic processes. Within that category, subjective credibilities of individual sets of sources could be assigned according to the credibility and applicability of each tectonic process.

The remaining zonation methods might be given credibilities according to the following line of argument—which, again, is presented merely as an example. Historical seismicity indicates where crustal stresses have been sufficient to generate earthquakes; crustal geology indicates, in a general way, where crustal structures (faults) might be uniformly distributed. These are equally justifiable bases for drawing area sources, and each might be judged to be twice as credible as the hypothesis that earthquakes are equally likely to occur anyplace. In summary, for this example only, the subjective credibilities would be as follows:

Sources based on tectonic processes	0.5
Sources based on historical seismicity	0.2
Sources based on crustal geology	0.2
Sources based on uniform hazard concepts	0.1
Total	1.0

For the tectonic process method, several sets of sources might be devised, each set having its own subjective credibility; the total credibility for these sets would sum to 0.5. Similarly, other methods might be represented by several sets of sources. This method of deriving credibilities is rather subjective. The credibilities are derived from the relative credibilities of different lines of scientific reasoning, and a fundamental tenet of seismic hazard and risk analysis is that better analyses and better decisions result when these credibilities are identified explicitly and assigned quantitatively. To be sure, *any* analysis of seismic hazard will assign subjective credibilities to scientific hypotheses, and, in the extreme case, a deterministic assessment will assign a credibility of unity to a preferred hypothesis and zero to others. As long as reasonable credibilities (not near 0 or 1) are assigned to alternative seismic sources, the total hazard estimation often is not highly sensitive to the exact choice of subjective credibilities for each zonation method.

Deriving seismic sources and quantitative credibilities that are based on different principles or a different expert judgment is useful for several reasons. First, it forces professionals to look explicitly at *all* methods of drawing seismic sources; if one or more methods are rejected, then they must be deliberate about the reasons. Second, it forces them to identify explicitly why they believe that certain methods are more capable of delineating future earthquake locations, and this exercise may reveal innate biases. Finally, the use of quantitative credibilities with justification allows the assessment to be reviewed by others, thereby adding credibility (of a different form) to the interpretations, even if the reviewer disagrees with them.

A few comments about the uniform seismic source concept are appropriate here. This method consists of drawing a single source for an entire area and assuming that the seismicity within it will be uniformly distributed in location, with the same magnitude distribution throughout. Such a distribution would appear highly unlikely; future seismicity would not be expected to exhibit such characteristics, even over the long term. However, this method also represents the concept that tectonic structures (on which future earthquakes will occur) exist in specific locations, but the locations are unknown. The uniform method is equivalent (with respect to mean hazard) to defining 100 sources representing possible structures, drawing these sources to cover the entire region, and assigning each a relative credibility of 0.01. Note, however, that the uniform source represents with U_R what is actually U_K. In a hazard assessment, the concept of a uniform seismic source may be quite useful. In the earlier example that used four methods of deriving seismic sources, it would be said that the first three specific methods (tectonic processes, historical seismicity, and crustal geology) have only a 90% credibility. There is a 10% chance that future seismicity may, because of processes that have not yet been recognized, occur in sources that have not yet been delineated, and no one knows where those sources might be.

Finally, one method of delineating the locations of future earthquakes is to avoid focusing on geologic and tectonic questions and instead "rebroadcast" historical seismicity—that is, assume that earthquakes will occur in the future where they have occurred in the past. Sometimes error terms are added to the locations of past events to reflect some uncertainty in their past and future locations. The U.S. Geological Survey (USGS) has used this method in calculating national hazard maps for the United States (USGS 2001). In the context of deriving area sources on the basis of all the data available (see the list of data and interpretations near the beginning of this section), this method is the simplest. Often, historical methods of this type result in hazard estimates that are similar, on average, to estimates based on more detailed geologic, geophysical, and tectonic interpretation. This is so because, in most applications, activity rates are derived from historical seismicity. All methods will generally indicate a higher hazard where rates have been high in the past. The key difference is that historical methods will miss regions where conditions are conducive to moderate-to-large earthquakes but where such earthquakes have not occurred historically. These regions will be identified by source methods that include geology, geophysics, and tectonics, at least insofar as those fields of study are reliable guides to understanding seismicity.

To make the best, most scientifically defensible estimates of seismic hazard, it is important to use *all* knowledge about earthquakes and tectonic processes, not just the historical seismicity. Here again the *use* of seismic hazard estimates to make design or mitigation decisions is critical: many decisions are important enough that they deserve, and should be defended by, the best scientific interpretations that can be prepared. In particular, detailed source derivations are necessary for critical engineering facilities such as power plants, dams, major bridges, tunnels, and large commercial facilities.

3.2 Earthquake Magnitude and Magnitude Scales

The second step in modeling seismicity is estimating the size of future earthquakes. The single most commonly used descriptor of an earthquake's size is its magnitude. Since the development of the first magnitude scale by Charles Richter (1935), this parameter has been adopted for a variety of uses, both well- and ill-conceived. The current importance of earthquake magnitude in seismic hazard studies should be evident; in the future, this descriptor will be useful as a baseline, comparative tool, even as more elegant and accurate descriptions of earthquake sources become available.

Richter's original magnitude scale is now known as the "local magnitude" scale. It was devised and calibrated to observations on a specific instrument (a Wood-Anderson torsional seismometer with an 0.8-sec. natural period and near-critical damping) and was intended for use in Southern California.

Since that scale was devised, other magnitude scales have been developed over the years to respond to different problems in seismology. Table 2 summarizes some of these magnitude scales, the ground motion period to which each scale is sensitive, and the saturation level of each scale (the approximate level at which observations are bounded for each scale as a result of physical properties of wave generation and instrument response).

Figure 4 (Boore and Joyner 1982) illustrates how these magnitude measures compare. Note that the saturation levels in Figure 4 differ in detail from those described in Table 2. Saturation of magnitude occurs because the energy in ground shaking saturates; that is, for large earthquakes, the ground motion energy recorded at one location does not continue to increase as the earthquake rupture area increases, except for very-long-period motion. Thus an earthquake with an 800-km rupture might be recorded as having the same magnitude as an event with a 400-km rupture. This effect has been estimated empirically, leading different researchers to observe different saturation levels.

Preference for the moment magnitude scale has grown in recent years, for several important reasons. Fundamentally, it is a measure of earthquake size that can be related to physical parameters of an earthquake such as the amount of fault slip and the energy radiated by seismic waves. The other magnitude scales have at most only an empirical tie to the physical process. Furthermore, moment magnitude is a measure (in concept) of a wave with an infinite period and

Table 2. Magnitude scales.

Designation	Symbol	Period (sec.)[a]	Saturation Level	Reference
Local magnitude	M_L	0.8	~ 6.8	Richter (1935)
Body-wave magnitude (short period)	m_b	1	~ 7	See, e.g., Kanamori (1983)
Body-wave magnitude (long period)	m_B	> 5	~ 8	Gutenberg (1945a)
Body-wave magnitude[b]	m_{bLg}, m_{Lg}	1	~ 7	Nuttli (1983)
Surface-wave magnitude	M_S	20	~ 8.3	Gutenberg (1945b)
Energy magnitude	M_e	4	None	Kanamori (1977)
Duration magnitude, coda magnitude	m_d, m_c	All	N/A[c]	Real and Teng (1973)
Moment magnitude	$\mathbf{M}$, M_w	4	None	Hanks and Kanamori (1979)

a   Approximate period of ground motion to which scale is sensitive
b   Body-wave magnitude determined from higher-mode (L_g) surface waves
c   Not applicable. Duration magnitude scales are used to study small earth-
    quakes, generally below magnitude 4.

does not saturate because of seismograph limitations. The latter point is not reason in itself to prefer this scale over others for seismic hazard studies, if the purpose is to determine the hazard from high-frequency ground motion. On the contrary, the saturation characteristics of other magnitude scales may, in certain situations, help avoid problems in estimating maximum magnitudes. That is, if a fault can generate a magnitude near the saturation level for a particular scale, then it would be feasible to adopt that scale without any worry about the largest moment magnitude that is possible.

The term "Richter magnitude" is commonly used by the news media in reporting an earthquake's numerical size. This popularized term acknowledges Richter's pioneering connection to the earthquake magnitude scale, but it often blurs seismological correctness. When an earthquake occurs, seismologists typically report a local magnitude (M_L) for shocks below ~6.5 and surface-wave magnitude (M_S)

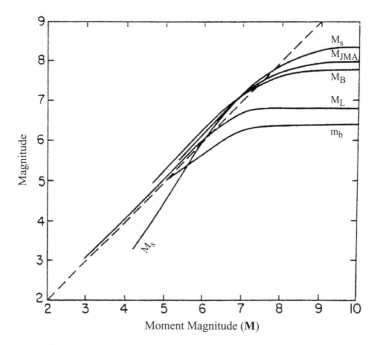

Figure 4. The relationship between moment magnitude and other magnitude scales (from Boore and Joyner, 1982). M_{JMA} is magnitude as reported by the Japan Meteorological Agency; other magnitudes are as listed in Table 2.

or moment magnitude (**M**) for larger values. Although the use of a uniform magnitude scale such as moment magnitude is desirable for all purposes, the popular use of "Richter magnitude" is likely to persist for some time. Coincidentally, as shown in Figure 4, moment magnitude is equivalent to Richter's local magnitude (M_L) below about magnitude 6½; for larger earthquakes, the advantage of using moment magnitude to convey true relative size is evident.

Whatever magnitude scale is chosen for seismic hazard analysis, it must be consistent with the method chosen for estimating earthquake ground motion (Section 4). That is, the seismicity description must be relevant to the estimation of earthquake effects. If seismicity data are available in several magnitude scales, then they must be converted to a single scale so that earthquake statistics will be meaningful.

Table 3 lists some relations that have been suggested among different magnitude scales, as well as among magnitude and seismic moment M_o, energy E, and epicentral MMI I_e. A note of caution is appropriate here: these are empirical, inexact relations. Any one earthquake may, upon comparison of magnitudes estimated independently on different scales, indicate values that are inconsistent with an average conversion equation. A directly determined magnitude value for an earthquake is preferred over an estimate derived from an alternative scale, unless the direct determination is suspect. Magnitudes estimated by converting values from other scales imply a larger uncertainty than if the preferred magnitude were obtained directly from instruments, and this uncertainty must be included when seismicity parameters are estimated.

This monograph does not further examine the differences among magnitude scales. The derivations that follow apply regardless of which scale is adopted for analysis. The magnitude symbols m and M used herein represent a specific or random value, respectively, of magnitude, without regard to any specific magnitude scale.

3.3 Magnitude Distributions

The final step in representing earthquake occurrences is to develop a distribution of earthquake magnitudes. Sections 3.3.1–3.3.6 discuss common magnitude distributions and some issues related to fitting these distributions to data.

3.3.1 Truncated Exponential Distribution Most applications of seismic hazard analysis use the exponential probability distribution (either alone or in conjunction with a "characteristic magnitude") to represent the relative frequency of different earthquake magnitudes. This is because magnitude-frequency statistics of historical earthquakes can often be represented by a truncated exponential distribution, and this function allows considerable analytical convenience in the hazard calculations.

The exponential distribution of earthquake magnitudes in a region can be expressed by the Richter (1958) relation:

$$\log_{10} n(m) = a - bm \tag{15}$$

or

$$n(m) = 10^a \, 10^{-bm} \tag{16}$$

Table 3. Examples of relations among various measures of earthquake size.

Region	Relation[a]	Range of Validity	Reference
Central U.S.	$I_e = 2m_b - 3.5$	$I_e \leq VII$	Nuttli (1974) Nuttli and Herrmann (1978)
Southeastern U.S.	$m_{bLg} = 1.13 \log_{10} A_{IV} - 0.45$	$\log_{10} A_{IV} < 4$	Nuttli et al (1979)
Southeastern U.S.	$m_{bLg} = 3.25 - 0.25 \log_{10} A_f + 0.098 (\log_{10} A_f)^2$	$\log_{10} A_f < 6$	Nuttli et al (1979)
Central U.S.	$m_{bLg} = 2.65 + 0.098 \log_{10} A_f + 0.054 (\log_{10} A_f)^2$	$\log_{10} A_f \leq 6$	Nuttli and Zollweg (1974)
Central U.S.	$M_S = 1.59\, m_{bLg} - 3.6$	$2.4 \leq M_S \leq 5.0$	Nuttli and Zollweg (1974)
Southern California	$\log_{10} M_o = 1.97 \log_{10} A_{VI} - 2.55$	$10^{23} < M_o < 10^{28}$ dyne-cm	Hanks et al (1975)
Southern California	$\log_{10} E = 2.0\, M_L + 8.1$	$2.0 \leq M_L \leq 7.0$	Thatcher and Hanks (1973)
California	$\mathbf{M} = 2/3 \log_{10} M_o - 10.7$	All values	Hanks and Kanamori (1979)
California	$\log_{10} E = 11.8 + 1.5\, M_S$	All values	Richter (1958)
Worldwide	$M_R^b = 1.3 + 0.6\, I_e$	$3.4 \leq M_R \leq 6.7$	Gutenberg and Richter (1942)
California	$M_R^b = 1 + 2/3\, I_e$	$4.5 \leq M_R \leq 7.6$	Gutenberg and Richter (1956)
California	$\log_{10} M_o^c = 17.53 + .63\, M_L + .10\, M_L^2$	$0 \leq M_L \leq 7$	Hanks and Boore (1984)
Northeastern North America	$m_{bLg} = 0.49\, I_e + 1.66$	$V \leq I_e \leq IX$	Street and Turcotte (1977)
Northeastern North America	$m_{bLg} = 1.13 \log_{10} A_{IV} - 0.32$	$A_{IV} \geq 10,000\ km^2$	Street and Turcotte (1977)

Table 3. *Continued.* Examples of relations among various measures of earthquake size.

Region	Relation[a]	Range of Validity	Reference
Utah	$m_b = 4.68 - 0.70 M_L + 0.15 M_L^2$	$3.2 \leq M_L \leq 6.0$	Griscom and Arabasz (1979)
California	$M = -3.02 + 1.74 \log A_f$	$4.5 \leq M \leq 8$	Hanks and Johnston (1992)
Global stable continental region	$\log M_o = 47.34 - 10.81 \log A_f + 1.17 \log^2 A_f$	$30,000 < A_f < 10,000,000$	Johnston (1994)
Global stable continental region	$\log M_o = 20.94 + 0.36 \log A_{VI} + 0.14 \log^2 A_{VI}$	$20 \leq A_{VI} \leq 2,000,000$	Johnston (1994)
Global stable continental region	$M = 1.14 + 0.24 m_{Lg} + 0.09333 m_{Lg}^2$	$3.1 < m_{Lg} < 7.3$	Johnston (1996)
California	$M = -3.02 + 1.74 \log A_f$	$20,000 \leq A_f \leq 2,000,000$	Hanks and Johnston (1992)
California	$M = 2.38 + 0.96 \log A_{VI}$	$3,000 \leq A_f \leq 600,000$	Hanks and Johnston (1992)
Eastern North America	$M = -0.39 + 0.98 m_b$ $M = 2.715 - 0.277 m_b + 0.127 m_b$	$m_b \leq 5.5$ $m_b > 5.5$	Atkinson and Boore (1995)
Eastern North America	$m_b = -10.23 + 6.105 M - 0.7632 M^2 + 0.03436 M^3$	$5 \leq m_b \leq 7.3$	EPRI (1993)

[a] I_e is MMI in the epicentral region, A_f is felt area in km^2, A_α is area within MMI α isoseismal in km^2, and E is radiated energy in ergs. See Table 2 for definitions of other symbols.

[b] "Richter magnitude" M_R in these equations is essentially M_S for values $\geq 6\frac{1}{2}$ and M_L for values $< 6\frac{1}{2}$.

[c] Quadratic fit to graphical data presented in reference

37

where n is the number of earthquakes of magnitude m or greater per unit of time, and a and b are constants. (Lowercase n is used here, in contrast to the original Richter uppercase notation, to be consistent with this monograph's notation scheme wherein uppercase letters designate random variables). For seismic hazard analysis, this is usually expressed in the equivalent form:

$$n(m) = v_o e^{-\beta m} \tag{17}$$

where $v_o = 10^a$ is the number of earthquakes per unit of time with $m \geq 0$, and $\beta = b \ln 10 \simeq 2.3b$. Often, a lower-bound m_{min} other than magnitude 0 is used; the equivalent expression is

$$n(m) = v_{m_{min}} e^{-\beta(m-m_{min})} \quad m_{min} \leq m < \infty \tag{18}$$

Equation 18 consists of $v_{m_{min}}$, the number of earthquakes per unit of time with $m \geq m_{min}$ (the mean activity rate for the seismic source being considered), and the complementary cumulative function $G_M(m)$ for earthquake magnitude:

$$G_M(m) = e^{-\beta(m-m_{min})} \quad m_{min} \leq m < \infty \tag{19}$$

for which the corresponding density and cumulative distribution functions are

$$f_M(m) = \beta e^{-\beta(m-m_{min})} \quad m_{min} \leq m < \infty \tag{20}$$

$$F_M(m) = 1 - \beta e^{-\beta(m-m_{min})} \quad m_{min} \leq m < \infty \tag{21}$$

The density function (equation 20) is $P[\bar{s}]$ in equation 4 when the source descriptor is earthquake magnitude.

In most seismic hazard analyses, the magnitude distribution is truncated at an upper-bound value m_{max}. This truncation may arise because the magnitude scale saturates (Table 3) or, more often, because it is felt that the seismogenic or seismotectonic zone in question cannot generate magnitudes above m_{max}. The best method of incorporating this upper-bound magnitude is to truncate and renormalize the probability density function, so that

$$f_M(m) = k\beta e^{-\beta(m-m_{min})} \quad m_{min} \leq m \leq m_{max} \tag{22}$$

where

$$k = [1 - e^{-\beta(m_{max} - m_{min})}]^{-1} \qquad (23)$$

The corresponding cumulative and complementary-cumulative distribution functions are

$$F_M(m) = k - ke^{-\beta(m - m_{min})} \qquad m_{min} \le m \le m_{max} \qquad (24)$$

$$G_M(m) = 1 - k + ke^{-\beta(m - m_{min})} \qquad m_{min} \le m \le m_{max} \qquad (25)$$

Some researchers have proposed truncating $F_M(m)$ instead of $f_M(m)$. This would require adding a delta function to $f_M(m)$ at m_{max}, which would represent a simple characteristic earthquake model. A characteristic earthquake model is better derived from geological or other considerations, as discussed below. Unless there are specific reasons to reject it, the truncated, renormalized density function (equation 22) is the preferred method of incorporating an upper-bound magnitude.

If equation 18 is modified to incorporate the upper bound, then the number of earthquakes $n(m)$ with magnitude $\ge m$ per unit of time is expressed as

$$n(m) = \nu_{m_{min}}[1 - k + ke^{-\beta(m - m_{min})}] \qquad m_{min} \le m \le m_{max} \qquad (26)$$

and this is the most common representation of the exponential magnitude distribution in a seismic source. The lower bound, m_{min}, is chosen on the basis of the minimum magnitude that will cause damage or loss and that must be considered for risk mitigation decisions. The remaining three parameters, ($\nu_{m_{min}}$, β, and m_{max}) must be estimated. In virtually all cases, except where extraordinarily long earthquake histories are available, historical seismicity is insufficient to estimate m_{max}. This statement also applies to the estimation of U_K in m_{max}. Instead, m_{max} and its distribution must be estimated by using geologic evidence (length of faults or tectonic structures), geophysical data (inferences about possible crustal stress), analogies to similar tectonic regimes, or other methods (including increasing the maximum historical earthquake by an amount based on professional judgment).

Historical seismicity is generally used to estimate the seismicity rate $\nu_{m_{min}}$ and β. Methods for doing so are described below. Regardless of how $\nu_{m_{min}}$ and β are estimated, the fitted distribution should always be compared graphically with the data. One way to do this is to plot the observed number (per unit of time) of earthquakes of magnitude m or greater versus m and then compare this plot with the fitted distribution (equation 26). An additional comparison can be made by plotting the observed *frequency* statistics (the number of earthquakes per unit of time in specific magnitude intervals) and comparing the fitted distribution to these statistics. This comparison is particularly appropriate if frequency statistics have been used to estimate parameters $v_{m_{min}}$ and β. The *predicted* frequency of magnitudes n_p in an interval Δm centered on m is (from equation 26)

$$n_p(m) = n(m - \Delta m/2) - n(m + \Delta m/2)$$

$$= v_{m_{min}} k e^{-\beta(m - m_{min})}(e^{\beta \Delta m/2} - e^{-\beta \Delta m/2}) \qquad (27)$$

To a reasonable approximation, the difference of exponentials in the above equation is equal to $\beta \Delta m$ (for typical applications, $b \simeq 0.9$ so that $\beta \simeq 2.07$ and $\Delta m \simeq 0.6$, and the error involved in this approximation is only 7%).[2] Making this approximation and taking logarithms of equation 27 gives

$$\ln n_p(m) = \alpha - \beta(m - m_{min}) \qquad (28)$$

or

$$\log_{10} n_p(m) = a' - b(m - m_{min}) \qquad (29)$$

where $\alpha = \ln(v_{m_{min}} k \Delta m \beta)$ and $a' = \log_{10}(v_{m_{min}} k \Delta m \beta)$. The logarithmic relationship between $n_p(m)$ and m makes the comparison of frequency data and equations straightforward. Frequency data are plotted on semilogarithmic axes (logarithmic frequency versus magnitude) at the *center* of the magnitude intervals used, and the fitted equation is plotted with $n_p(m_{min}) = 10^{a'}$ and slope $-b$.

As a practical matter, sometimes $b \simeq 0.8$, so that $\beta \simeq 1.84$; $m_{max} \gg m_{min}$, so that $k \simeq 1$; and Δm is about 0.6. When this is so, $k \Delta m \beta$ is close to 1, and as a result the intercept of the frequency distribution $n_p(m_{min})$ is close to the rate of earthquake activity $v_{m_{min}} = n(m_{min})$. That is, the frequency of earthquakes in the interval $m_{min} \pm \Delta m/2$ is approximately equal to the frequency of earthquakes of magnitude m_{min} or greater. This is not a general result; it depends on the conditions stated above.

---

[2] Typically, M is proportional to $\sim 0.6 I_e$, as shown in Table 3. Most catalogs contain many earthquakes for which M has been estimated from I_e, so choosing $\Delta m = 0.6$ avoids the condition in which some bins have low or high counts just because of a discrete intensity scale.

3.3.2 Fitting Truncated Exponential Distributions to Data

Several methods are available to fit parameters of the exponential distribution to data. The most appropriate method is one that accounts for magnitude data represented as numbers of events in magnitude intervals (this is the usual representation of historical seismicity) and also accounts for zero observations.

One approach used by investigators is least-squares regression analysis. It consists of representing historical seismicity as the annual occurrence rate for selected magnitude intervals or the exceedance rate for prescribed magnitudes and fitting constants in equation 15 to these data. Several variations of least-squares regression analysis are possible, including regressions on frequency or cumulative data and weighting or not weighting the observed frequency at each magnitude level by the number of observations. There are many objections to using regression analysis for these applications. When regression analysis is applied to cumulative data, the assumption of independent observations is violated, because rates at lower magnitudes include events observed at higher magnitudes. For both cumulative and frequency data, the observations do not follow a Gaussian distribution, but this distribution is an underlying assumption of least-squares regression. Applying the logarithmic recurrence relation (equation 15) cannot account for zero observations, either above a given magnitude or in a specific interval. For all these reasons, least-squares regression analysis should be avoided.

A better approach to estimating β and $\nu_{m_{min}}$ is the maximum-likelihood method. This method accounts for data represented in magnitude intervals and for zero observations. If a complete description of z historical earthquake magnitudes $m_1, m_2, \dots m_z$ all $\geq m_{min}$ is available for some representative time interval, then the likelihood function for β is defined as

$$l(\beta \mid m_1, m_2, \dots m_z) = P[m_1, m_2, \dots m_z \mid \beta] \qquad (30)$$

Under the usual assumptions that successive earthquakes and their magnitudes are independent, that there is no upper bound, and that equation 20 is the density function for magnitude, the likelihood function is

$$l(\beta) = \prod_i \beta \exp[-\beta(m_i - m_{min})] \qquad (31)$$

41

which can be expressed as

$$l(\beta) = \beta^z \exp[-\beta \sum_{i=1}^{z} (m_i - m_{\min})]$$ (32)

Taking the derivative of $l(\beta)$ with respect to β, equating this to 0 to maximize the likelihood function, and solving for β leads to the simple expression

$$\beta = (\bar{m} - m_{\min})^{-1}$$ (33)

where $\bar{m}$ is the average magnitude of the data. This provides an easy, approximate check on a value of β calculated from a computer program that accounts for other assumptions, as discussed below.

When an upper-bound magnitude $m_{\max}$ is introduced, equation 22 gives the appropriate density function for magnitude. Substituting this into equation 30 and equating $dl/d\beta$ to 0 leads to

$$\frac{1}{\beta} = \bar{m} - m_{\min} + \frac{(m_{\max} - m_{\min})e^{-\beta(m_{\max} - m_{\min})}}{1 - e^{-\beta(m_{\max} - m_{\min})}}$$ (34)

Equation 34 is solved recursively for the maximum-likelihood value of β. When $m_{\max}$ is more than about 2 magnitude units above $m_{\min}$, the maximum-likelihood value of β from equation 34 is close to that for the unbounded case.

The maximum-likelihood value of the activity rate $v_{m_{\min}}$ can be assessed once a distribution of earthquake occurrences in time is assumed. Under the Poisson assumption that successive earthquake occurrences are independent in time, and for z events observed during time t, the likelihood function for $v_{m_{\min}}$ is

$$l(v_{m_{\min}}|z \text{ events in } t) = P[z \text{ events in } t|v_{m_{\min}}]$$ (35)

or

$$l(v_{m_{\min}}|z \text{ events in } t) = \frac{(v_{m_{\min}}t)^z e^{-v_{m_{\min}}t}}{z!}$$ (36)

Equating $dl/dv_{m_{\min}}$ to 0 leads to the result

$$v_{m_{\min}} = z/t$$ (37)

which says that the most likely value for $v_{m\text{min}}$ is the observed rate of activity. This result holds for the Poisson process and for a wide variety of other distributions of earthquake occurrences in time. For example, many models (including chaotic processes) are consistent with the assumptions that an earthquake may occur with probability p in time t', the probability of multiple occurrences in t' is negligible, and successive main shock occurrences are independent. Under these assumptions, the number of earthquakes is distributed according to a binomial distribution. Then the likelihood function is

$$l(p|z \text{ events in } t) = (p)^z (1 - p)^{n-z} \tag{38}$$

where $n = t/t'$ is the number of discrete time periods in t. Equating dl/dp to 0 leads to

$$p = z/n \text{ and } v_{m\text{min}} = p/t' = z/t \tag{39}$$

which is the same result as for equation 37.

In practical applications, several complications usually arise. Data are often available as independent magnitude estimates for each event, but they are summarized as the numbers of earthquakes (per decade, for example) in different magnitude intervals. A typical case is one in which magnitudes for preinstrumental earthquakes have been estimated from reported intensities, and the magnitude intervals for the summary are chosen to represent one-unit intensity increments. For data in magnitude intervals, the maximum-likelihood β-value solutions (equations 33 and 34) for exact magnitude data are only approximate. The approximation is acceptable when the magnitude interval is small, but the interval may be as large as 0.67 when magnitudes are estimated from intensities (typical relations are described in Section 3.5).

A second practical complication is that the *periods of completeness* are different for each magnitude interval: data for smaller magnitudes may be complete for years or decades, but data for larger magnitudes may be complete for several centuries. The reason for this is, of course, sociological. Large historical shocks affected a wide area and would have been recorded as an extraordinary phenomenon even several centuries ago. Small local earthquakes might have affected a sparsely populated area and might not have been recorded in local reports, or those reports might have been lost or overlooked in a historical data search. A derivation of the maximum likelihood values for β and v is given in Appendix A for this important case.

An important factor to recognize in estimating seismicity parameters is the uncertainty in the magnitude estimate for historical earthquakes, particularly preinstrumental shocks. These events may initially be characterized by the highest MMI value assessed for earthquake-related effects (see Section 3.6). The use of deterministic conversions from MMI values to m will underestimate the true activity rate, sometimes by a factor of 2 or more.

An example is useful to illustrate this effect. Suppose that the earthquake catalog in an area contains earthquakes designated solely by their epicentral intensity I_e and that the relationship between $\overline{m}$ (the mean magnitude) and I_e is

$$\overline{m} = 1.3 + 0.6\,I_e \qquad (40)$$

This relationship was developed by Gutenberg and Richter (1942) from worldwide data, as indicated in Table 3. There is considerable uncertainty (U_R) in the magnitude values for individual events when I_e is given, and a typical standard deviation is $\sigma_m = 0.6$. Under the assumptions that magnitudes are exponentially distributed with $\beta = 2$ and that equation 40 is used, intensities will also be exponentially distributed with $\beta_I = 2 \times 0.6 = 1.2$.[3]

A scientist or engineer may be interested in earthquakes with $m \geq 4.6$. Since there are earthquake data in the form of epicentral intensity I_e, $m = 4.6$ corresponds to I_e of MMI levels V–VI (or 5.5 on the arabic scale) when equation 40 is used. (Note that intensities are defined only for integer values, but decimal values are useful to illustrate quantitative points through examples). It is desirable to calculate the rate of events with $m > 4.6$ or $I_e > 5.5$.

Make the following assumptions:

- The original size measure available for each earthquake is epicentral intensity I_e, and earthquakes are distributed exponentially according to I_e.
- Magnitudes for each event when I_e is given follow a Gaussian distribution with mean $\overline{m}$ (from equation 40) and $\sigma_m = 0.6$.

---

3 This follows from a deterministic substitution of equation 40 into equation 17 for the number of earthquakes $\geq m$:

$$n(m) = \nu_o \exp(-\beta m)$$
$$n(I_e) = \nu_o \exp[-\beta(1.3 + 0.6I_e)]$$
$$ = \nu_o' \exp(-0.6\beta I_e)$$

where $\nu_o' = \nu_o \exp(-1.3\beta)$ is the number of earthquakes with $I_e \geq 0$.

With these assumptions, Table 4 summarizes the calculated statistics of 1,000 earthquakes with MMI values of III–VIII and intervals whose width is 0.2 MMI units. Column 1 indicates epicentral intensity I_e for the center of each intensity interval, column 2 indicates the corresponding value of mean magnitude $\overline{m}$, and column 3 shows the number of earthquakes (out of 1,000) that are expected in that interval. These numbers were calculated from equation 17, with $\nu_o = 270,426$ and $\beta = 2$, which gives $n(m \geq 2.8) = 1,000$. For each $\overline{m}$ and under the assumption of a Gaussian distribution with $\sigma_m = 0.6$, column 4 shows the probability that $m > 4.6$, and column 5 indicates the expected number of earthquakes with $m > 4.6$ (column 3 times column 4) given that value of I_e and $\overline{m}$. The total at the bottom of column 5 is the total expected number of events with $m > 4.6$ (from all intensity values). This is the "exact" estimate of $n(m > 4.6)$, given the two assumptions stated above. Dividing the total by a time period would give the activity rate for earthquakes with $m > 4.6$.

Using a deterministic version of equation 40 would lead to counting only events with MMI $\geq$ VI as having $m > 4.6$, and these events are indicated in column 6 of Table 4. The total of these events underestimates the true count (and the true activity rate) by a factor of more than 2.

A simple result, proposed first by Veneziano and Van Dyck (EPRI 1986), can accurately account for the effect of uncertainty in the estimated magnitude. This result consists of using, for statistical purposes, a magnitude (conventionally termed "m-star") calculated as

$$m^* = \overline{m} + 0.5\beta\sigma_m^2 \qquad (41)$$

where $\beta = b$ log 10 of the magnitude distribution. Magnitude m^* is estimated for each interval in column 7, and these magnitude values are used *as if there were no uncertainty in m^**, to calculate the number of events with $m^* > 4.6$. The number of such events is shown in column 8; the total closely matches the correct total at the bottom of column 5.

In an actual catalog, the use of equation 41 is straightforward. Magnitude m^* is estimated by using equation 41 for each event, then events are counted in specific m^* intervals and divided by the period of completeness to estimate the rate of activity in that interval. The intervals should be centered on m^* values converted from integer MMI values. This accommodates various conversion methods and

Table 4. Summary of the expected number of earthquakes when intensity is converted to magnitude.

MMI	1 I_e	2 $\overline{m}$	3[a] $n[I_e,\overline{m}]$	4 $P[m > 4.6]$	5 "Exact" $n[m > 4.6]$	6 "Deterministic" $n[\overline{m} > 4.6]$	7[b] m^*	8 "Approximate" $n[m^* > 4.6]$
III	2.6	2.86	213.5	.002	.4	.0	3.22	.0
	2.8	2.98	168.0	.003	.6	.0	3.34	.0
	3.0	3.10	132.1	.006	.8	.0	3.46	.0
	3.2	3.22	103.9	.011	1.1	.0	3.58	.0
	3.4	3.34	81.8	.018	1.5	.0	3.70	.0
IV	3.6	3.46	64.3	.029	1.8	.0	3.82	.0
	3.8	3.58	50.6	.045	2.3	.0	3.94	.0
	4.0	3.70	39.8	.067	2.7	.0	4.06	.0
	4.2	3.82	31.3	.097	3.0	.0	4.18	.0
	4.4	3.94	24.6	.136	3.3	.0	4.30	.0
V	4.6	4.06	19.4	.184	3.6	.0	4.42	.0
	4.8	4.18	15.2	.242	3.7	.0	4.54	.0
	5.0	4.30	12.0	.309	3.7	.0	4.66	12.0
	5.2	4.42	9.4	.382	3.6	.0	4.78	9.4
	5.4	4.54	7.4	.460	3.4	.0	4.90	7.4
VI	5.6	4.66	5.8	.540	3.1	5.8	5.02	5.8
	5.8	4.78	4.6	.618	2.8	4.6	5.14	4.6
	6.0	4.90	3.6	.691	2.5	3.6	5.26	3.6
	6.2	5.02	2.8	.758	2.2	2.8	5.38	2.8
	6.4	5.14	2.2	.816	1.8	2.2	5.50	2.2

Table 4. *Continued.* Summary of the expected number of earthquakes when intensity is converted to magnitude.

	1	2	3[a]	4	5	6	7[b]	8
MMI	I_e	$\bar{m}$	$n[I_e,\bar{m}]$	$P[m > 4.6]$	"Exact" $n[m > 4.6]$	"Deterministic" $n[\bar{m} > 4.6]$	m^*	"Approximate" $n[m^* > 4.6]$
VII	6.6	5.26	1.8	.864	1.5	1.8	5.62	1.8
	6.8	5.38	1.4	.903	1.2	1.4	5.74	1.4
	7.0	5.50	1.1	.933	1.0	1.1	5.86	1.1
	7.2	5.62	.9	.955	.8	.9	5.98	.9
	7.4	5.74	.7	.971	.7	.7	6.10	.7
VIII	7.6	5.86	.5	.982	.5	.5	6.22	.5
	7.8	5.98	.4	.989	.4	.4	6.34	.4
	8.0	6.10	.3	.994	.3	.3	6.46	.3
	8.2	6.22	.3	.997	.3	.3	6.58	.3
	8.4	6.34	.2	.998	.2	.2	6.70	.2
Totals:			1,000		54.9[c]	26.6[d]		55.4[d]

[a] Calculated from equation 17: 270,426 exp(-2m)

[b] Calculated from equation 41: $m^* = \bar{m} + 0.5(2)(.6)^2$

[c] Exact total of expected number of earthquakes with m > 4.6

[d] Approximations to total expected number of earthquakes with m > 4.6

uncertainties (from I_e, felt area, other magnitude scales, and so on) in a unified procedure that produces unbiased estimates of both activity rates and b values. Veneziano and Van Dyck (EPRI 1986) also provide a procedure for incorporating the uncertainty caused by direct estimates of an instrumental magnitude. This procedure uses an m^* calculated as in equation 41 but with the sign changed. Because instrumental values of σ_m are generally small, this correction is small, and it is accurate to use $m^* = \overline{m}$ for direct instrumental measurements of the desired magnitude values.

Table 4 illustrates why deterministic conversions from intensity to magnitude underestimate the true rate of activity. As shown in column 4, the MMI = IV events, for example, with $\overline{m}$ in the 3.4–4.0 range, indicate a small but important probability that the actual magnitude exceeds 4.6 (from 0.029 to 0.136, depending on $\overline{m}$). The large number of MMI = IV earthquakes means that there will be a significant number with $m > 4.6$ (column 5 of Table 4). Of course, there also are earthquakes with $\overline{m} > 4.6$ and a small probability that $m < 4.6$, but there are fewer of these larger earthquakes, which results in an underestimation of the total rate if a deterministic conversion is used.

In an actual application, the effect of using m^* instead of $\overline{m}$ will usually be less than a factor of 2, because not all events in the catalog will be estimated from I_e. However, other conversion formulas have their own uncertainties in estimating m, and it is important to account for these in estimating activity rates and b values.

As an example, the effect of m^* can be observed in the seismicity of the New England coast, as shown in Figure 5 (Seeber and Armbruster 1991). This is an area of moderate seismicity, by eastern U.S. standards, and it has a history of earthquakes dating from 1627 (Seeber and Armbruster 1991). Summaries of historical seismicity for the area are shown in Table 5 (for magnitude $\overline{m}$) and Table 6 (for magnitude m^*). For this example, historical earthquakes with an epicentral intensity I_e but no independent magnitude assessment were converted to a body-wave magnitude by using $m_b = 0.7 + 0.6\,I_e$ (Table 3). This results in magnitude intervals of 0.6 magnitude units.

Note that the number of earthquakes per unit of time in each magnitude interval decreases as one goes back in history. This is a common observation, the result of incomplete reporting for the early years and for the lower magnitude levels. Years for which the reporting is considered complete are indicated in the table; choosing these intervals is subjective.

Demographic data, if available, should be considered in choosing completeness intervals. The completeness interval for any given magnitude or intensity level should be equal to or longer than intervals for smaller earthquakes, because larger shocks affect larger areas and are more likely to be reported and documented in the earlier years. For some magnitudes, intervals different from those in Tables 5 and 6 could be chosen without greatly affecting the observed rate of earthquake occurrence. Where a real uncertainty exists for appropriate periods of completeness, several analyses should be conducted by using different completeness periods to ascertain the effect on seismic hazard and on decisions resulting from the hazard analysis. Finally, note that less than half of the earthquakes in the entire historical record are used in the final analysis to select parameter values; this is not an uncommon fraction of data to use in determining seismicity parameters.

Figure 6 shows the annual frequency of earthquakes of magnitude m or greater, plotted against magnitude m. Two sets of data are shown: the data labeled "$\overline{m}$" use the expected magnitude and earthquake counts summarized in Table 4, and the data labeled "m^*" use earthquakes summarized in Table 5. In both cases, the data are plotted at the lower end of the interval, because Figure 6 represents cumulative frequencies (the annual number of events $> m$). Error bars are shown corresponding to $\pm 1\sigma$, where σ in the number of events was calculated as $\sqrt{n}/t$, consistent with a Poisson process.

The comparison in Figure 6 shows the effect of using m^* instead of $\overline{m}$ in the rate and b-value calculations. Magnitude m^* gives higher rates predominantly for smaller events where only the epicentral intensity is valuable for magnitude estimations. For older, larger earthquakes, more data are usually available (for example, the felt area is often reported), and these events are studied in more detail, thus the uncertainty in m often is lower. As a result, the m^* analysis, which is more accurate, gives a steeper slope than the $\overline{m}$ analysis. This is a common but not universal result.

These comparisons illustrate typical results from the maximum-likelihood procedure for estimating seismicity rates and b values. Although the process of fitting rates and b values can be automated to a considerable degree, it is strongly recommended that the analyst plot observations and mathematical fits to the observations. Many ideas for more appropriate analyses will result from such plots, including alternative intensity-to-magnitude conversions, magnitude

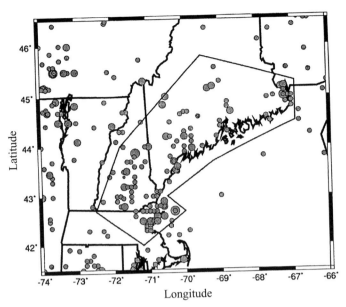

Figure 5. Historical seismicity in New England, 1670–1984; used for sample calculations. The dot size is proportional to magnitude (Seeber and Armbruster catalog, 1991).

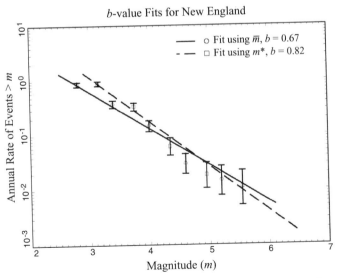

Figure 6. Maximum likelihood fits for New England m^* and $\bar{m}$ data.

Table 5. Historical earthquake summary for New England, using $\overline{m}$ conversion.

MMI	IV	V	VI	VII	VIII
Magnitude Range[a]	2.80–3.40	3.40–4.00	4.00–4.60	4.60–5.20	5.20–5.80
1620–1629	0	0	1	0	0
1630–1639	0	0	0	0	0
1640–1649	1	0	0	0	0
1650–1659	0	1	0	0	0
1660–1669	1	0	0	0	0
1670–1679	0	0	0	0	0
1680–1689	1	0	0	0	0
1690–1799	0	0	0	0	0
1700–1709	1	0	0	0	0
1710–1719	0	0	0	0	0
1720–1729	0	0	0	1[b]	0[b]
1730–1739	3	2	0	0	0
1740–1749	1	0	0	1	0
1750–1759	2	0	0	0	1
1760–1769	5	0	1	0	0
1770–1779	0	0	0	0	0
1780–1789	1	0	0	0	0
1790–1899	0	0	0	0	0
1800–1809	6	1	0	0	0
1810–1819	0	1	3	0	0
1820–1829	3	2	1	0	0
1830–1839	1	0	0	0	0
1840–1849	2	0	1	0	0
1850–1859	5	3	1	0	0
1860–1869	0	0	0	0	1
1870–1879	8[b]	1[b]	1[b]	0	0
1880–1889	11	4	1	0	0
1890–1899	2	1	2	0	0
1900–1909	3	3	1	0	1
1910–1919	7	2	2	0	0
1920–1929	14	4	1	0	0
1930–1939	3	2	0	0	0
1940–1949	3	1	3	0	1
1950–1959	2	1	1	1	0
1960–1969	3	3	1	0	0
1970–1979	1	2	1	0	0
1980–1984	0	4	0	1	0

[a] Body-wave magnitude $\overline{m}$ estimated from MMI for preinstrumental shocks by using $\overline{m} = 0.7 + 0.6\,I_e$

[b] First interval for which the earthquake count is considered complete

Table 6. Historical earthquake summary for New England, using m^* conversion.

MMI	IV	V	VI	VII	VIII
Magnitude Range[a]	3.15–3.75	3.75–4.35	4.35–4.95	4.95–5.55	5.55–6.15
1620–1629	0	0	1	0	0
1630–1639	0	0	0	0	0
1640–1649	1	0	0	0	0
1650–1659	0	1	0	0	0
1660–1669	1	0	0	0	0
1670–1679	0	0	0	0	0
1680–1689	1	0	0	0	0
1690–1799	0	0	0	0	0
1700–1709	1	0	0	0	0
1710–1719	0	0	0	0	0
1720–1729	0	0	0	1[b]	0[b]
1730–1739	5	0	0	0	0
1740–1749	1	0	1	0	0
1750–1759	2	0	0	0	1
1760–1769	5	0	1	0	0
1770–1779	0	0	0	0	0
1780–1789	1	0	0	0	0
1790–1899	0	0	0	0	0
1800–1809	6	1	0	0	0
1810–1819	0	4	0	0	0
1820–1829	3	3	0	0	0
1830–1839	1	0	0	0	0
1840–1849	2	1	0	0	0
1850–1859	6	3	0	0	0
1860–1869	0	0	0	0	1
1870–1879	8[b]	2[b]	0[b]	0	0
1880–1889	12	4	0	0	0
1890–1899	2	3	0	0	0
1900–1909	3	3	1	0	1
1910–1919	7	4	0	0	0
1920–1929	14	5	0	0	0
1930–1939	3	2	0	0	0
1940–1949	3	3	1	1	0
1950–1959	2	2	1	0	0
1960–1969	4	2	1	0	0
1970–1979	3	1	0	0	0
1980–1984	3	1	1	0	0

[a] Body-wave magnitude m^* estimated from the MMI for preinstrumental shocks by using equation 40

[b] First interval for which the earthquake count is considered complete

distributions, completeness intervals, and combinations of data from different sources.

3.3.3 Alternative Exponential-Type Magnitude Distributions

Several magnitude distributions other than the truncated exponential distribution (equations 22 through 25) are available for modeling earthquake magnitudes. These distributions, when plotted as the cumulative number of events (on a logarithmic scale) versus magnitude, have been used to account for the nonlinearity of earthquake magnitude statistics. Note that the truncated exponential distribution, when plotted in the complementary cumulative form of equation 25, exhibits nonlinearity as well. Alternative distributions may be useful to model magnitude scales that are nonlinear with respect to moment magnitude (see Figure 4). Appendix B describes several alternative distributions.

3.3.4 Characteristic Magnitude Distribution

A final magnitude distribution worth considering is that of "characteristic" earthquakes. Many faults, among them the San Andreas, in California exhibit seismicity and crustal strain, indicating that an exponential or other continuous distribution encompassing all magnitudes is not appropriate. The continuous distribution may be adequate for events up to, say, $m = 6$–7. Larger earthquakes may occur with a characteristic magnitude (say, $m = 7.5$–8) whose frequency of occurrence is higher than obtained by extrapolating from the smaller-magnitude earthquakes. In this case, two truncated exponential distributions could accurately model the understanding of future events: a distribution between $m_{min} = 5$ and $m_{max} = 7$ with a standard β value, and a separate distribution between $m_{min} = 7.5$ and $m_{max} = 8.0$ with $\beta = 0$ representing the equal likelihood of a characteristic event magnitude in that range. The rate $\nu_{m_{min}}$ for the first distribution would probably be computed from historical seismicity; the rate for the characteristic event might be estimated with paleoseismicity and crustal strain data along with substantial judgment. Characteristic earthquake distributions can and should be incorporated into seismic hazard calculations where they are thought to be appropriate.

One form of the characteristic magnitude model is illustrated in Figure 7 (Schwartz and Coppersmith 1984). In this form, the characteristic part of the distribution is 0.5 magnitude units wide. The frequency of the characteristic part of the distribution equals the frequency of the exponential part at $m = m_{max} - 1.5$. Note that the complementary cumulative distribution of the characteristic model is nonlinear on a semilog plot of frequency versus magnitude.

53

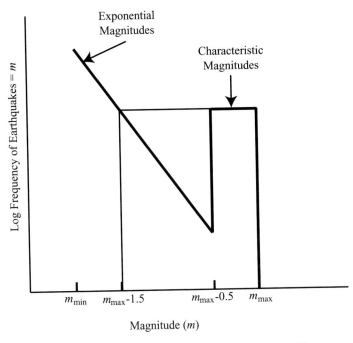

Figure 7. Characteristic magnitude model proposed by Schwartz and Coppersmith (1984).

Another form of the characteristic magnitude model includes no U_R in magnitude and assumes that all energy is released by earthquakes having the same magnitude. The USGS hazard map of California used this model for major faults. These faults, such as the San Andreas, were divided into segments, and various adjacent segments were combined and assumed to rupture with a characteristic magnitude that was estimated on the basis of the length of the combined segments. The USGS Working Group on California Earthquake Probabilities (WGCEP 1999) took a similar approach, using a mean magnitude for identified fault segments and an uncertainty of $\sigma = 0.12$.

The best magnitude distribution to adopt in any particular application depends on which magnitudes are most critical for the seismic hazard analysis and which ones therefore influence the seismic risk mitigation decision. One good way to understand this sensitivity is through deaggregation of the hazard, which is discussed in Section 5.

The idea is that, if magnitudes of about 7.5–8 cause the major contribution to seismic hazard, then there is no need to agonize over what distribution best fits magnitudes 5–6.5. The time required to select a multiparameter distribution, fit it to available data, and incorporate the distribution into the hazard calculations may be better spent on other aspects of the analysis. When the large magnitudes dominate the seismic hazard, and the truncated exponential distribution is suspected of being unrealistic, then alternative distributions should be investigated in depth. For most regions of the world, available data are insufficient to categorically accept or reject a given model; the best procedure is often to select several distributions that represent a range of interpretations, conduct the hazard analysis with each distribution, and examine the results. If the final hazard results are sensitive to the choice of distribution, then this sensitivity should become clear; a final result can be obtained by applying subjective weights to the distributions if the uncertainty (U_K) about the appropriate distribution cannot be resolved.

3.3.5 Clusters Moderate-to-large earthquakes sometimes occur in clusters—for example, in the central United States in 1811–12 and central Italy in 1997. In a given region, if an earthquake cluster is suspected that consists of multiple events with magnitude $> m$ in a short time period, then the rate v_m should represent the cluster's rate of occurrence. The hazard analysis will use $P[\bar{s}]$ in equation 4 to represent the probability of two events and their magnitudes, three events and their magnitudes, and so on. $P[l]$ in equation 4 will include the location probability for multiple events, and equation 4 will thereby include the hazard from clustered events. Often a model of clustered earthquakes will be given a credibility of less than 100%, because there is not 100% certainty that all moderate-to-large earthquakes will occur in clusters. To repeat previous advice, what is known about earthquake occurrences should guide the hazard analysis, not vice versa.

3.3.6 Foreshocks and Aftershocks An implicit assumption in deriving magnitude distributions is that earthquakes in a catalog are independent events. Clearly, foreshocks and aftershocks violate this assumption, so they are generally removed from the catalog before processing begins. Dependent events (foreshocks and aftershocks) can be treated with separate distributions, which will increase somewhat the frequency of occurrence of a seismic hazard. However, arguments against including such distributions are that (1) the magnitudes of foreshocks and aftershocks are by definition smaller than the main shock, and thus the associated motions will generally be smaller; (2) if a main shock damages an industrial facility, then the facility will be shut down, leading to less damage during aftershocks; and (3) structural damage ascertained via empirical data (including insurance payments) already includes the effects of dependent events, to the extent that they have caused additional damage during past earthquakes. As a result, the standard procedure in PSHA is to include only main shocks in deriving magnitude distributions.

3.4 Stress Drop and Seismic Moment

Although earthquake magnitude is the traditional measure of earthquake size, it leaves much to be desired. Other, more physical characteristics allow the linking of earthquake size with the amount of fault slip during events and with the associated ground motions. The two most important characteristics are stress drop and seismic moment. The former helps in understanding the ground motion generated during an earthquake (Section 4). The latter helps in estimating earthquake occurrence rates for a given slip rate on a fault, in conjunction with assumptions about the distribution of earthquake sizes.

The stress drop $\Delta\sigma$ is the change in average stress over the faulted surface during an earthquake. The *static* stress drop is a measure of this stress change from the condition before the earthquake occurs to the condition after the fault has ruptured. In the simplest representation of the faulting process, the fault rupture initiates at a single point and progresses across the fault surface (in two dimensions) until the driving stress is sufficiently low and the static friction across the unruptured surface is sufficiently high that the rupture can no longer propagate. The fault surface itself may be quite heterogeneous. In such a case, the stress across a fault surface will change dramatically as a function of time and of location on the surface during the rupture. At any point on the fault surface, the stress across the fault surface may increase as the rupture approaches and may reach its highest level just before rupture occurs at that point. As the rupture front passes, the stress will drop to a low level, and the fault may continue to move at some low-stress level for a few seconds. Finally, fault slip at the point will cease, and the stress may recover to some level that is slightly higher than the level during sliding. The difference between the maximum and minimum stress across the fault averaged over the whole fault surface is called the *dynamic* stress drop. Figure 8 illustrates static and dynamic stress drop. Note that only stress *differences* across the fault can be estimated from observations of earthquakes; *absolute* levels of stress cannot be determined from observations of the dynamics of faulting or the ground motion produced. Stress drops are conventionally expressed in units of bars, where one bar = 10^6 dyne/cm$^2 \simeq 1$ atmosphere of pressure, or in units of megapascals, where one MPa = 10 bars $\simeq$ 10 atmospheres of pressure. Although stress drop is easy to define, it is often difficult to measure unambiguously; examples are given in the discussion by Atkinson and Beresnev (1997). Figure 8 is very much a simplification: the stress history will vary significantly across the fault surface; this variation depends on the depth, locations of asperities, and general heterogeneities in the crust. Fault ruptures are complicated processes indeed.

Seismic moment is a representation of the forces in the earth's crust that are causing energy release during an earthquake. These forces, which vary in a complex way in space, can be simplified into an

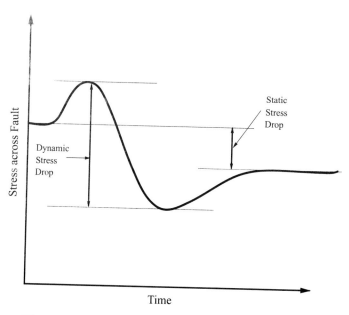

Figure 8. Stress across a fault at one location as an earthquake occurs.

equivalent double couple (Figure 9). At distances far from the source, the low-frequency displacement resulting from the complicated force pattern can be accurately approximated by this double-couple representation. This is because crustal earthquakes are an elastic rebound phenomenon caused by the release of shear stresses across a fault.

The moment from one couple of the pair is termed the seismic moment M_o, conventionally expressed in units of dyne-cm or Newton-meters. (In deference to the standard symbol for seismic moment, the use of M_o deviates from this monograph's practice of using uppercase letters for random variables). Seismic moment can be related to properties of the crust and of the faulting process by

$$M_o = \mu(rupture\ area)(average\ rupture\ displacement) \qquad (42)$$

where μ is shear rigidity of the crust (typically 3×10^{11} dyne/cm^2 or 3×10^{10} N/m^2), the rupture area is the entire rupture surface, and the rupture displacement is averaged over that surface.

Stress drop, particularly dynamic stress drop, is related to details of the faulting process and affects high-frequency characteristics of the generated ground motion. Thus an important advantage of using a stress-drop-seismic-moment representation of earthquake sources is that $\Delta\sigma$ and M_o provide a physical basis for estimating strong ground motion at both high and low frequencies, as described in Section 4. The more traditional use of magnitude alone requires empirical estimates of ground motion.

Seismic moment is a measure of the total energy release during an earthquake, which affects the long-period characteristics of ground motion. M_o is preferable to magnitude for expressing earthquake size, for several reasons. One reason is that M_o is an equivalent physical representation of the forces at work that cause earthquakes, whereas magnitude is solely a convenient relative scale relating the amplitudes of certain wave types or instrument responses to one another. Another reason is that the definition of seismic moment does not imply a saturation level, as do most magnitude scales. As a practical matter, this latter characteristic may be of limited benefit in seismic hazard applications, because the usual interest is in moderate-to-high-frequency (>1 Hz) aspects of the ground motion (with important exceptions for long-span bridges, highrise buildings, and base-isolated structures).

Fault Surface

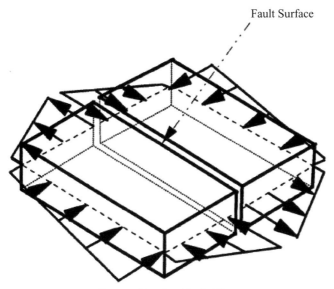

Forces Causing Fault Slip

Fault Surface

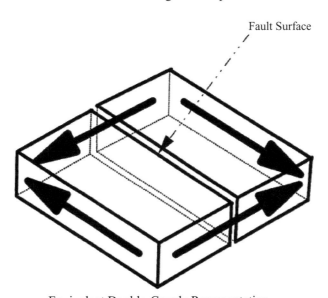

Equivalent Double-Couple Representation

Figure 9. Double-couple representation of crustal forces released during a strike-slip earthquake caused by the release of shear stresses on faults.

A benefit of characterizing earthquakes by their seismic moment is that estimates of total slip rate on a fault can be made and compared with independent estimates or observations. If a fault with area a_T is identified, then the total average rate of slip on the fault surface is (from equation 42)

$$\dot{s} = \dot{M}_o / \mu a_T \qquad (43)$$

where $\dot{M}_o$ is the rate of release of seismic moment. If a magnitude distribution and rate of occurrence have been observed for the same fault area, then these can be converted into $\dot{M}_o$ (as described below), $\dot{s}$ can be estimated, and this estimate can be compared with others—perhaps estimates made via paleoseismic, geologic, or geodetic measurements. Agreement will imply support for the resulting recurrence relationship; disagreement should prompt an examination of the assumptions and data for inconsistencies.

The typical relationship between M_o and m is

$$\log_{10} M_o = cm + d \qquad (44)$$

where, for moment magnitude **M** (in dyne-cm; see the 1979 Hanks and Kanamori relation in Table 2), $c = 1.5$ and $d = 16.05$. When a transformation of variables is used, the density function for seismic moment can be derived from the density function for magnitude (equation 22), yielding a geometric probability distribution:

$$f_{M_o}(M_o) = k \frac{\beta}{\gamma} \exp[\beta (m_{min} + d/c)] M_o^{-(1+\beta/\gamma)} \qquad (45)$$

where m_{min} is the minimum magnitude and $\gamma = c \ln 10$. The rate of release of seismic moment on the fault is computed as

$$\dot{M}_o = \int_{M_{o,min}}^{M_{o,max}} M_o \nu_{m_{min}} f_{M_o}(M_o) dM_o \qquad (46)$$

where $M_{o,min}$ and $M_{o,max}$ are the lower- and upper-bound seismic moments corresponding to m_{min} and m_{max}. Substituting the density function for M_o into equation 46 and integrating gives

$$\dot{M}_o = \frac{\nu_{m_{\min}} \, k\beta \exp[\beta(m_{\min} + d/c)]}{\gamma - \beta} \left(M_{o,\max}^{1 - \beta/\gamma} - M_{o,\min}^{1 - \beta/\gamma} \right)$$

(47)

where $\gamma \neq \beta$. Equation 47 implicitly assumes that all of the moment release comes from earthquakes between $m_{\min}$ and $m_{\max}$, even if $m_{\min}$ is significantly greater than 0, and this is a good approximation for typical b values of approximately 0.9. For example, when $b = 0.9$, 92% of the moment release comes from magnitudes between $m_{\max}$-2 and $m_{\max}$, and 98% comes from magnitudes between $m_{\max}$-3 and $m_{\max}$. For high b values or low $m_{\max}$ values, the analyst may wish to set $M_{o,\min} = 0$ in equation 47 to account for events with $m < m_{\min}$. If $\beta = 0$, such as for characteristic events within a range of 7.5–8, then the calculation of $\dot{M}_o$ simplifies to

$$\dot{M}_o = \frac{\nu_{m_{\min}}}{\gamma} \frac{M_{o,\max} - M_{o,\min}}{m_{\max} - m_{\min}}$$

(48)

(In equation 47, note that $k\beta$ goes to $[m_{\max}-m_o]^{-1}$ as β goes to 0). Suppose that β and $\nu_{m_{\min}}$ have been estimated from historical seismicity on a fault. With $\dot{M}_o$ from equation 48, the slip rate $\dot{s}$ in equation 43 can be estimated and compared with other estimates that might be available (for example, from stream offsets, geodetic measurements, or consideration of that particular fault and its relationship to crustal plate motions).

If the estimates differ, then several factors might have caused this. A long-term slip rate $\dot{s}$ computed from geologic data or crustal plate motion is a long-term average; the slip rate over several decades or centuries might vary substantially from this. For example, in the decades after a great earthquake, a large fraction of crustal stress may have been relieved, thus $\dot{s}$ may tend to be lower than its long-term average. The opposite may occur if the last earthquake on the fault occurred in the distant past. A complicating factor is that a substantial fraction of crustal deformation may occur aseismically, and thus the geologic slip rates would give upper bounds on the rate of earthquake occurrence.

If it is believed that the long-term slip rate will apply over the next few decades, then the historical seismicity may still underestimate this rate in cases where the historical data do not include the occurrence of a large earthquake. The concept of a characteristic earthquake becomes important in this case; the low-level historical seismicity may exhibit an exponential distribution with magnitude, but it cannot be used to estimate the recurrence of large events. In this case, the slip rate that is not explained by historical data can be ascribed to characteristic earthquakes; their rate of occurrence can be estimated by choosing a minimum and maximum size and a value for β and inverting equations 43 and 47 to calculate $v_{m_{min}}$ as a function of the unexplained slip rate $\dot{s}$

$$v_{m_{min}} = \dot{s}\mu a_T \frac{\gamma(1 - \beta/\gamma)}{k\beta \exp[\beta(m_{min} + d/c)]} \left(M_{o,max}^{1 - \beta/\gamma} - M_{o,min}^{1 - \beta/\gamma} \right)^{-1}$$

(49)

for the exponential magnitude distribution with parameter β. This approach can also be used for a characteristic magnitude model with $\beta = 0$. Equation 49 allows the slip rate to be converted to an activity rate for input into seismic hazard calculations.

The slip rate for the San Andreas Fault can serve as an illustration. The long-term average slip rate on the section north of San Francisco (denoted the "northern San Andreas Fault") is approximately 2.4 cm/yr, on the basis of trenching and geodetic data. Seismicity parameters can be estimated for this illustration as follows. The moment magnitude **M** of the 1906 earthquake is estimated to be 7.7, on the basis of a seismogenic rupture length of 430 km, a rupture width of 10 km, an average displacement of 3 meters, and equations 42 and 44. Recent historical seismicity for $5 \leq \mathbf{M} \leq 7$ indicates $v_{5.0} = 0.1$ and $b \approx 0.75$; for the magnitude range $5.0 \leq \mathbf{M} \leq 7.0$, inverting equation 49 indicates a slip rate of 0.09 cm/yr. In addition to the exponential part of the distribution, characteristic magnitudes of 7.5–7.8 are modeled, with a rate v_{char} of 0.008/yr (one event every 125 years, on the average). With a b value of 0, inverting equation 49 indicates a slip rate of 2.17 cm/yr. The seismicity model is summarized as follows:

Magnitudes	b value	M range	$\dot{s}$
Exponential	0.75	5.0–7.0	0.09 cm/yr
Characteristic	0	7.5–7.8	2.17 cm/yr
All	—	5.0–7.8	2.26 cm/yr

This model is close to the target slip rate of 2.4 cm/yr. Using a characteristic magnitude range of 7.54–7.8 would give an exact match of slip rates. The characteristic magnitudes account for most of the total slip rate. This does not necessarily indicate that they are the dominant contribution to hazard or risk: with certain annual frequencies and ground motion sensitivity, the exponential part of the magnitude distribution could be more important than the characteristic part. Also, the characteristic slip rate depends on $\mathbf{M}_{max}$; raising it from 7.8 to 7.9, for example, increases $\dot{s}$ from 2.26 to 2.67 cm/yr. Therefore, if the slip rate is well controlled geologically, then it can be a diagnostic tool to help determine the range of characteristic magnitudes, including $\mathbf{M}_{max}$.

An actual application would use a much more detailed model of fault behavior, including segmentation, contributions of various characteristic magnitudes to $\dot{s}$, time since the last event, and fault interaction (as in WGCEP 1999). The present example illustrates the interaction of activity rates on the basis of historical seismicity, $\mathbf{M}_{max}$, $\dot{s}$, and characteristic magnitudes in deriving a comprehensive, consistent model of seismicity for a fault.

3.5 Earthquake Occurrences in Time

The necessary assumptions about earthquake occurrences in time are deceptively simple. At the most basic level, only a mean rate of occurrence v_j is needed for each source j, this being the rate for all earthquakes of interest (e.g., m > 5). This rate is used in calculating seismic hazard (equation 4).

How that rate is estimated can vary from the simple to the complex. At one extreme, the number of recorded earthquakes on that source can be counted and then divided by the time period of observation to estimate v_j, as in equation 37. At the other extreme, fault interactions, seismic history, and plate motions can be studied to estimate earthquake occurrences on major faults and thus establish a rate; for example, WGCEP (1999) estimated the probabilities of occurrence for a 30-year period. The most appropriate method for estimating rates of occurrence is the model with the most credibility, with significant doses of U_K if necessary.

Detailed models of random processes have been applied to earthquake occurrences, including renewal models, Markov and semi-Markov models, time- and slip-predictable models, and trigger models. With a few exceptions, these applications are limited by a short history of earthquakes with which to calibrate them, or by judgmental grouping of data from different regions to obtain a larger database. Cornell and Winterstein (1988) examined a range of time- and magnitude-dependent earthquake occurrence models. They concluded that the memoryless (Poisson) model is adequate, except where a single fault dominates the seismic hazard, the time since the last earthquake occurrence exceeds the mean recurrence interval, and the fault exhibits a very regular interval of earthquake occurrence. Such situations are rare, and, for the large majority of cases, the mean rate of activity and its U_K uncertainty are sufficient for seismic hazard calculations.

3.6 Fault Rupture Characteristics

When faults are known to cause earthquakes or are suspected of doing so, they should be modeled as seismotectonic sources in the hazard analysis. There are two benefits of such modeling. First, the movement of the earth's crust across a fault surface is the generating mechanism for ground vibrations observed during an earthquake. A physically realistic modeling of the generating mechanism allows a more accurate estimation of the associated ground motions. For example, many developers of ground motion equations use the distance between the site of interest and the closest point of rupture as the most relevant distance measure. This measure is usually more relevant than the hypocentral distance, epicentral distance, or distance to some arbitrarily specified "energy center" at the center of the rupture. For a small-magnitude event with small dimensions, the choice will not make much difference. If the rupture extends over several tens or hundreds of kilometers, however, then the shortest distance to the rupture is more appealing intuitively and leads to better understanding of empirical ground motion data.

A second benefit of specifying faults as earthquake sources is that surface displacement can be estimated if the faults are deemed capable of rupturing the surface. This is an important consideration in the design or analysis of structures that straddle faults and might suffer damage during surface rupture.

3.6.1 Length of Rupture To determine the shortest distance between a site of interest and a fault rupture, the length (or area) of the rupture must be estimated. The methods for doing so are primarily empirical, relying on field observations after past earthquakes for calibrating models.

Table 7 summarizes some relations between rupture length and magnitude. The dependence is a function of the type of faulting and the region (interplate or intraplate tectonic mechanisms). The empirical data exhibit substantial scatter, and this should be considered in the hazard analysis.

3.6.2 Fault Displacement The displacement of a fault during rupture can affect a facility that straddles a surface fault trace or strand. As discussed in Section 2, the hazard analysis can be applied to fault displacement to determine the probabilities that various displacement amplitudes will be exceeded. Informed decisions can then be made on the siting, design criteria, and safety of important facilities that might be affected by fault displacements.

Table 7 presents several relationships that allow estimation of fault displacement during earthquakes. Substantial scatter results from attempts to derive such relationships from empirical data, because at least two factors contribute to scatter (and perhaps bias) in observations. First, field observers tend to identify the location on the fault trace that has *maximum* displacement and report this value. The *average* displacement along the entire rupture length of the fault is lower and exhibits less scatter (Wells and Coppersmith 1994).

Second, fault movements in the time period of hours and days after a major shock tend to increase the observed displacement anywhere along the fault. Those subsequent movements, which may result from aftershocks or fault creep, increase the scatter and bias in estimates of fault displacement that are based on empirical observations. This is not to say that such estimates are not useful; on the contrary, they are often the only viable methods available, but they must be applied with a realistic understanding about their accuracy.

3.7 Intensity

Macroseismic intensity scales characterize the severity of ground shaking at a specific location by considering noninstrumental ("macroseismic") observations of how the shaking affects people, artificial structures, and natural surroundings at the location. The intensities assigned to a particular earthquake may vary from quite high (indicative of violent shaking) near the fault rupture, to low (imperceptible) at large distances. The primary use of macroseismic intensity observations in seismic hazard analysis is to estimate the magnitudes (or seismic moments) of preinstrumental shocks, either from the maximum reported intensity (loosely designated the epicentral

Table 7. Relations among magnitude, rupture length, rupture area, and displacement.

Data	Fault Type	Equation	Dispersion	Reference
World-wide	Strike-slip	$\log RL = -3.55 + .74\mathbf{M}$	$\sigma_{\log RL} = 0.23$	Wells and Coppersmith (1994)
World-wide	Reverse	$\log RL = -2.86 + .63\mathbf{M}$	$\sigma_{\log RL} = 0.23$	Wells and Coppersmith (1994)
World-wide	Strike-slip	$\log RL = -4.10 + .80M_s$	$\sigma_{\log RL} = 0.20$	Bonilla, Mark, and Lienkaemper (1984)
World-wide	Reverse	$\log RL = -1.96 + .50M_s$	$\sigma_{\log RL} = 0.20$	Bonilla, Mark, and Lienkaemper (1984)
World-wide	Strike-slip	$\log AD = -6.32 + .90\mathbf{M}$	$\sigma_{\log AD} = 0.28$	Wells and Coppersmith (1994)
World-wide	All	$\log AD = -4.80 + .69\mathbf{M}$	$\sigma_{\log AD} = 0.36$	Wells and Coppersmith (1994)
World-wide	Strike-slip	$\log MD = -3.90 + .48M_s$	$\sigma_{\log MD} = 0.26$	Bonilla et al. (1984)
World-wide	Strike-slip	$\mathbf{M} = \log A + 3.98$ $(A \leq 537 \text{ km}^2)$ $\mathbf{M} = 1.33 \log A + 3.07$ $(A > 537 \text{ km}^2)$	$\sigma_{\mathbf{M}} = 0.03$ $\sigma_{\mathbf{M}} = 0.04$	Hanks and Bakun (2002)

Notes: RL is surface rupture length in km, AD is average displacement at the surface in meters, MD is maximum displacement at the surface in meters, A is rupture area in km², and the log is base 10. These relations were derived from crustal earthquake data and should not be used for subduction zones.

intensity I_e) or from the area within certain isoseismals. An additional use is to characterize earthquake effects and ground motion attenuation in regions with few strong-motion instruments. Also, some intensities are assigned on the basis of strong-motion records, primarily for emergency response and damage estimation.

The intensity scale used in the United States is the MMI scale, which was developed by Wood and Neumann (1931) and modified by Richter (1958). Little work has been done since then to improve this scale. Recent efforts have been made to calibrate instrumental response to MMI levels, for applications in rapid emergency response and loss estimation after earthquakes. Appendix C lists the unabridged MMI definitions. Often, a shortened version of the MMI scale is published and used for intensity assessment, which can lead to errors in borderline cases. The Rossi-Forel (RF) scale was used in the United States to assign intensities (e.g., for the 1906 San Francisco earthquake) before the MMI scale was published, so an analyst who relies on early intensity reports must be careful to determine what scale was used.

The European Macroseismic Scale (EMS) (Grunthal 1998) deserves special mention in regard to intensity scales. This scale, derived collaboratively in 1998 among researchers in Europe, has the following features:

- Five grades of earthquake damage are defined in detail for different building types, ranging from slight damage to total destruction.
- Six vulnerability classes are defined, and building types are subdivided into vulnerability classes according to their level of earthquake-resistant design.
- The adjectives "few," "many," and "most" are defined quantitatively by the fraction of structures affected.

With these features, the intensity levels are defined as the effects on *few*, *many*, or *most* people, or as the grade of damage experienced by *few*, *many*, or *most* buildings in a vulnerability class. The EMS gives intensity values that are very similar to those obtained via the MMI scale. As compared with the MMI scale, the EMS allows a more objective evaluation of earthquake effects and damage and reduces the bias that an analyst might introduce. Table 8 shows a very general correspondence between the MMI and EMS scales. Adoption of the EMS by the United States and other nations would greatly facilitate the comparison of observed shaking from earthquakes that occur in different parts of the world.

Intensity "data" (i.e., inferences based on historical descriptions of earthquake effects) have often been criticized when used as input into numerical, quantitative analyses of seismic hazard. The intensity scale values, critics point out, were originally designated by Roman numerals to prevent the inference of a cardinal difference between specific values. Applying numerical analyses and extrapolation to such data, critics say, is unwarranted and unjustified. Observing intensities in current times and correlating them to instrumental data is not necessarily consistent with interpretations of earthquake effects from long ago, when the documentation was more incidental and less scientific (by current standards). Indeed, the sophistication and omnipresence of current news media ensure that many more people are aware of the "earthquake problem" and are quick to report any personal experiences. Finally, observations of current seismic effects in California and elsewhere do not necessarily correspond to equivalent levels of seismic shaking in earlier times in other parts of the world, when structures were of different strengths, ages, and dynamic characteristics. A primary cause of these differences is the changing environment of recent times, which is not accounted for in intensity scales devised 70 years ago. Highrise buildings are much more abundant now and much more flexible. Modern airtight windows have closer tolerances with standard framing than older sliding-sash windows. Waterbeds allow users more sensitivity to seismic motions, and a proliferation of swimming pools in warm climates leads to exaggerated reports of seismic effects as compared with the same kind of event earlier in the twentieth century.

Although such criticisms have merit, the fact remains that many important earthquakes occurred around the world in preinstrumental times, and many earthquakes still occur in regions where strong-motion instruments are sparse or nonexistent. The best way to understand these earthquakes is through intensities. It is possible to compare the damage and felt areas of modern shocks with older ones and to characterize ground motion attenuation with distance where no strong-motion records exist. Even though the available scales are crude and can lead to errors and misinterpretations, no better set of intensity measures has been devised. In short, intensity scales offer an inexact but useful means of characterizing earthquakes for which no instrumental data are available.

Table 8. General correspondence between the
MMI and EMS[a] scales.

Description	MMI	EMS
Not felt	-	I
Felt by very few	I	II
Felt indoors by few	II	III
Moderate vibration felt	III	III
Hanging objects swing	III	IV
Felt indoors by many	IV	IV
Glassware and china clatter	IV	V
Entire building trembles	V	V
Small objects shift	V	VI
Plaster falls	VI	VI
Furniture shifts	VI	VII
High damage to weak structures	VII	VII
Moderate damage to ordinary structures	VII	VIII
High damage to ordinary structures	VIII	VIII
Moderate damage to well-built structures	VIII	IX
General panic	IX	IX
Damage to most masonry and frame structures	IX	X
High damage to well-built structures	X	X
Most masonry structures destroyed	XI	XI
Most buildings destroyed	XII	XII

[a] Grunthal (1998)

Another important use for intensity scales is in making estimates of damage and loss from earthquakes (see Section 6). With the large uncertainties (U_K) that are generally involved in such estimates (uncertainties in the number and types of structures, secondary losses, relationship of structural response to damage, and earthquake effects for a given event), the precision offered by intensity scales is often sufficient for estimates that apply to a large group of structures.

When historical data exist only in the form of earthquake intensities, the best way to proceed is to use the intensity data (the epicentral intensity I_e, the felt area, the area within a certain isoseismal, or a combination of these) to estimate magnitudes for preinstrumental events. The hazard analysis can then proceed via an estimation of activity rates $v_{m_{min}}$ for seismic source zones as described in Section 3.3, recognizing that the estimation of magnitude from intensity involves substantial (but quantifiable) uncertainties (U_K).

It is best to avoid the alternative approach of deriving activity rates for I_e, attenuating ground motions to site intensity I_s, and conducting the hazard analysis for I_s. There are so many unknowns in the conversion of I_s to ground motions—involving the adoption of empirical relations from one region to another—that this method should be avoided. The hazard should be estimated via I_s only if damage or loss is determined directly from I_s. Any application of this type should always work with I_s observations in a city or locale and should not rely on isoseismals to estimate intensity.

Table 3 indicates some relationships proposed for estimating magnitude values (on various scales) from epicentral MMI values (I_e) and from the areas enclosed within specific isoseismals. To develop this table, recent seismicity was used for which both intensity and magnitude were known; a relationship was then derived between the two. If there is uncertainty or differing opinions about the proper relationship for a given region, then several relationships should be adopted to investigate the seismic hazard sensitivity. If necessary, subjective weights reflecting different credibilities should be applied for final results and decisions.

At close distances, peak accelerations of ¹/₂ g will
be the norm for **M** ≃ *6.5, rather than the exception.*

Tom Hanks, 1976

4 ESTIMATING EARTHQUAKE
GROUND MOTION

Estimating seismic ground shaking is an important step in an-
ticipating earthquake effects on people and structures. This section
examines the characteristics of ground motion, how these characteristics are commonly estimated, and how some common problems in
ground motion specification can be avoided. More details about
ground motion characteristics can be obtained from Stewart et al.
(2001) and the references contained therein.

4.1 Importance of Earthquake Shaking
Earthquakes can cause damage, injury, and loss of life in four ways:
1. Vibratory ground motion may cause damage to natural and
   artificial structures and may cause ground failures, any of
   which may inflict injury and loss of life.
2. Rupture of the fault at the ground surface and underground
   may cause damage to structures in the immediate area.
3. Upheaval or subsidence in the fault region may cause damage, perhaps in conjunction with ocean or river waters.
4. Tsunamis or seiches may inundate coastal regions or other
   locations near bodies of water, causing damage and loss of life.
Of these four, seismic ground shaking causes the most damage and
loss worldwide, by far.

Three basic steps are required for estimating and using ground
shaking functions in seismic probability analyses. First, the important
characteristics of the ground motion must be identified. The character-

71

istics of interest depend on the structures or effects being considered in the analysis. For example, evaluating the safety of a two-story unreinforced brick structure will require designation of the high-frequency amplitudes of motion, whereas assessing the percentage of damage to a ten-story reinforced-concrete, moment-resisting frame structure will require determination of ground motion energy of about 1 Hz. If old, unreinforced masonry (URM) buildings are under study, then the MMI may have to serve as the measure of ground motion.

Second, the probability distribution of the selected characteristic must be estimated as a function of earthquake source properties and location of the energy release with respect to the site. This is $P_j [C > c|\bar{s} \ at \ l]$ in equation 4. When data for the ground motion characteristic are available for a wide range of $\bar{s}$ and l, this estimation process is a more or less straightforward procedure (although substantial judgment is required for several steps). If data are not available, for instance because of infrequent seismicity or poor instrument coverage in a region, then future ground motions may have to be estimated via theoretical methods, historical observations of intensity, or analogies to similar regions. In such cases, good engineering judgment and intuition are often as important as mathematical analysis in deriving ground motion estimates.

The third step is to use equation 4 to calculate the frequency with which various levels of ground motion will be exceeded during time t. The scatter in ground motion estimates is always large; empirical distributions of quantitative ground motion amplitudes, conditional on source characteristics and distance, often exhibit a coefficient of variation of 0.6–0.8. This is a major uncertainty that contributes to seismic hazard calculations. Some early studies assumed that there would be no scatter in the ground motion estimates, leading to completely erroneous estimates of seismic hazard.

Ground motion characteristics at a site, conditional on a given earthquake, can be estimated in several ways, which depend on the earthquake source characteristics available. Figure 10 is a flow diagram of two possible methods. First, the earthquake source characteristics are specified, preferably through quantities such as magnitude, seismic moment, and stress drop. In that case, method B is used, and either the peak motion characteristics or the response spectrum at the site is estimated by using a ground motion equation. If peak motion characteristics have been estimated, then the response spectrum can be derived via spectral amplification factors. Last, the

72

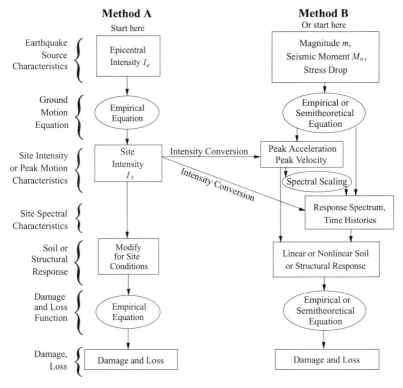

Figure 10. Steps in estimating site ground motion characteristics, soil or structural response, damage, and loss.

response spectrum or time histories are used in soil or structural models to calculate structural response, and a damage function allows estimation of damage and loss.

If the source characterization is expressed as epicentral intensity I_e, then a choice is available. The preferred alternative is to convert I_e to magnitude or seismic moment and follow the steps in method B. In this conversion, all intensity observations (e.g., areas within various isoseismals as well as epicentral intensity) should be used to estimate magnitude.

A less desirable alternative is to start with method A, compute a site intensity I_s through an empirical equation, and use an intensity conversion to estimate peak motion or spectral characteristics (method B). This alternative has several disadvantages, however. The primary one is that I_s is a qualitative measure of ground motion (see Section 3.6), so translating it into a response spectrum for design involves significant uncertainties (both U_R and U_K). That is, the same site intensity I_s may be associated with very different spectral amplitudes and shapes.

For some cases, such as estimating the losses for a portfolio of structures, method A is acceptable. In these applications, I_s is used because damage and loss for many structural types can be estimated from statistics and experience.

In general, the most direct method of estimating the final desired parameter from the source characteristics is the most preferable. It is better, for example, to go from magnitude directly to spectral acceleration than to use peak motion parameters as an intermediate step. The reason is that any intermediate variable introduces variabilities, complications, and possible biases in the analysis.

Sections 4.2 and 4.3 describe empirical and semitheoretical methods for estimating ground motion characteristics, because these are the two most common methods. They fit into the overall response- and damage-estimation problem, as represented by the ellipses in Figure 10. Empirical and semitheoretical methods are used to estimate site intensity, peak motion characteristics, or spectral characteristics (spectral acceleration or velocity) as a function of earthquake source characteristics and distance.

4.2 Empirical Ground Motion Equations

Empirically based estimates of ground motion characteristics are the oldest estimates in seismic hazard analysis, dating from the 1960s. They are popular for regions where many data are available, and they typically have the following type of form:

$$\ln A = c_o + f(m) + f(r) + f(soil) + \varepsilon \qquad (50)$$

or

$$I_s = c_o + f(I_e, m) + f(r) + f(soil) + \varepsilon \qquad (51)$$

where A is ground motion amplitude, which could be a peak motion parameter or spectral amplitude; I_s is site intensity; "soil" is some quantitative, perhaps bivariate function of soil type; c_o is a constant; and ε is a random variable taking on a specific value for each observation. Some equations involve inseparable terms in magnitude m (or epicentral intensity, I_e) and distance r, as well. Examples of typical equations are given below.

Boore, Joyner, and Fumal (1997) estimate spectral velocity with the following equation:

$$\log A = c_1 + c_2(\mathbf{M} - 6) + c_3(\mathbf{M} - 6)^2$$
$$+ c_5 \log r_{JB} + c_6 \ln(v_s / v_a) + \varepsilon \tag{52}$$

where $\mathbf{M}$ is the moment magnitude, $r_{JB} = (d + h)^{1/2}$, d is the shortest distance to the surface projection of the rupture, h is a depth term determined by regression, and v_s is the shear wave velocity in the upper 30 meters compared with a reference velocity v_a.

Campbell (1997) estimates PGA first, then spectral acceleration from PGA:

$$\ln(\text{PGA}) = c_1 + c_2\mathbf{M} + c_3 \ln \sqrt{r^2 + [c_4 \exp(c_5\mathbf{M})]^2}$$
$$+ (c_6 + c_7 \ln r + c_8\mathbf{M})f$$
$$+ (c_9 + c_{10} \ln r)s + \varepsilon \tag{53}$$

$$\ln(SA) = \ln(\text{PGA}) + c_1 + c_2 \tanh[c_3(\mathbf{M} - 4.7)]$$
$$+ (c_4 + c_5\mathbf{M})\, r + c_6 s$$
$$+ c_7 \tanh(c_8 D)(1 - s_h) + f_{SA}D \tag{54}$$

where r is the shortest distance to the rupture surface, f is a binary variable (i.e., 0 or 1) indicating fault type, s is a binary variable indicating soil type, D is depth to basement rock, and f_{SA} is a defined function for spectral acceleration.

Sponheur (1960) used the following form:

$$I_s = I_e - c_3 \log(\sqrt{r_s^2 + h^2} / h)$$
$$+ c_4 \alpha \sqrt{r_s^2 + h^2} - h + \varepsilon \tag{55}$$

where r_s is horizontal distance to the epicentral region, h is depth, and α is a region-specific attenuation term that may depend on azimuth from the epicenter to the site.

The coefficients of equations 52 through 55 are estimated from observations of A, I_s, $\mathbf{M}$, r, soil type, and other parameters via linear or nonlinear least-squares regression analysis, as appropriate for the equation form. An important drawback of this approach is that it violates many of the implicit assumptions of least-squares regression analysis:

- Observations of A are not independent. Often, two horizontal components of an accelerograph record are used, and these observations are correlated by common source, path, and site effects. Multiple records are used from one earthquake, and these are correlated by common source and, perhaps, by path effects. Multiple records from the same site but different events are used, and these are correlated by common soil conditions.

- The form of the equation may not be correct. In particular, a tendency of A to reach limits at near-source distances ("saturation") may imply that the magnitude dependence is not independent of distance (i.e., the m and r terms may not be separable as in equation 50). Also, the dependence of A on r near the source may be more complicated: the dependence may be affected by source azimuth, rupture directivity, and other effects, especially for long-period motions. As a result, errors in the predicted values of A may not be homoskedastic with magnitude and distance (i.e., the scatter in observations around the predicted value depends on what m and r values are used; the predictions may be biased for some m and r values).

These problems are compounded by the available data. Many ground motion records from a few earthquakes may dominate the data set, particularly for recent years—when strong-motion networks are more dense. Also, ground motion records are not well distributed with respect to magnitude and distance: small earthquakes produce triggered records only at short distances, and large earthquakes produce many more records at long distances than short distances because of purely geometric effects (there is more area and usually more instrumentation between, say, 50 and 55 km than between 0 and 5 km). Additional variables, such as the foundation size of the building where the instrument is located, may be important and may bias the results.

Several procedures can be utilized to overcome these problems. Alternative forms for the ground motion function should be examined, including a nonlinear dependence of $\ln A$ on m and mixed terms involving both m and r. Binary variables can be used to examine the dependence of ground motion on foundations and other variables. In general, variables indicating qualitative conditions (such as soils and foundation types) should not be allowed to have three values (e.g., 0, 1, and 2); a preponderance of data in two categories and the assumed form will dominate predictions in the third category without regard to data in that category. For data concentrated in a few magnitude and distance ranges, weighting of observations can be pursued. One weighting scheme applies weights that are inversely proportional to the number of records from each earthquake, so that each event has the same total weight. An alternative scheme, with great intuitive appeal for specific applications, applies weights according to the importance of specific magnitudes and distances in the hazard analysis. This requires a recursive procedure: a trial set of weights is used to derive the ground motion function, a hazard analysis is performed to determine which magnitudes and distances are the most important, the weights are revised so that observations close to those magnitudes and distances are heavily weighted, and the hazard is reanalyzed. The process stops when the set of weights agrees with the importance of observations from the perspective of hazard.

One method that has been used successfully, particularly when a few well-recorded earthquakes dominate the magnitude dependence, is to perform an initial regression using the form

$$\ln A = \sum_i b_{2i} z_i + b_3(r + r_c) + b_4 r + b_5 s + \varepsilon \qquad (56)$$

where z_i is a binary variable that is set to 1 if the observation of A is from the ith earthquake or is set to 0 otherwise. This produces a set of coefficients b_{2i}, one for each earthquake i included in the data set. An overall magnitude dependence can then be derived by regressing the b_{2i} values on magnitude:

$$b_{2i} = b_1 + b_2 \mathbf{M} + \varepsilon \qquad (57)$$

The summation term in equation 56 is then replaced by the right side of equation 57. The advantage of this two-step process is that the magnitude dependence of $\ln A$ is determined by weighting each earthquake equally, so that a couple of well-recorded events do not dominate the magnitude dependence. Note that uncertainty in $\ln A$ in the first regression must be modified by uncertainty in the second relationship, to properly express uncertainty in individual observations. Regressions of this type were proposed by Joyner and Boore (1981).

The inclusion of correlation among observations (e.g., from common earthquakes) can be handled more elegantly and efficiently through regression analysis by using a random effects model; examples of applications are in Brillinger and Priesler (1985) and Abrahamson and Youngs (1992). This is an iterative procedure that requires the numerical solution of a likelihood function within the iteration, but it gives ground motion estimates that include the variance attributable to the random effect being modeled (in this case, caused by earthquake-to-earthquake variability).

One point should be obvious but still needs to be stated: all data should be carefully selected. More accurate results will come from using half the available data, carefully screened to avoid inapplicable, erroneous, questionable, or biased observations, than from uncritically throwing all data together for statistical analysis. Errors can come from many sources: malfunctioning equipment, late triggers, inaccurate knowledge of soil or foundation conditions, high noise levels, poor record processing, or simple misidentification. The careful assignment of uniformly determined magnitudes, distances, and soil types is equally important. In all cases, plots showing observed and predicted values of ground motion should be prepared, so that possible problems with data can be identified. Of course, a fundamental rule is that data should not be discarded just because they disagree with predictions.

Note that the ground motion equations such as equation 50 estimate mean log (amplitude), the exponent of which corresponds to the median amplitude, not the mean amplitude. Typical ground motion distributions have positive skewness, and a lognormal distribution is often assumed, so the mean amplitude lies above the median amplitude by the factor $\exp(-\sigma^2/2)$, where σ is the standard deviation of log (amplitude).

Before adopting a published ground motion equation, it is essential to know whether the equation estimates ground motion for a randomly oriented horizontal component, the larger of the two horizontal components, or something else—like peak particle motion. The mean ratio of a larger/random component is typically 1.13. The correct choice depends on the application, but typically the randomly oriented component is used for horizontal ground motion.

For most regions of the world with numerous instrumental records of earthquakes or with a well-studied catalog of historical events with intensities, empirical ground motion equations have already been developed and published. Thus the seismic hazard or risk analyst will not have to develop his or her own equations. The analyst must, however, choose from available equations or weight their credibilities explicitly, so it is important to understand the strengths and weaknesses of one equation versus another.

One is never sure of having the "correct" functional form of a ground motion equation. Indeed, as one cynic has said, "All current forms of ground motion equations are incorrect, as they will all be replaced in ten years." This statement points out the importance of including multiple equations in the analysis and showing that (1) the range of currently available forms is included (and weighted), or (2) the decisions to be made from the hazard and risk analysis are robust with respect to the form of the ground motion equation.

How well an equation recognizes the limitations of regression analysis and seeks to reduce their effects should influence how the analyst assesses that equation's credibility. One useful procedure when equations are otherwise equally valid is to determine the M and r ranges that are most critical to hazard analysis, develop a set of strong-motion data relevant to the study site, and compare the chosen equations with data in the critical M and r ranges. Equations that fit the critical data better are given high weight, and equations that fit less well are given low weight. Weights can be calculated proportionally to the inverse of the residual variance of the data around each equation, to achieve the desired weighting.

Figures 11 through 13 illustrate predictions of ground motion on rock for moment magnitude $M = 6.5$ using four recent ground motion equations, compared with observations on rock from $6.0 \leq M \leq 7.0$, scaled to $M = 6.5$, recorded in the western United States. Scaling to a single magnitude reveals the residual variation in the data when compared with equations predicting ground motion for that same magnitude; the scaling is discussed below, in conjunction with Figures 14 and 15. The ground motion measures plotted are PGA and spectral acceleration (SA) at 10 and 1 Hz.

Some interpretation and assumptions are needed to plot predictive equations on a comparable basis. Various distance measures are used in the estimation equations, such as distance to the rupture surface, distance to the seismogenic part of the rupture, and distance to the surface projection of the fault rupture. Here it is assumed that a vertical fault ruptures to within 3 km of the surface, and predictions are plotted against distance to the rupture surface

Peak Ground Acceleration on Rock for **M** = 6.5

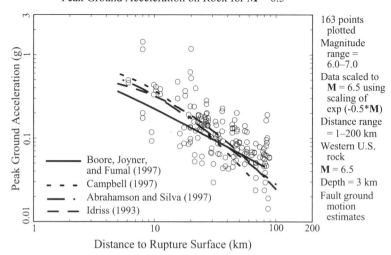

Figure 11. PGA on rock for **M** = 6.5 from four equations compared with data from **M** = 6.0–7.0. A depth of 3 km was used to plot the distance to the rupture surface for the Boore-Joyner-Fumal (1997) relation.

10-Hz Spectral Acceleration on Rock for **M** = 6.5

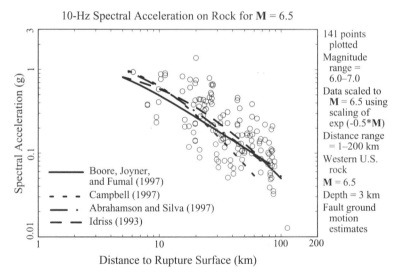

Figure 12. *SA* (10 Hz) on rock for **M** = 6.5 from four equations compared with data from **M** = 6.0–7.0.

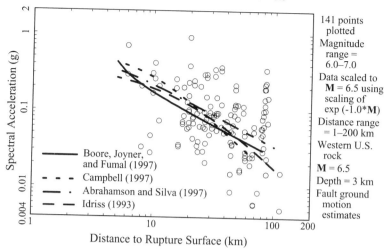

Figure 13. *SA* (1 Hz) on rock for **M** = 6.5 from four
equations compared with data from **M** = 6.0–7.0.

using, for appropriate equations, a designation of "all ruptures" (not
just strike-slip ruptures, because the data are mixed). With these
assumptions, the estimates and data can be plotted and evaluated
on a comparable basis.

Notwithstanding a few exceptions, the striking conclusion about
these comparisons is that the predictive equations generally pass
through the center of most of the data. The estimates agree best where
data are abundant (at about magnitude 6.5 and distances of 20–80
km) and agree least where extrapolations are involved. In particular,
empirically based methods yield large differences in estimates at short
distances where data are relatively sparse. These differences result
from different functional forms assumed for the equations and from
the data and fitting procedures used by the cited authors. If the events
critical to the hazard assessment are about **M** = 6.5 and *r* = 20–80
km, then the choice among estimating equations will make little difference; if larger magnitudes or shorter distances are critical, then
the choice may be crucial.

Figure 14 shows 10-Hz *SA* data from $10 \leq r \leq 30$ scaled to $r = 20$ km
(using $\ln A \propto r^{-1}$) versus **M**, and Figure 15 shows a similar plot for
$5 \leq r \leq 15$ scaled to $r = 10$ km (again using $\ln A \propto r^{-1}$). Both plots

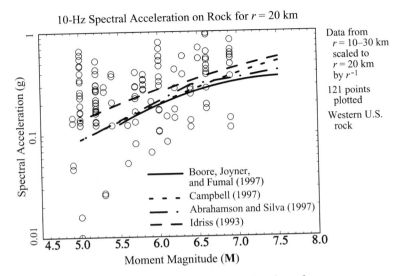

Figure 14. *SA* (10 Hz) on rock for *r* = 20 km from four equations compared with data from *r* = 10–30 km.

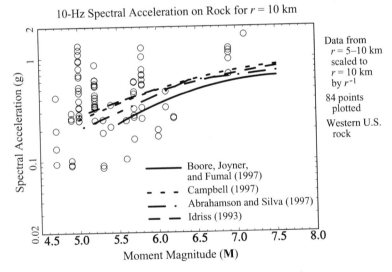

Figure 15. *SA* (10 Hz) on rock for *r* = 10 km from four equations compared with data from *r* = 5–15 km.

include estimates from the four empirically based ground motion equations. Although the data are very scattered, particularly for small magnitudes, the equations lie near the center of the data for $\mathbf{M} < 7$. For larger magnitudes, the equations are not constrained by the sparse data, and estimates depend on the mathematical form and the fitting process. If these magnitudes are critical to the hazard and risk analysis, then we are well advised to use multiple equations to span the range of interpretations. Note that the slope of ln SA versus $\mathbf{M}$ is about 0.5, which prompted the scaling of the PGA and 10-Hz SA data plotted in Figures 11 and 12 by the factor of exp $[-0.5 \, (\mathbf{M} - 6.5)]$, to scale them to $\mathbf{M} = 6.5$. For 1 Hz, the scaling factor exp $[-1.0 \, (\mathbf{M} - 6.5)]$ was used. Note also that the slope of ln SA versus r in Figures 11 through 13 is about -1, which prompted the scaling of data in Figures 14 and 15 by the factors $(20/r)^{-1}$ and $(10/r)^{-1}$.

A last observation from Figures 11–15 is that the scatter in observations is quite large. Typical coefficients of variation are 0.6–0.8, as discussed in Section 4.4.

The lognormal distribution is usually adequate to characterize uncertainties in most measures of ground shaking. Figure 16 shows errors in the estimated values of PGA, which are calculated as ln (observed value/estimated value), plotted on normal-probability paper. For this figure, the estimates were made by using the Idriss (1993) equation. The linearity of the logarithmic data on normal-probability paper strongly confirms the use of a lognormal distribution to characterize deviations of individual values from estimated levels, at least within the limits of ± 2 standard deviations.

The scatter in observations can be reduced if additional factors that affect ground motion are known and taken into account in the estimation procedure. Some of these factors are as follows:
- Detailed site geology
- Type of faulting
- Topography
- Size of the building that houses the instrument
- Elevation of the instrument inside the building
- Interaction of the building and supportive soil
- Directivity effects of rupture propagation
- Azimuth of the horizontal component with respect to arriving seismic energy

Accounting for additional factors, either by segregating data or adding more independent variables on the right side of equation 50,

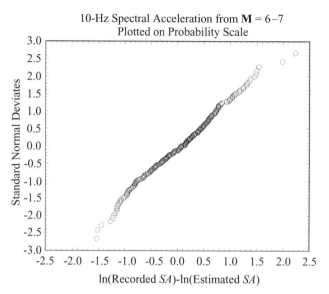

Figure 16. Log errors for *SA* (10 Hz) from Figure 12, using Idriss (1993) equation plotted on a normal probability scale.

may reduce the apparent scatter in observations. Several points must be kept in mind, however. First, standard statistical tests (e.g., on the significance of computed coefficients) should be used with care to evaluate coefficients and residuals. The question is whether the calculated coefficients are meaningful. Conclusions from standard statistical tests are confounded because the tests assume that observations are independent, which is not so for most strong-motion data, as discussed above. Second, the mathematical form used to quantify the above effects should be chosen carefully, lest intermediate or extrapolated values produce results unsubstantiated by data. Third, the predictive model should be plotted throughout its range of *m* and *r*, to ensure that it is reasonable. At least one researcher has been embarrassed by a quadratic magnitude dependence that showed decreasing ground motion with magnitude for a large *m*. Fourth, only variables that are known and can be specified *before* an earthquake should be included in the predictive equation. Using what are actually random properties of an earthquake source (properties that might be known *after* an earthquake) in the ground motion estimation artificially reduces the apparent scatter, requires more complex analysis, and may introduce errors because of the added complexity.

An example is useful to illustrate this point. Suppose a site lies a distance r^* along the strike from a strike-slip fault that will produce an earthquake of known magnitude (Figure 17, part A) with a unilateral rupture. The only unknown feature of the event is its direction of propagation, which is as likely to be toward the site as away from it. The goal is to determine the seismic hazard at the site in terms of $P[A > a^*]$ during the next earthquake.

The most straightforward way to achieve this is to gather data from similar sites located on strike from similar events whose propagation direction is known, then derive a ground motion equation for sources of the type e_1 (a rupture away from the site) and e_2 (a rupture toward the site). Figure 17, part B shows two such functions. The hazard for the site located r^* from the fault is then calculated by the total probability theorem

$$P[A > a^* \,|\, e_1 \text{ or } e_2 \text{ at } r^*] = P[A > a^* \,|\, e_1 \text{ at } r^*]P[e_1]$$
$$+ P[A > a^* \,|\, e_2 \text{ at } r^*]P[e_2] \quad (58)$$

which is the just the average probability of exceeding a^* from the two events, since $P[e_1] = P[e_2] = 0.5$. The probability distributions for events e_1 and e_2 are illustrated in Figure 17, part C.

A simpler analytical method is possible, if certain conditions are met. All the acceleration data can be treated together in producing a ground motion equation for an event e, without specifying the rupture direction. The resulting function is shown as a dashed line in Figure 17, part B. For the site at distance r^*, the hazard is then calculated as

$$P[A > a^* \,|\, e_1 \text{ or } e_2 \text{ at } r^*] = P[A > a^* \,|\, e \text{ at } r^*] \quad (59)$$

Equation 59 gives the same result as equation 58, and this is illustrated in Figure 17, part C: the probability density function for acceleration during an earthquake of unspecified rupture direction is just the average of the density functions for the two events e_1 and e_2.

Two conditions must be met for these kinds of simplifications to work. First, the characteristic that one wishes to ignore (that is, not treat explicitly) in the ground motion estimation must be unpredictable for future earthquakes. Second, the available ground motion data that the estimates will be based on must reflect future events and their probabilities. As long as these conditions are met, even approxi-

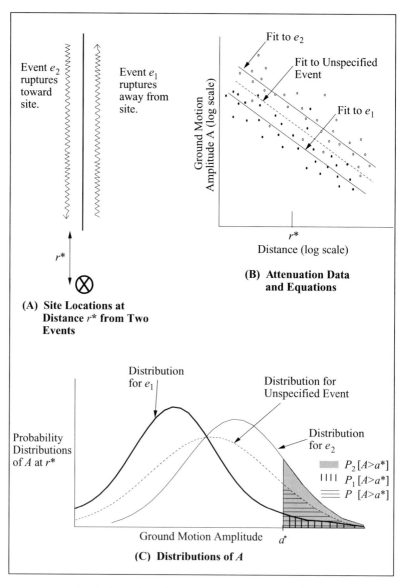

Figure 17. Seismic hazard analysis for a site at distance r^* along the strike from a fault producing two events: e_1 ruptures away from the site, and e_2 ruptures toward the site.

mately, ground motion estimates (and hazard analyses) can and should be kept simple.

Several contrary examples in which these conditions are not met come quickly to mind. First, if the ground motion equations are not well calibrated in the region of interest (i.e., if the data illustrated in Figure 17, part B are absent), then it will be more justifiable to treat the direction of fault rupture explicitly than to rely on extrapolation from more distant data. This is the practical reason for fault studies that take fault rupture directivity into account explicitly: distant data cannot accurately represent fault directivity effects at short distances, and short-distance data are sparse, so directivity must be accounted for explicitly.

Second, on average, the ground motions generated by a fault depend on the style of faulting (strike-slip, normal, reverse, thrust, or oblique), so a site near a fault trace should not be treated as though the style of faulting were unknown. Ground motion data should be segregated by fault type, and the appropriate data should be used in the prediction. This example does not meet the previously described condition of being an unpredictable characteristic.

Third, suppose that the faults in an area are covered by alluvium, making their exact locations unknown, and they are treated by using a large area source. If 90% of these faults are suspected of moving in the reverse sense, and if half the ground motion records consist of strike-slip fault data and the other half consist of reverse-slip fault data, then these data must be segregated, and the hazard analysis must be performed by explicitly accounting for fault type in the ground motion prediction.

Fourth, a fundamental factor is that ground motions are not usually recorded from earthquakes with the same magnitude distribution that is expected to affect hazard and risk at all sites. This is the reason why PSHA makes the ground motion estimate (equation 50) a function of m, conditions on m in the hazard integral (equation 4), and thereby treats magnitude dependence explicitly. The same is true for the distance parameter.

Fifth, most researchers agree that the use of epicentral or hypocentral distance in ground motion estimation is not as accurate at short distances as a measure like the shortest distance to the rupture surface. The issue that frequently arises is this: when fault locations are unknown, should epicentral (or hypocentral) locations and distances be used in the hazard analysis, without worrying about the possible locations of fault ruptures? Or should the analyst account explicitly for all possible fault and rupture locations and use the shortest distance to the rupture surface in the hazard calculations? To investigate this, the following suppositions can be made about earthquake motions affecting the site shown in Figure 18, part A:

- An earthquake of only one size can occur with an epicenter as shown in part A, and the event can rupture in one of eight possible directions.
- Historical earthquakes have ruptured in equal numbers in all eight directions, and future ruptures are equally likely in any direction.
- Available ground motion data (upon which a ground motion equation is based) are representative of ground motions at the site during historical earthquakes at distance Δ from the site.
- Uncertainty (U_R) in ground motion for a given rupture distance is relatively small, so that U_R in acceleration for a given epicentral distance results primarily from U_R in the distance to the rupture. (These are aleatory uncertainties, because it has been assumed that the fault can rupture in eight possible directions).
- Ground motion amplitude a^* is exceeded only when the earthquake ruptures in directions 6, 7, or 8 (closest to the site).

Given these assumptions, how can the probability be calculated that a ground motion of amplitude a^* will be exceeded at the site during the next event?

Two methods are possible. To take explicit account of rupture location, use the "exact" ground motion function that is based on the rupture distance shown in Figure 18, part B and calculate the probability of exceeding a^* as

$$P[A > a^* \mid next\ earthquake] \ = \ \sum_i P[A > a^* \mid e_i]P[e_i] \qquad (60)$$

$$= 1 * \frac{1}{8} + 1 * \frac{1}{8} + 1 * \frac{1}{8}$$

$$= \frac{3}{8}$$

where only ruptures e_6, e_7, and e_8 contribute to the summation, because all the other ruptures cause amplitudes that are less than a^*.

Alternatively, work with epicentral distance Δ and the "apparent" ground motion function shown in Figure 18, part C. For this

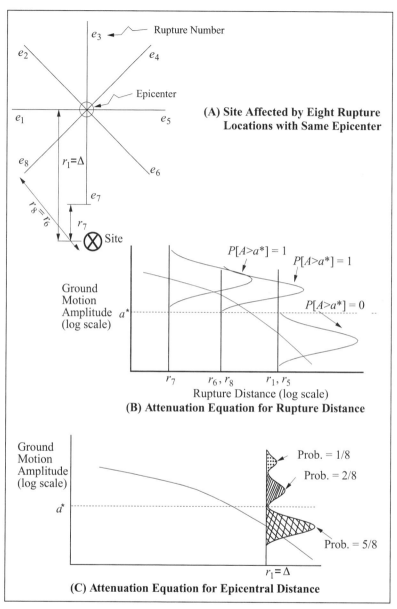

Figure 18. Seismic hazard analysis for a site affected by earthquakes with a known epicenter but unknown rupture location.

portion of the figure, the distribution of acceleration at distance Δ is caused by some events propagating toward the site and some away from the site. In this case, the hazard at the site is calculated directly as

$$P[A > a^* | \Delta] = \frac{3}{8} \tag{61}$$

which is the same as when rupture locations are taken into account explicitly.

Why does the same hazard result when "rupture distance" and "epicentral distance" are used? Because, in a ground motion equation, accounting for a source characteristic that is unpredictable for future earthquakes and integrating over all possible values indicates the same hazard as when the characteristic is ignored and contributes to unexplained scatter in ground motion amplitudes. As mentioned above, the characteristic must be represented in the scatter of ground motion data in the correct proportion, and the characteristic must be unpredictable. It should be evident that introducing additional uncertainty—in ground motion scatter, earthquake size, rupture orientation, or epicentral location—does not change the above conclusion.

The key to making the correct hazard calculations in the previous example is using the right ground motion estimation in each calculation. If the wrong function is used, then errors will of course result, and this has led some analysts to make fundamental errors in hazard calculations. Examples of such errors are as follows:

- If the hazard analysis (Figure 2, part D) is performed with epicentral distance, then using "rupture distance" ground motion estimates (Figure 2, part C) will underestimate the hazard.
- If the hazard analysis (Figure 2, part D) is performed with rupture distance, then using "epicentral distance" ground motion estimates (Figure 2, part C) will overestimate the hazard.
- Whether an epicentral- or rupture-distance ground motion equation is selected (Figure 2, part C), comparing a hazard analysis (Figure 2, part D) on the basis of epicentral versus rupture distance will always show that the rupture-distance method leads to a higher hazard. The reason is that the rupture-distance method calculates shorter distances than epicentral distances, and ground motion estimates usually increase with decreasing distance. Thus, epicentral-distance hazard analyses will appear unconservative by comparison. This has led some analysts to erroneously conclude from such

comparisons that, when fault locations and azimuths are unknown, epicentral-distance methods are flawed.

As a practical matter, ground motion estimation functions may be more readily available in one form than another, and this may govern the choice of which analytical method to adopt.

4.3 Stochastic Methods of Estimating Ground Motion

Stochastic methods estimate ground motions during an earthquake on the basis of physical properties of the energy release and the travel path of seismic waves. From the characteristics of the process in time, an estimate can be made of spectral response, peak motion parameters, or any other desired measure (including nonlinear response).

These methods are appealing, for two reasons. First, they provide a theoretical link between the physical characteristics of the earthquake source and the resulting field of ground motions. This link is not available in strictly empirical methods, although theoretical considerations are certainly used to guide the form of the equation used in the regression analysis and to constrain the permissible values of the coefficients. Second, and as a consequence of the first consideration, stochastic methods can be used in regions for which there are few ground motion data; empirical methods would fail in such regions. This application is particularly important in low-seismicity intraplate regions where, for example, stochastic methods can examine the importance of different assumptions about dynamic stress drops that have been identified by seismological studies.

The standard stochastic method represents the far-field shear-wave energy generated by the earthquake source as a band-limited random process. Limits on the bandwidth result from the corner frequency of the earthquake source (i.e., an abrupt change in the spectral amplitude at the lower end, related to the dimension of the source) and from limits on the highest frequencies that the source can produce and that can propagate through the earth's crust (at the upper end). An additional limit on the high frequencies may be imposed by near-surface rock or soil properties and the frequencies they can transmit.

The stochastic method is based on a set of assumptions about the source spectrum and about the effects of path and site conditions, which can be summarized with a few concepts. Detailed equations implementing these concepts are in Appendix D, and Boore (2003) gives a comprehensive description with numerous references. An overview of the basic steps is given here and is illustrated in Figures 19–21.

91

First, the Fourier amplitude of ground motion (usually ground acceleration) at frequency f is represented as

$$a'_{gm}(f) = c\, a'_s(f)p(f,r,q,v_s,...)$$ (62)

where a'_s is the Fourier representation of acceleration at the earthquake source (called the "source spectrum"); p is a path factor that accounts for attenuation by the travel path and near-surface rock; c is a constant that apportions energy into three components and accounts for the effects of a free surface; and r, q, and v_s are properties of the travel path. Figure 19 shows typical shapes for a'_s, $p(f_n...)$, and a'.

The power of the ground motion is estimated with the one-sided spectral density function g_a from the locally averaged Fourier amplitudes:

$$g_a(f) = |\overline{a'_{gm}(f)}|^2 /\pi s$$ (63)

where s is the duration of strong motion. Many definitions of strong-motion durations have been proposed; a good summary is in Bommer

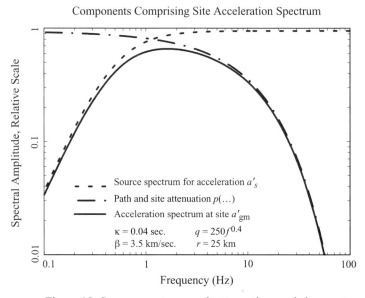

Figure 19. Source spectrum, path attenuation, and site spectrum.

92

and Martinez-Pereira (1999). The definition in equation 63 is meant to be the duration over which strong-motion characteristics are stationary.

Second, to calculate a response spectrum at frequency f_n, the spectral density function of a linear oscillator response can be used, as follows:

$$g_x(f) = g_a(f) \mid h_x(f; f_n, \xi) \mid^2 \tag{64}$$

where $h_x(f; f_n, \xi)$ is the transfer function of a single-degree-of-freedom (SDOF) linear oscillator with natural frequency f_n and damping ratio ξ. Figure 20 shows typical shapes for g_a and h_x. From g_x, the root-mean-square (RMS) response of the oscillator can be determined as

$$\sigma_x = [2\pi \int_0^\infty gx(2\pi f)df]^{1/2} \tag{65}$$

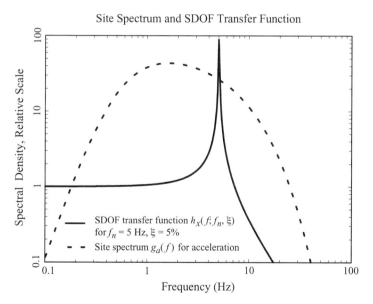

Figure 20. Site spectral density function and SDOF transfer function for 5 Hz.

Finally, the peak response, the *SA*, is estimated as

$$SA(f_n) = \sigma_x \, p_f(f_n, s) \qquad (66)$$

where p_f is a peak factor (the ratio of peak to RMS response) that depends on natural frequency and duration s. Figure 21 illustrates σ_x, p_f, and *SA* for an oscillator with $f_n = 1$ Hz subjected to a ground motion of 30 sec. duration. Note that σ_x applies only to the strong-motion part of the record, which for this example lasts from 5 sec. to 15 sec.

So, in concept, the application of stochastic methods is straight-forward. Start with a source spectrum modified for path and surficial rock conditions (equation 62 and Figure 19), convert to the power spectral density of an oscillator (equations 63–64 and Figure 20), compute the RMS response of the oscillator (equation 65 and Figure 21), and estimate spectral acceleration with a peak factor (equation 66). To

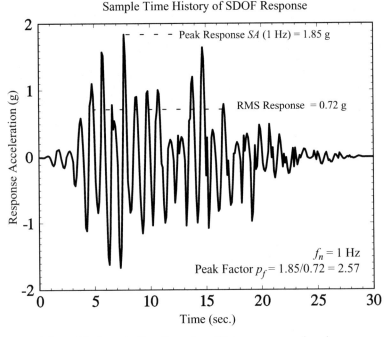

Figure 21. Sample function of oscillator response showing σ_x, p_f, and *SA*.

model a soil site with an equivalent linear soil model, transform the rock spectral density into a soil spectral density by using a format similar to equation 64. To use a fully nonlinear model of soil (or structural) response, generate sample functions of motion from the spectral density for input to the nonlinear model.

For illustration purposes, it is useful to adopt some reasonable assumptions, calculate ground motion using the stochastic method, and compare the calculated ground motion with empirical data. For this purpose, the following parameter values are assumed:

$\mathbf{M} = 6.5$
Density $\rho = 2.7$ gm/cm^3
Shear-wave velocity $v_s = 3.5$ km/s
Stress drop $\Delta\sigma = 60$ bars
Site attenuation $\kappa = 0.04$ sec.
Path attenuation $q = 250\, f^{0.4}$
Surface amplification $c(f)$
$\quad = 2.024 + 0.65 \ln (f) + 0.263\,[\ln (f)]^2 \qquad 0.5 \le f < 5$ Hz
$\quad = 3.75 \qquad\qquad\qquad\qquad\qquad\qquad 5$ Hz $\le f$

The surface amplification factor $c(f)$ quantifies the rock amplification curve illustrated in Appendix D, Figure D3. For estimates of SA, the simplified equations in Appendix D are used; i.e., equation D15 is used to estimate root-mean-squared SA, the peak factor is obtained from equation D17, and PGA is assumed to be equal to SA at $f = 33$ Hz.

Figures 22 through 24 compare estimates from the stochastic model with strong-motion data from both hard and soft rock sites for PGA and for SA at frequencies of 10 and 1 Hz. In these plots, distance is measured from the rupture surface of the fault, which is assumed to be equivalent to the point-source distance for the stochastic model. As in Section 4.2, data from $6 \le \mathbf{M} \le 7$ have been scaled to $\mathbf{M} = 6.5$ for these plots by using $SA \propto \exp(0.5\,\mathbf{M})$ for the high frequencies and $SA \propto \exp(1.0\,\mathbf{M})$ for $f = 1$ Hz. The stochastic model provides a good estimate of the median level of ground motion over the frequency range and for very short distances ($r \simeq 3$ km), recognizing that data at very short distances are pretty sparse. The stochastic estimates in these plots stop at $r \simeq 3$ km, which is consistent with the assumption that the seismogenic portion of a fault's rupture lies at depths of at least 3 km. Even if a fault ruptures to the surface, the shallower segments do not release significant energy.

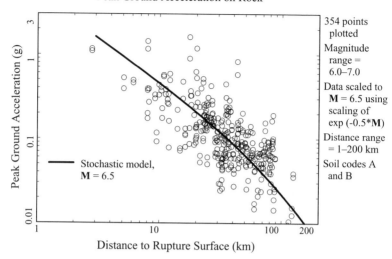

Figure 22. PGA on rock for **M** = 6.5 from a stochastic model compared with data from **M** = 6.0–7.0.

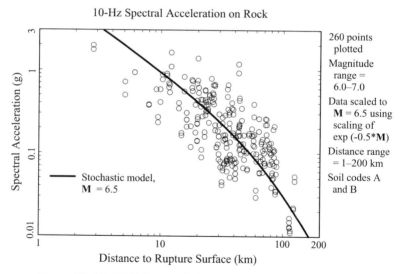

Figure 23. *SA* (10 Hz) on rock for **M** = 6.5 from a stochastic model compared with data from **M** = 6.0–7.0.

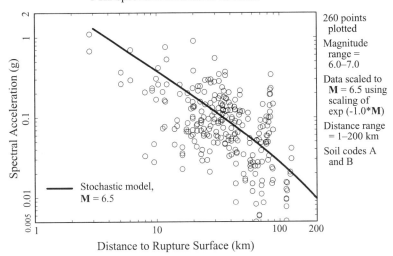

Figure 24. *SA* (1 Hz) on rock for **M** = 6.5 from a
stochastic model compared with data from **M** = 6.0–7.0.

Parameters of the stochastic model are usually established by
"inversion" from data, meaning that some parameters of the model—
such as the density of the earth's crust—are fixed (that is, they are
estimated from other studies), and others are adjusted to obtain the
best fit to the data (either by varying parameters manually or by using least-squares regression analysis). Therefore, be careful in comparing model parameters from different studies. Estimates of κ, for
example, will depend strongly on what q model has been used and
on whether surface amplification $c(f)$ has been included. Unless the
same model has been used in all studies, differences in model parameters cannot always be interpreted as physical differences.

The stochastic model for seismic hazard and risk analysis is commonly applied by using the full equations in Appendix D—that is,
equations D22 and D19 for RMS *SA* and peak factor, respectively.
Nonlinear or equivalent-linear soil amplification programs are used
to establish the response of surficial rock and soil layers as a function of ground motion amplitude. In such cases, closed-form expressions for *SA* are not available. It is usual in these applications to
predict ground motions for a range of magnitudes and distances, and

97

then fit coefficients for simplified equation forms to the generated estimates. This allows simpler equations to be used in the seismic hazard and risk analysis, while justifying the equations with the full theory behind the stochastic model. Users need not develop their own software for the stochastic model, as public domain programs are available (Silva and Lee 1987, Boore 1996).

As stated at the beginning of this section, the most important application of the stochastic model is in estimating ground motions in regions for which strong-motion data are sparse. For such regions, use seismological data from weak ground motions (i.e., from small or distant earthquakes) to establish critical parameters of the model ($\Delta\sigma$, κ, q, and source depth) and rely on the established applicability of the stochastic model in regions with abundant data to justify its use.

4.4 Ground Motion Uncertainties

Uncertainties in ground motion estimation can be distinguished by two categories: aleatory uncertainties in random effects U_R and epistemic uncertainties in knowledge U_K. Below are some useful examples.

U_R uncertainties that affect the ground motion include the dynamic effects of rupture propagation, random characteristics of the energy release (such as its overall dynamic stress drop and the variation of that drop across the rupture area), scattering of seismic waves by heterogeneities in the earth, random interference effects of incoming waves at the site, and any other effects that cannot be predicted. These uncertainties are usually not modeled explicitly but are represented by scatter in the ground motion predictions around the median value.

Ground motion modeling typically involves U_K uncertainties in choosing the "correct" or most appropriate median empirical ground motion equation for a region, the dynamic effects that soils at a specific site have on strong shaking, the average parameters (e.g., dynamic stress drop) to use in the stochastic model, and which U_R uncertainties to assume. The apparent complexity of having U_K uncertainties about U_R uncertainties should not be intimidating. The U_R uncertainty in the ground motion (the scatter in the ground motion equations) is just another parameter in the seismic hazard or risk calculations that contributes to the annual frequency of exceedance, and it is logical that any such parameter would have U_K uncertainty. It might be desirable to estimate this U_K uncertainty from statistics, but there are other considerations, as discussed below.

Note that stress drop $\Delta\sigma$ has been deliberately mentioned under both U_K and U_R uncertainties. A tectonic region such as the Basin and Range province of the United States that is under extensional stress will generate normal-faulting earthquakes with a different average static and dynamic stress drop than events in California or the eastern United States, where the tectonic regimes differ. For the Basin and Range province, there will probably be some U_K uncertainty about what *average* $\Delta\sigma$ (the average over many earthquakes) should be used in the stochastic ground motion model. In addition, even if the appropriate *average* $\Delta\sigma$ for the Basin and Range province were known, each future event will have a random $\Delta\sigma$, and this is U_R uncertainty.

The fundamental understanding about U_K and U_R uncertainties in ground motion comes from the large scatter in observations, even when they are normalized by magnitude, distance, and other parameters. This scatter is evident in the plots presented in Figures 11–15. If this scatter were not so large, and if *SA* could be predicted within ± 5% at a site given m, r, and site characteristics, then the ground motion section of this monograph could be very short indeed. This section would consist of presenting *the* ground motion equation, and the analyst could focus on U_K and U_R uncertainties for seismicity only.

It would be tempting to estimate the U_R uncertainty in ground motions from observations and then estimate U_K uncertainty in this parameter with statistical methods. The problem is that most statistical methods assume independent observations, and ground motion data are correlated, as discussed in section 4.2. This is why, even with hundreds of ground motion observations, different researchers report different scatter in normalized ground motion data. In addition, an important component of scatter in groun d motion data comes from site amplification/deamplification of the ground motion: different sites with ostensibly the same characteristics affect ground motion differently, contributing to scatter in the normalized observations. Therefore, some of the variability observed in normalized ground motion data is properly treated as U_K uncertainty caused by site characteristics. Studies relevant to this issue have been undertaken by Brune (1999), who observed precarious rocks near the San Andreas Fault and concluded that they had not experienced ground motions with PGA > 0.4 g, even though multiple $\mathbf{M} = 8$ earthquakes had occurred on the fault over the last 10,000 years. This PGA equals the median ground motion estimates from published ground motion equations, implying that the U_R uncertainty is small. To extend this conclusion to other sites without similar observations, U_R and U_K uncertainty in ground motion must be partitioned in a defensible way. However the U_R and U_K uncertainties are partitioned, the *mean frequency* of exceedance will be the same, although—as Anderson and Brune (1999) point out—the *probability* of exceedance will be affected when exposure time is long in relation to the earthquake recurrence interval. Fortunately for most seismic hazard applications, the exposure time is shorter than the earthquake recurrence interval. The first major seismic hazard study to differentiate ground motion (U_R and U_K) uncertainty this way was the Diablo Canyon, California probabilistic risk assessment (PG&E 1988). If this strategy is adopted, then the partitioning of uncertainty between U_R and U_K for ground motion necessarily involves substantial judgment, because quantitative conclusions about how much uncertainty is caused by unknown effects of site characteristics are almost certainly site-dependent.

A common parameter for quantifying scatter in ground motion observations is $\sigma_{\ln(SA)}$, since $\ln(SA)$ is usually found to be normally distributed. Figure 25 illustrates $\sigma_{\ln(SA)}$ versus period for several empirical ground motion equations for $\mathbf{M} = 6.5$. The standard deviation of $\ln(SA)$ can be translated into the coefficient of variation (COV) of ground motion with the assumption of the lognormal distribution by using

$$\text{COV} = \frac{\sigma_{SA}}{mean_{SA}} = \sqrt{\exp[\sigma^2_{\ln(SA)}] - 1} \qquad (67)$$

This equation implies, for example, that for a typical $\sigma_{\ln(SA)}$ of 0.6, the COV of SA is 0.66—that is, the standard deviation of SA is 66% of the mean. This is a large uncertainty. To state confidence levels in predicted values of SA, it is easiest to first work in logarithms and then translate into acceleration units. For example, if a median SA of 0.5 g is predicted for a given set of conditions and $\sigma_{\ln(SA)} = 0.6$, then (for the normal distribution) 84% of observations will lie below the mean-plus-one-standard-deviation level (of $\ln[SA]$). This translates into an acceleration of

$$\exp[\ln(0.5\text{g}) + 0.6] = 0.91\text{g} \qquad (68)$$

This is substantial uncertainty, and it illustrates why the estimation of ground motion remains a challenging (and humbling) task.

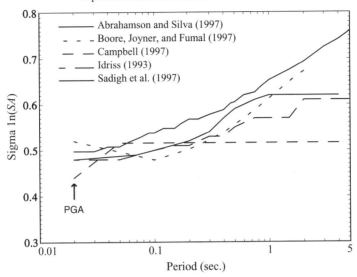

Figure 25. $\sigma_{\ln(SA)}$ versus period for **M** = 6.5 for five ground motion equations.

From Figure 25, ground motion uncertainty quantified by $\sigma_{\ln(SA)}$ is generally found to be larger at long periods. The reason is that long-period ground motions are more deterministically related to properties of the source function. Long-period waves are sensitive to large-scale discontinuities on the rupture surface. High-frequency (short-period) ground motion at a site, on the other hand, generally represents contributions from several or many smaller-scale fault asperities. Furthermore, the high-frequency motion is influenced by two effects: (1) source properties, such as rupture dynamics and directivity, that will not be identical for dislocations at the many different asperities; and (2) a high degree of scattering of short-period waves traveling from individual asperities to the site as they encounter small-scale heterogeneities in the crust. (Long-period waves are not scattered much by small-scale heterogeneities in the crust, and there is less averaging of directivity and other effects at long periods). The net result of this overall averaging of short-period waves is a reduction in $\sigma_{\ln(SA)}$.

101

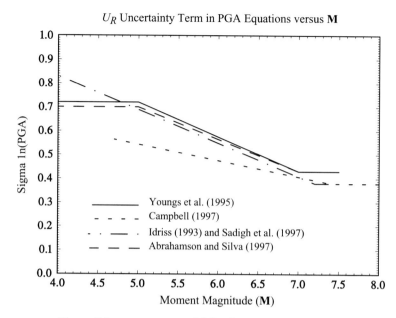

Figure 26. $\sigma_{\ln(PGA)}$ versus **M** for four attenuation equations.

Figure 26 shows $\sigma_{\ln(PGA)}$ as a function of magnitude, reported by several investigators who have examined this dependence, for PGA. The observations show that $\sigma_{\ln(PGA)}$ is larger for small magnitudes than for large magnitudes. At first glance, this appears to contradict Figure 25: if small-scale, short-wavelength energy has less statistical scatter, then why should small-magnitude earthquakes, with smaller source dimensions, show more statistical scatter than large-magnitude earthquakes? The answer lies in the source size. Small m events may involve only one coherent dislocation, whereas large m events involve multiple dislocations, and the largest peak ground motion from multiple subevents will have a smaller COV (sigma/mean) than the COV for a single dislocation.

Note that recordings from the 1999 Chi-Chi, Taiwan earthquake (**M** = 7.7) indicate higher U_R uncertainty than Figure 26 shows for that magnitude. These data may lead ground motion researchers to rethink their models of $\sigma_{\ln(SA)}$ versus magnitude in the future.

Some historical perspective is always useful. Figure 27 shows values of $\sigma_{\ln(PGA)}$ reported in the literature from empirical ground

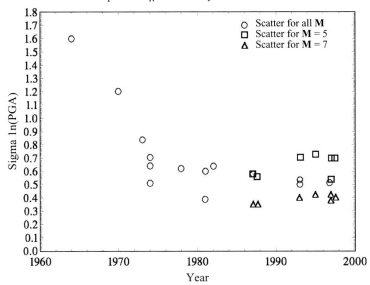

Figure 27. $\sigma_{\ln(PGA)}$ reported in literature from 1964–1998.

motion equations based primarily on California data. Early equations from the 1960s indicated $\sigma_{\ln(PGA)} > 1.0$, and more recent models have reduced this to 0.4–0.7 (the amount depends on **M**), primarily because better forms of equations have been developed. These better forms use mixed **M** and r terms to achieve magnitude-dependent distance scaling and distance-dependent magnitude scaling, particularly at short distances. These equations also use more predictive variables such as fault type, site category, and building size (the size of the building where the instrument was located) than earlier equations did, and these extra predictive variables reduce the residual scatter.

One important conclusion from Figure 27 is that U_R uncertainties in ground motion have not been reduced at all in the last 15 years: $\sigma_{\ln(PGA)} \simeq 0.4$ for **M** = 7 and $\simeq 0.7$ for **M** = 5. These plateaus in uncertainty will probably not be reduced unless data are restricted to a specific region and/or site characteristic.

Note that, even though more data are now available, the mere quantity of data has not reduced the scatter of ground motion prediction since the 1960s. If an original set of data is representative of a region, and if analysts continue using the same predictive equation, then adding more observations will not change the estimate of σ much at all. The way to reduce σ is to pursue additional data in connection with more detailed models (such as models that include the effect of a specific soil type) so that specific effects caused by certain (predictable) conditions can be quantified.

Beware of the temptation to reduce U_R uncertainties by smoothing spectral amplitudes over a frequency bandwidth, thereby reducing frequency-to-frequency scatter. Unless the structure under study responds to the entire frequency bandwidth, frequency-to-frequency scatter must still be added to predict spectral accelerations and structural response, and the most accurate way to do this is to predict each spectral acceleration directly. Arguments that smoothed spectral accelerations are more "robust" are misguided.

A final note of caution about adding predictive variables is appropriate. It is tempting to use as many characteristics of the earthquake as possible to reduce scatter in ground motion. However, for the resulting scatter estimate to be meaningful, these characteristics must be variables that can be *predicted*. If the direction of rupture propagation is used as a variable (i.e., propagation toward the site versus away from the site), then this will underestimate the observed scatter unless the rupture direction for the next event can be predicted, as explained in the example of this effect in Section 4.2. The alternative, which is to condition on the variable for the attenuation equation and to integrate over its possible values during the seismic hazard calculations, is appropriate when observed data do not contain a representative distribution of that variable.

The expected occurrence of about four great earth-quakes per century in the California region by no means excludes the possibility that double that number might occur in a given century, or that a whole century might pass without even one.

Beno Gutenberg and Charles Richter, 1944

5 SEISMIC HAZARD ANALYSIS

5.1 *Introduction*

In PSHA, as in many undertakings, there is no substitute for experience. With that in mind, this section proceeds to study the details of a PSHA application by looking at a real (albeit simplified) example. This PSHA of the ground shaking hazard in Berkeley, California is performed to review typical results and their sensitivities.

A PSHA should be viewed as a *process* by which probabilistic results (in this case, annual frequencies versus ground motions, along with uniform hazard spectra) are calculated and documented. Just as an earthquake is not defined by the peak acceleration at only one site, a PSHA does not consist of only the final hazard curves or spectra. For example, if parameter x is determined to be very critical to the results, then a complete evaluation and inclusion of the uncertainty in x must be part of the PSHA. Equally important, if parametric studies show that parameter y has no influence on the hazard, then documentation of those studies should also be included.

The following PSHA is not exhaustive or definitive, and it does not examine all the parameters that might be appropriate (for example, uncertainties in fault geometry). Rather, the focus is on the PSHA process, how one evaluates alternative assumptions, and whether they should be included. It is preferable here to present a clear, understandable use of the PSHA process via a few demonstrations than to present a comprehensive, detailed examination of the critical influences on PSHA at one unique site. Earthquakes are complex phenomena, and no single site can provide a demonstration of all the important influences.

In this vein, the present example examines a number of assumptions about faults and area sources, some of which might be viewed as unrealistic or unjustified for the case at hand. For instance, some of the maximum magnitude (M_{max}) values assigned to the Hayward fault, which runs through Berkeley, might be deemed unsupportable by the potential rupture area. If, however, there is a high sensitivity of hazard to M_{max} (and there certainly is), be aware of that sensitivity and treat uncertainty in M_{max} completely. It is with this perspective and goal that this section examines the seismic hazard in Berkeley.

5.2 Basic Seismic Hazard Calculations

The starting point of PSHA calculations for Berkeley (122.3° W, 37.9° N) is the interpretation of fault sources and seismicity in California by the USGS (WGCEP 1999, USGS 2001). These data consist of 42 active fault segments within 50 km of Berkeley and background seismicity modeled as earthquakes occurring at points with spacing of 0.1° longitude and latitude. Figure 28 shows the nearby faults.

For seismicity on the faults, the starting point is the WGCEP (1999) interpretation, which assumes a characteristic model of seismicity— that is, a range of characteristic magnitudes M_{CH} can occur on each fault with a specified annual frequency. For the Hayward fault, which not surprisingly is the dominant contributor to seismic hazard, the PSHA will model only the northern segment of the fault, for simplicity in the sensitivity studies presented here. The WGCEP interpretation is actually more complicated than this, consisting of seven segments of the Hayward and Rodgers Creek faults that can rupture separately, but the simplification of using only one segment is adequate for this PSHA. The entire Hayward fault is 85 km long, and the northern segment is about half that length. The seismogenic zone is assumed to extend from the surface to a 12-km depth, and a vertical fault is assumed. The slip rate assigned to the northern segment of the fault is 9 mm/yr (WGCEP 1999).

For seismicity in the background region, the PSHA uses the rates of activity developed by the USGS, a b value of 0.9, a maximum magnitude M_{max} of 6.5, and a minimum magnitude of 5.0 at each 0.1° grid

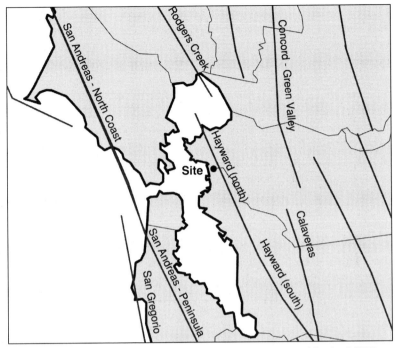

Figure 28. Faults in the Berkeley vicinity that were used in the PSHA.

point. To be consistent with the definitions of distance used in the ground motion equations (which are described next), the PSHA generates a rupture length for each earthquake centered at each grid point by using a random azimuth and a length estimated as $RL=10^{(-2.57\,+0.62\mathbf{M})}$, which comes from Wells and Coppersmith (1994). With these rupture lengths, the proper distance to the site can be determined for each ground motion equation.

The ground motion equations are as follows:
- Abrahamson and Silva (1997), rock, fault type 0
- Boore, Joyner, and Fumal (1997), rock, strike-slip faulting
- Campbell (1997), soft rock, depth to basement = 0.8 km
- Idriss (1993), rock, strike-slip faulting
- Sadigh et al. (1997), rock, strike-slip faulting

Each of these equations was assigned a weight of 0.2. For the single-hypothesis analysis described below, these equations were used to calculate five ground motion values for each magnitude and site-rupture distance, and the (logarithmic) average of the five equations was taken as the mean log ground motion. Similarly, the standard deviations of ln [ground motion] from the five cited approaches were averaged. This gave the equivalent of a single ground motion equation for the single-hypothesis analysis.

Figures 29 and 30 show the hazard contribution from the individual faults and background seismicity for PGA and 1-Hz *SA*, respectively, for the base case, single-hypothesis analysis (that is, without inclusion of uncertainties in parameters, and using the single average ground motion equation as described above). As expected, the northern segment of the Hayward fault dominates the hazard at all but the lowest ground motions (i.e., it dominates at ground motions of about 0.1 g and greater).

Subsequent sections examine the hazard from the fault and from the background seismicity separately. Faults and area sources reflect different interpretations of seismicity, and the proper inclusion of uncertainties requires the consideration of different parameters for each. In addition, the process of deaggregating the hazard to determine which events are dominant is best done in the context of a single fault or area source, although combined deaggregation plots provide useful insight.

5.3 Anatomy of Fault Hazard

It is clear from Section 5.2 that the predominant hazard in Berkeley comes from the Hayward fault, and it is instructive to find out what interpretations of seismicity on the fault are most influential. This exploration of hazard examines the range of interpretations and effects that might be available for *any* fault, so that the review is not restricted to only those that have credibility for the Hayward fault. Though some of the interpretations examined here might not apply to the Hayward fault, this study exposes any sensitivity of hazard to those interpretations so that, for a PSHA done elsewhere, those potential sensitivities will be evident.

First, consider as a base case model a Hayward fault description that consists of a northern segment with a pure characteristic magnitude model (i.e., events occur with only one magnitude, $M_{CH} = 6.9$) and a slip rate of 9 mm/yr. This M_{CH} equals the estimated magnitude of the 1868 earthquake that ruptured the southern half of the Hayward fault, and it equals the "floating earthquake" that the WGCEP (1999) assigned to the fault. The recurrence period for the base case with a fault length of 43 km, fault width of 12 km, and slip rate $\dot{s}$ of 9 mm/yr

PGA Hazard at Berkeley by Source

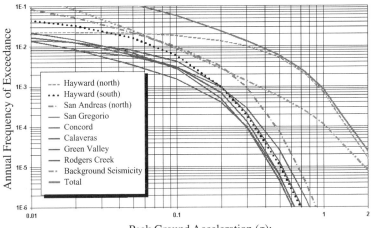

Peak Ground Acceleration (g);
Average of Five Ground Motion Equations

Figure 29. Contribution to the PGA hazard in Berkeley, for each
fault and background seismicity.

1-Hz Hazard at Berkeley by Seismic Source

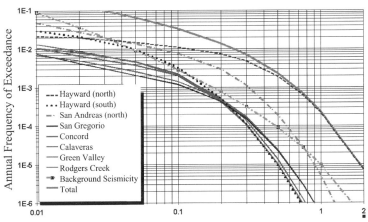

1-Hz Spectral Acceleration (g);
Average of Five Ground Motion Equations

Figure 30. Contribution to the 1-Hz *SA* hazard in Berkeley, for
each fault and background seismicity.

109

can be calculated as follows (see equation 42):

$$\dot{M}_o = \mu \, a_T \, \dot{s}$$
$$= (3 \times 10^{10} \text{ N/m}^2)(43 \text{ km x } 12 \text{ km})(9 \text{ mm/yr})$$
$$= 1.4 \times 10^{17} \text{ N-m/yr}$$

The $\mathbf{M}_{CH}$ value of 6.9 implies a seismic moment of

$$M_o = 10^{1.5\mathbf{M} + 16.05}$$
$$= 2.5 \times 10^{26} \text{ dyne-cm}$$
$$= 2.5 \times 10^{19} \text{ N-m}$$

$$recurrence\ interval = moment\ per\ event\ /\dot{M}_o$$
$$= 180 \text{ years}$$

which is almost identical to the estimated recurrence interval of 184 years for all earthquakes involving the northern segment (WGCEP 1999). This recurrence interval can also be calculated as the inverse of the activity rate, equation 47, by putting in the correct values for the variables.

Table 9 lists some alternative models of seismicity on the Hayward fault. The base case model with $\mathbf{M}_{CH} = 6.9$ is listed as model 1. Other models explore the effects of other magnitude distributions. These models consist of two variations of a "characteristic only" model, which has a range of magnitudes with $\Delta\mathbf{M} = 0.5$ magnitude units, and four variations of a "standard characteristic" model, which uses a characteristic magnitude for large events and an exponential distribution for smaller magnitudes, as illustrated in Figure 7. Model 8 examines the effects of using a pure exponential magnitude distribution in place of the characteristic model.

Figure 31 compares results for the base case (model 1) with models 2, 4, and 6 in Table 9. These other models give hazards similar to the base case, because the seismicity description is similar. Model 2 uses a range of magnitudes ($\mathbf{M} = 6.7$–7.2) instead of a pure characteristic model ($\mathbf{M} = 6.9$), model 4 adds the exponential part of the magnitude distribution at low magnitudes, and model 6 uses the entire Hayward fault geometry, not just the northern segment. None of these differences causes major changes in the hazard, and this could be expected since the rate of occurrence of the characteristic events ($\mathbf{M} = 6.7$–7.2, centered on 6.95) is similar for models 2, 4, and 6 (see the last column of Table 9). The hazards for models 4 and 6 are somewhat higher at low and moderate ground motion values (PGA < 0.5 g), because the additional small magnitudes add hazard for the lower ground motions, while not accounting for much tectonic slip. That

Table 9. Alternative seismicity models for the Hayward fault.

Model	Fault Segment	Slip Rate	M_{CH}	M Distribution	Characteristic Recurrence Interval (yrs)	Characteristic Recurrence Interval on North Segment (yrs)
1	North	9 mm/yr	6.9	Pure characteristic	180	180
2	North	9 mm/yr	6.7–7.2	Characteristic only	242	242
3	North	9 mm/yr	6.9–7.4	Characteristic only	483	483
4	North	9 mm/yr	6.7–7.2	Standard characteristic	256	256
5	North	9 mm/yr	6.4–6.9	Standard characteristic	92	92
6	Entire fault	9 mm/yr	6.7–7.2	Standard characteristic	128	256
7	North	4.5 mm/yr	6.3–6.8	Standard characteristic	128	128
8	North	9 mm/yr	None	M 5–7.2 exponential	None	None

111

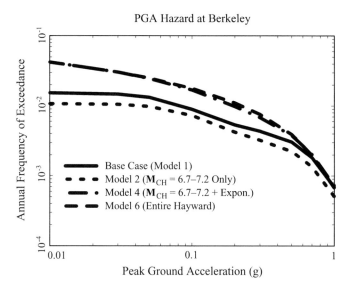

Figure 31. PGA hazard in Berkeley from the Hayward fault for the base case model and similar models.

is, for a fixed slip rate (9 mm/yr on this fault), adding small-magnitude events does not decrease the rate of occurrence of the characteristic events much, but it does add some hazard at low and moderate ground motion amplitudes.

Figure 32 shows a different set of results from models that *do* make a difference in seismic hazard. The base case model is shown, along with models 3, 5, 7, and 8. In what might seem a counterintuitive result at first glance, model 3 (with a higher magnitude range) implies somewhat less hazard than the base case, and model 5 (with a lower magnitude range) implies somewhat more hazard than the base case.

The reason for this result is related to the specification of activity by slip rate. Once the slip rate is estimated, a higher characteristic magnitude range will imply a lower recurrence rate and a longer recurrence interval. $\mathbf{M} = 7.4$ earthquakes must occur less often than $\mathbf{M} = 7.2$ earthquakes to explain a 9 mm/yr slip rate on a fault, and the lower recurrence rate reduces the hazard (it more than compensates for the larger ground motions implied by $\mathbf{M} = 7.4$ versus $\mathbf{M} = 7.2$). Table 9 shows the recurrence intervals for these models. Here is an example of why associating a large magnitude with a fault is not always "con-

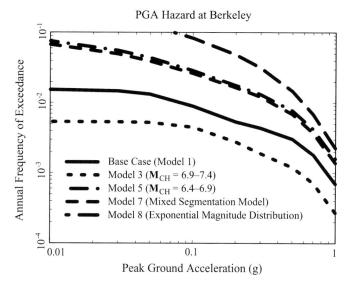

Figure 32. PGA hazard in Berkeley from the Hayward fault for the base case model and other models that give different results.

servative." Note also that changing the characteristic magnitude range by only 0.2 magnitude units has an important effect on the estimated hazard. Thus, the estimation of M_{CH} must *not* be treated lightly.

As further proof of this last statement, model 7 (with $\dot{s} = 4.5$ mm/yr) gives almost the same hazard as model 5. The reason is that, for model 7, M_{max} has been reduced by 0.1 unit, from 6.9 to 6.8. This means that a change of 0.1 magnitude unit in M_{max} is equivalent to a 50% change in slip rate, emphasizing again the importance of M_{max} and M_{CH} in hazard estimates.

Model 8, the exponential magnitude model, implies significantly more hazard than any of the characteristic models, just because the large rate of occurrence of small and moderate events needed to explain a slip rate of 9 mm/yr implies high hazard. To reiterate a perspective stated previously, this is not to say that an exponential model is credible; in fact, a comparison of predicted seismicity from the exponential model with historical seismicity around the Hayward fault would rule out the exponential model as a credible assumption, given a slip rate of 9 mm/yr.

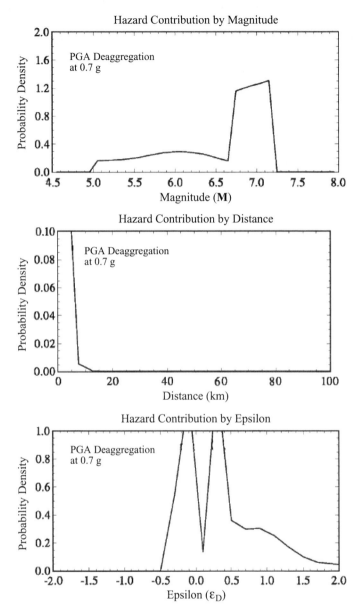

Figure 33. Deaggregation of the 0.7 g PGA hazard
from the Hayward fault, for model 5.

Figure 33 shows the deaggregation of PGA hazard at 0.7 g (approximately the 475-year ground motion) by magnitude, distance, and ground motion epsilon value (using ε_C, which is described in the next paragraph), for the model 4 analysis. This figure shows that characteristic earthquakes ($\mathbf{M} \simeq 7$) at short distances ($r \simeq 10$ km) dominate the hazard. For events at these distances, ε_C is in the range of -0.5 to +1, meaning that the dominant ground motions are within 1σ of the median. A close examination of Figure 33 in fact shows two peaks in the ε distribution, one centered at -0.2 and the other centered at +0.3. From the area of these two peaks (~ 0.6 total) and a comparison with the magnitude distribution (the top plot in Figure 33), it can be deduced that the peaks coincide with the area (~ 0.6) from $\mathbf{M} = 6.7$–7.2, which corresponds to $\mathbf{M}_{CH}$ for the Hayward fault. Why are there two peaks in the deaggregation of ε instead of one? Further examination reveals that, for $\mathbf{M} \simeq 7$ at $r = 1.8$ km (the distance to the Hayward fault), three of the ground motion equations estimate PGA as being greater than about 0.7 g, and two estimate PGA as < 0.7 g. Figure 34 shows predictions from the five ground motion equations. For deaggregation of hazard at 0.7 g, the three higher equations will

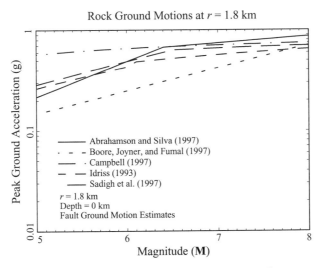

Figure 34. Comparison of predicted PGA values from five ground motion equations versus magnitude, for $r = 1.8$ km. The calculations assume that the rupture occurs at the surface.

115

have $\varepsilon \simeq -0.2$, and the two lower equations will have $\varepsilon \simeq +0.3$, leading to the bimodal ε distribution shown in Figure 33.

Deaggregation using ε_C assigns all weight to an ε value equal to $(x - \bar{x})/\sigma_x$, where x is the logarithm of the amplitude that is being deaggregated, $\bar{x}$ is the mean log amplitude, and σ_x is the standard deviation of log amplitude. An alternative is to assign weights to all ε values between ε_C and $+\infty$, because all such ε values will produce an exceedance of x. This is denoted ε_D (for "density," since the weights are assigned according to the normal density function).

To compare these two deaggregation methods, Figure 35 shows the deaggregation of a 0.7 g PGA hazard using the density definition of epsilon, ε_D, instead of the complementary cumulative definition, ε_C, shown at the bottom of Figure 33. The ε_D values for each earthquake occurrence and mean ground motion are smoothed out over higher ε values, which smooths out the peaks in ε_C from Figure 33 and makes the deaggregation by ε_D less diagnostic. Deaggregation by ε_D is more theoretically "pure," however, in that ε_D measures density function contributions from the ground motion distribution, just as $\mathbf{M}$ and r measure density function contributions from the magnitude and distance distributions, respectively. A true cognoscente of PSHA will appreciate this subtlety but will choose the deaggregation method that offers the most insight into seismic hazard.

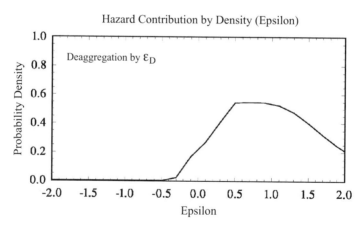

Figure 35. Deaggregation of the 0.7 g PGA hazard from the Hayward fault, using model 5 and showing distribution ε_D.

116

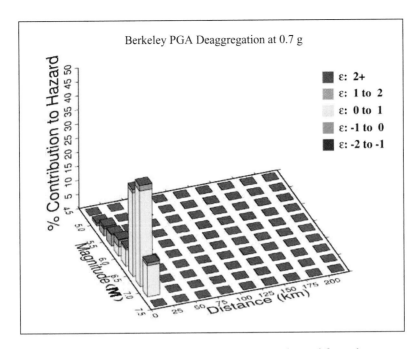

Figure 36. Deaggregation of the 0.7-g PGA hazard from the Hayward fault by **M**, r, and ε_C.

A 3-dimensional plot deaggregating the hazard by magnitude, distance, and ε_D gives a composite perspective, as illustrated in Figure 36. This figure shows that the primary contributions to hazard from the Hayward fault are at short distances, as expected, and that ground motions with $\varepsilon > 0$ are generally necessary to exceed 0.7 g.

Deaggregation plots (Figures 33, 35, and 36) are useful for two purposes. First, they show which magnitudes, distances, and epsilons contribute most of the seismic hazard, and this indicates where to concentrate efforts for better models. Figure 36, for example, shows that **M** $\simeq 6.5$ at $r < 25$ km is critical, so it might be desirable to examine further the effects of fault directivity. Figure 36 also shows that truncating the ground motion equation at $\varepsilon = 1\sigma$ would not affect the hazard very much for a PGA of 0.7 g. Second, secondary parameters for design, such as the duration of strong shaking, can be derived from the dominant m and r. This makes it possible to represent the ground motion—for example, with time histories—in a realistic way.

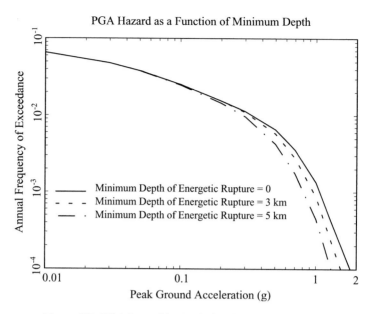

Figure 37. PGA hazard in Berkeley from the Hayward fault: sensitivity to minimum depth of energy release on the fault.

The comparison of these ground motions in Figure 34 assumed that the Hayward fault ruptured to the surface, and distances for each ground motion equation were calculated under that assumption. Two of the equations assume implicitly that, although the rupture may proceed to the surface, the energetic strain release that drives strong ground motion occurs at a minimum depth, on the order of 3–5 km. If this supposition is correct, should it be applied to the remaining three ground motion equations, and if so, what is the effect on the hazard? Figure 37 shows the PGA hazard curves, assuming a 0-km depth to the energetic rupture (the base case), a 3-km depth, and a 5-km depth. The differences are small at low ground motions, but they imply about a 20% difference in ground motion at 1×10^{-3} hazard (from 0–5 km of depth). This assumption should be examined further, by comparison with data and perhaps communication with the ground motion equation authors, before finalizing the PSHA.

Figure 38 compares hazard results for 1-Hz SA, using models compared in Figure 32 for PGA. Figure 39 illustrates the deaggregation

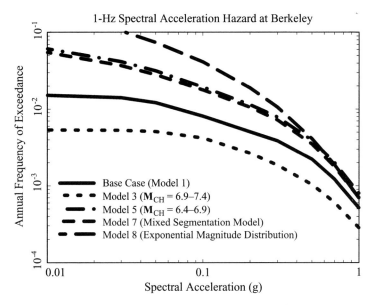

Figure 38. 1-Hz *SA* hazard in Berkeley from the Hayward fault, for the base case model and other models that give different results.

of hazard for 0.5 g *SA* at 1 Hz. This deaggregation is similar to that for PGA (Figure 33), in that characteristic magnitudes on the Hayward fault ($\mathbf{M} \simeq 7$) dominate the hazard.

This similarity of results for PGA and 1-Hz *SA*, with respect to sensitivity to different model assumptions and deaggregation of hazard, should not be considered universal. There are many sites where high- and low-frequency ground motion hazards are dominated by different faults or area sources and where consideration of alternative models must be different. A specific, separate investigation into high- and low-frequency effects and sensitivities is warranted at all sites.

Except for model 7, the basic slip rate of 9 mm/yr has not been varied, but it is clear from the derivation of activity rate ν from slip rate (see equation 47) that annual frequency is directly proportional to slip rate. Thus, uncertainties in slip rate will translate directly into uncertainties in annual frequencies, and changes in the mean slip rate will translate directly into changes in the mean hazard. It should also be clear that changes in *b* value have only a minor effect on

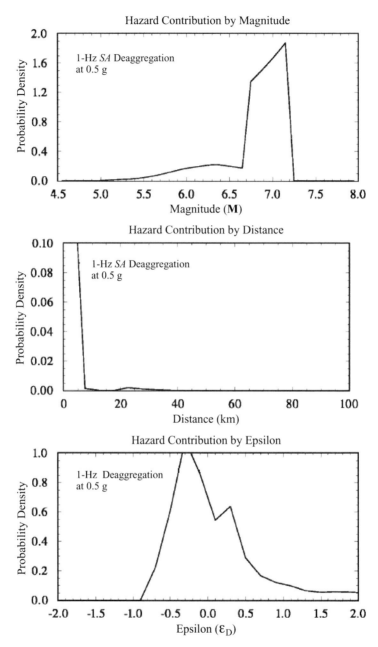

Figure 39. Deaggregation of 1-Hz *SA* hazard from the Hayward fault, for model 5.

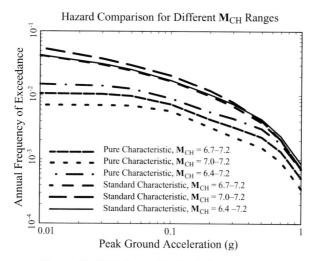

Figure 40. PGA hazard in Berkeley for pure and standard characteristic models, with different ranges for M_{CH}.

hazard when the standard characteristic model is used, because the exponential part of the distribution usually contributes only a small part of the hazard (see the top graph in Figures 33 and 39).

For a fixed value of M_{max}, the range of the characteristic magnitude part of the distribution will affect the hazard if the "pure characteristic" model (i.e., a model without an exponential portion) is used rather than the "standard characteristic" model. This is illustrated in Figure 40, which compares M_{CH} ranges of 0.5 (the base case), 0.2, and 0.8 for both the pure and standard characteristic models, using the same value of M_{max}. For the pure characteristic model, decreasing the range to $\Delta M = 0.2$ decreases the hazard, because the average magnitude increases and the recurrence rate decreases. Increasing the range to $\Delta M = 0.8$ has the opposite effect. For the standard characteristic model, changes in the range of M_{CH} are buffered by the exponential part of the distribution (less slip explained by M_{CH} means more slip attributed to small and moderate magnitudes), so changes in ΔM have less effect on the hazard. Note, of course, that this conclusion cannot be pushed too far: Figure 32 shows that decreasing ΔM to 0 and thereby creating a pure exponential distribution increases the hazard significantly.

An important conclusion about fault sources and the characteristic magnitude model is that the most critical seismicity parameters to estimate correctly are the maximum magnitude, the characteristic magnitude range (and whether a range is assumed), and the slip rate or recurrence interval. Details of the tectonic model and magnitude distribution, such as the fault segmentation and the b value of the exponential part of the distribution, are not so critical. But the importance of fault segmentation models must *not* be underrated. On the contrary, understanding fault segmentation and its uncertainty is the key to estimating slip rates and M_{max} values in an accurate and defensible way. Once that is done, however, the details of how faults are segmented may have little effect on the hazard.

On the ground motion side, it is absolutely critical to achieve consistency between the magnitude and distance definitions used in the ground motion equations and the definitions generated by the seismicity model in the PSHA. Issues such as the distance definition and the minimum depth to the energetic part of the rupture can affect ground motions by significant amounts.

With these observations in mind, a final calculation of seismic hazard in Berkeley is made from faults, by assuming the following distribution on slip rates, M_{max}, and depth of energy release:

slip rates: 6, 9, and 12 mm/yr (equal weights)

M_{max}: 7.2, 7.0, and 6.8 (equal weights)

depth of energy release: 0 km

Figure 41 shows the mean and fractile hazard curves from these uncertainties, compared with the single hazard curve from a single hypothesis on fault parameters. (This single hypothesis assumes a slip rate of 9 mm/yr and $M_{max} = 7.0$; that is, the central values listed above). The multihypothesis analysis shows a wide range in hazard, particularly at the higher ground motions, but the mean annual frequency of this analysis is close to that of the single-hypothesis analysis, at least down to 10^{-3}. This comparison points to the importance of including parameter uncertainties in a full seismic hazard analysis in order to understand how uncertain the results are.

Figure 42 plots the seismic hazard from the multihypothesis case in a commonly used format: the uniform hazard spectrum (UHS), so called because the spectrum—or, in this case, spectra—are plotted for a uniform annual frequency of exceedance. For this plot, the annual frequencies are 2.1×10^{-3} (the 475-year motion) and 1×10^{-4} (the 10,000-year motion).

122

PGA Hazard at Berkeley from Faults

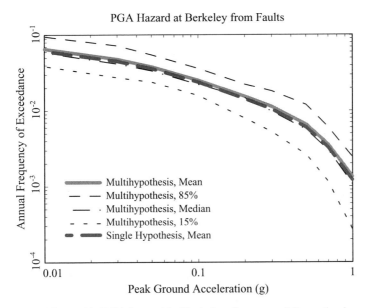

Figure 41. PGA hazard in Berkeley from a multihypothesis
analysis and mean hazard from a single-hypothesis analysis.

Uniform Hazard Spectra

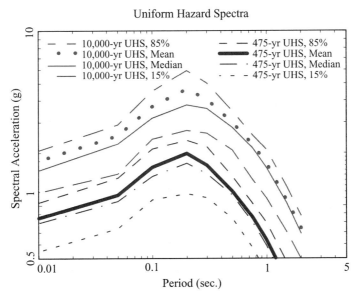

Figure 42. Uniform hazard spectra for 475-year and
10,000-year return periods.

This figure shows the mean, 15%, median, and 85% spectra for each return period. A characteristic of these results is that the mean UHS falls significantly above the median, meaning that the distribution of hazard has a positive skewness, toward larger values—that is, there is a long upper tail to the distribution.

This discussion has not examined the effects of uncertainties in fault geometry. It should be clear that these effects will be most important for a site near a fault, where changes in geometry will have a large effect on the distance from site to rupture. A particularly important uncertainty to consider is that of a nonvertical fault; if the site is on the hanging wall of a fault that produces oblique-slip earthquakes, then ground motions and hazard will be higher than for a vertical fault. As always, the guiding principle should be to consider all reasonable alternatives, assign them credibilities by using all relevant data (including interpretations in the context of modern plate tectonics), and include the alternatives in the PSHA.

Likewise, this discussion has not considered the effect of fault directivity. This directivity most affects the component of motion perpendicular to the direction of fault rupture and is important for frequencies below about 2 Hz. Somerville et al. (1997) showed that the effect of fault directivity can be to increase ground motions by more than a factor of 2 at very long periods (> 2.5 sec.). Of course, to produce an unbiased analysis, it should not be assumed that *all* earthquakes rupture toward the site: some ruptures will propagate away from the site, and other ruptures will be bilateral. A good PSHA will reflect all these possibilities.

A complication that arises when more than one fault contributes significantly to the hazard is the issue of *correlation* of uncertain fault parameters. It is simplest to assume that parameters such as $\dot{s}$ and $\mathbf{M}_{max}$ are uncorrelated. Although this might be valid for $\mathbf{M}_{max}$, the assigned values of $\dot{s}$ on faults might be negatively correlated at plate margins: a high slip rate on one fault would imply a low slip rate on another, thus maintaining a well-constrained plate margin slip rate, for example. These correlations must be built into the PSHA to calculate the correct uncertainty in the hazard. This can be handled by using global alternatives, with each alternative representing all faults and a consistent set of slip rates among them. The family of alternatives then represents the uncertainty in how a plate margin slip rate is apportioned among the faults. Ground motion equations on separate faults are often correlated; if one ground motion equation applies to one fault, then it probably applies to all faults in the region, so perfect correlation of ground motion equations for multiple faults is often an appropriate assumption. Even this rule has exceptions, however. If one empirical equation is based on a plethora of near-source data, and a second equation is well-constrained at distances of 50 km, then it may be appropriate to assign different weights to the different equations for separate faults and to treat them as being uncorrelated.

5.4 Anatomy of Hazard from Area Sources

A full PSHA includes uncertainties and alternative hypotheses in seismicity defined by area sources as well as faults. The simplified PSHA described in Section 5.2 is expanded here to include uncertainties in activity rates, b values, maximum magnitudes, and ground motion equations. A major difference between faults and area sources is that the characteristic magnitude distribution is generally not considered for area sources. Statistical distributions based on sufficient historical data usually show that seismicity in broad regions can be modeled by a truncated exponential distribution or one of its variants, as discussed in Section 3.

The seismicity grid used by the USGS is not a standard area source. Conventionally, area sources are defined as regions of homogeneous tectonic and/or crustal stress regimes in which the distributions of future earthquakes can be assumed to be homogeneous for calculating probabilities today. This does *not* mean that future seismicity will be uniform in space or time, or that specific faults will not be discovered in the future that may localize seismicity within the area source. Rather, it means that, given today's knowledge, and for purposes of making informed decisions about earthquake risks, the knowledge about a region's earthquake potential is homogeneous ("homogeneously bleak," the critics would say); thus, a homogeneous distribution reflects that state of knowledge.

A full PSHA will model uncertainties in the boundaries and parameters of area sources. This is one example of modeling what is really U_K (i.e., it is not known where the active faults are and where future earthquakes will occur) with U_R (i.e., future earthquake locations are treated as being random in space). The justification is that, in the foreseeable future, this epistemic uncertainty will not be resolved in most places, and the distinction is necessarily arbitrary in any case (as discussed in Section 2).

125

Table 10. Treatment of uncertainties for background
source and ground motion.

Model/	Simple Analysis		Full Analysis	
Parameter	Value	Weight	Value	Weight
Activity rate	USGS values	1.0	USGS values x 0.5	0.3
			USGS values	0.4
			USGS values x 1.5	0.3
b values	USGS values	1.0	USGS values x .87	0.3
			USGS values	0.4
			USGS values x 1.13	0.3
Maximum magnitude	6.5	1.0	6.0	0.3
			6.5	0.4
			7.0	0.3
Ground motion equation	Average ground motion	1.0	Abrahamson et al. (1997)	0.2
			Boore et al. (1997)	0.2
			Campbell (1997)	0.2
	Average σ	1.0	Idriss (1993)	0.2
			Sadigh et al. (1997)	0.2

Table 10 lists the parameters whose uncertainties are addressed in this section. The USGS activity rates for each cell in the background were somewhat arbitrarily assumed to have a 50% uncertainty, with weights of 0.3. This corresponds to a standard deviation in rates of a factor of ± 40%, which is typical. The b values were assumed to be uncertain by a factor of ± 13%, corresponding to a standard deviation of 10%, which is typical for b values. Finally, the maximum magnitude in the background zone was assumed to be 6.5 ± 0.5, with weights of 0.3 assigned to the extreme values. This, again, is a common uncertainty for maximum magnitudes in area sources. For calculations of hazard, the five ground motion equations were assigned equal weights, and (as discussed previously) the site-to-rupture distance was calculated to a randomly oriented fault centered at each background grid point.

Comparisons of hazard curves between the single-hypothesis case and the multihypothesis case are shown in Figures 43 and 44 for PGA and 1-Hz *SA*, respectively. For these comparisons, the single-hypothesis analysis indicates hazard estimates similar to the mean of the multihypothesis case, down to an annual frequency of 10^{-3} or so. For

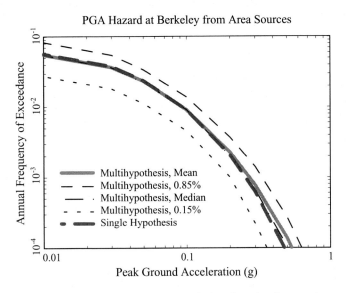

Figure 43. PGA hazard in Berkeley from background seismicity, for single-hypothesis and multihypothesis cases.

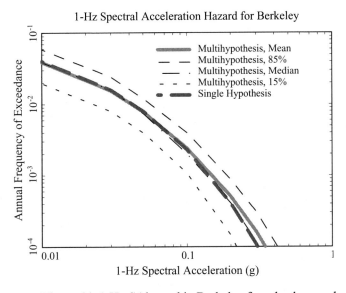

Figure 44. 1-Hz *SA* hazard in Berkeley from background seismicity, for single-hypothesis and multihypothesis cases.

127

lower annual frequencies (higher ground motions), the mean hazard from the multihypothesis calculation is slightly higher. This illustrates why the use of mean models and parameters in a seismic hazard analysis only approximates the mean hazard, especially for small annual frequencies. The error is about a factor of 50% in annual frequency at 10^{-4} and becomes progressively worse for higher ground motions.

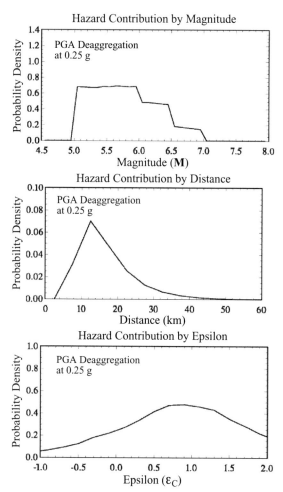

Figure 45. Deaggregation of PGA hazard in Berkeley, for PGA = 0.2 g, from the multihypothesis case.

Figures 45 and 46 show the deaggregation of hazard by **M**, *r*, and ε_C for PGA = 0.25 g and 1-Hz *SA* = 0.15 g, respectively (these are the ground motion amplitudes associated with an approximately 1,000-year return period, or annual frequency of 10^{-3}). These are distributions for the multihypothesis case; similar distributions are obtained for the single-hypothesis hazard, except that the magnitude

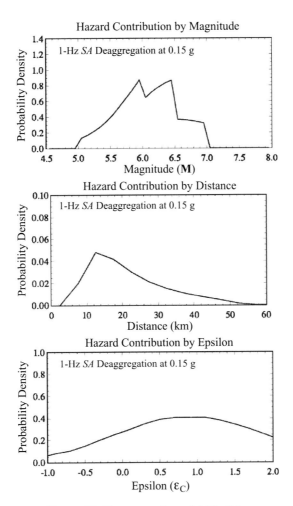

Figure 46. Deaggregation of 1-Hz *SA* hazard in Berkeley, for *SA* = 0.1 g, from the multihypothesis case.

distribution is smooth and is truncated at **M** = 6.5. When the two figures are compared, the 1-Hz *SA* distribution (Figure 46) shows the stronger influence of larger magnitudes and slightly longer distances, because long-period waves show less saturation with magnitude and attenuate more slowly with distance. The ε_C distributions for both PGA and 1-Hz *SA* show that ground motions from the median to 1.5σ above the median dominate the contribution to hazard. This means that not only does an earthquake have to occur close to the site, but the ground motion from the shock generally must be higher than average to cause the 1,000-year ground motion.

The difference in deaggregation plots (Figures 45 and 46) means that different earthquakes dominate the hazard at high frequencies (PGA) and lower frequencies (1 Hz). The difference is more apparent at some sites where close, small magnitudes may dominate the high frequencies, but larger magnitudes from a distant fault may dominate the lower frequencies. In such cases, two or more "design events" may be required to properly derive a time history for detailed structural analysis and design at a chosen return period. Detailed procedures for such applications have been published (for example, see Bommer et al. 2000 and REI 2002), and these procedures will not be addressed further here.

It is important to understand what contributes to the uncertainty in hazard that is shown in Figures 43 and 44. This can be achieved by isolating the changes in hazard caused by changes in one model or parameter and plotting individual hazard curves or percentiles of hazard associated with changes in this model or parameter. Plots of this type are shown in Figures 47 and 48, indicating the sensitivity to changes in the ground motion equation, maximum magnitude, activity rate, *b* value, and source depth. For this example, the major contributors to uncertainty in the hazard are differences among ground motion equations and uncertainty in the activity rate of the background seismicity.

The background has been treated as an area source, but it has one important difference from conventional area sources: it lacks boundaries. If conventional area sources (with boundaries) are modeled, then the site's location should be examined with respect to nearby boundaries. It would be rare to have an area source with a perfectly certain boundary. From arguments of symmetry, a site located on an area source boundary will have half the annual frequency of exceedance of any ground motion amplitude from that source, as compared with a site located well within the source. A compensating factor is that, if a source boundary is moved to exclude a site, then

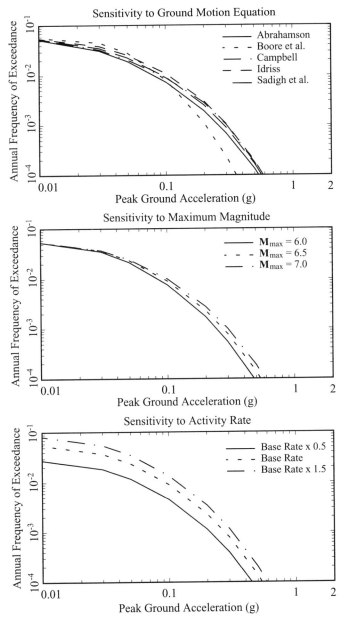

Figure 47. Sensitivity of PGA hazard in Berkeley to changes in the ground motion equation, maximum magnitude, and activity rate.

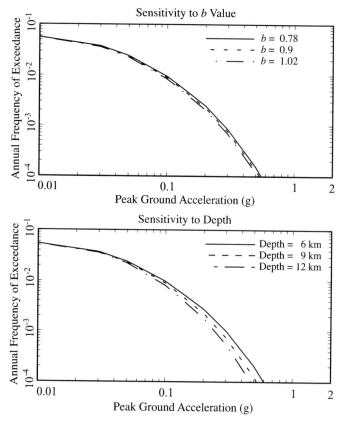

Figure 48. Sensitivity of PGA hazard in Berkeley to changes in *b* value and source depth.

another source usually occupies that space. To state this another way, few sites are located in a seismicity vacuum.

As indicated earlier, there are always exceptions to rules about which are the governing models and parameters in a seismic hazard analysis, so the results shown here should not be regarded as universal. Other sites may have the maximum magnitude and depth governing the seismic hazard calculations. Perhaps the only universal rule is that sensitivity studies as illustrated in Figures 47 and 48 should always be conducted, first to determine what models and parameters are most critical, and second to ensure that sufficient effort is made to develop a credible representation of those models and parameters.

One subtlety that has not been discussed so far is the *correlation* of uncertain models and parameters from location to location in the background. In fact, the discussion of uncertainty in the hazard has assumed perfect correlation of the five models and parameters in space. This is certainly justifiable with respect to uncertainty in the ground motion equation: one equation would be expected to be valid throughout the region, but it is uncertain what that equation is, and the weights on the five models reflect that uncertainty. With respect to m_{max}, activity rate, b value, and depth, the interpretation is not so clear-cut, as discussed below.

The uncertainty in m_{max} is traditionally regarded as being perfectly correlated within an area source; in fact, this is often assumed by definition. That is, an area source is defined as a region within which seismicity conforms to the same distribution, including the same distribution of m_{max}. Thus if $m_{max} = 7$ at one location in the source, then $m_{max} = 7$ at all locations within the source. A more general definition of area sources allows the mean rate to vary spatially within the source, but other parameters (m_{max} and b value) are fixed or are perfectly correlated.

With respect to the USGS background zone used here as an example, the definitions are a bit nonstandard, because the area source was not chosen as a result of its tectonic or geologic similarity. The background zone is a "none-of-the-above" region representing earthquakes that are not associated with mapped faults. So a reasonable interpretation of this background zone might allow less-than-perfect correlation in space among values of m_{max}. A similar argument would apply to activity rate ν and to the b value. For seismicity at depth h, a perfect correlation has been assumed, but it would be just as defensible (and perhaps more defensible) to model depth as a *random* phenomenon, allowing earthquakes to occur at all depths in the background with an assumed distribution.

The correlation between ν and the b value deserves some special mention. As discussed in Section 3, these parameters are often estimated by using historical seismicity with maximum-likelihood or least-squares fits of parameter values to historical data. Inevitably, the rate ν and the b value are correlated: if the b value is low (meaning a shallow slope for the magnitude distribution), then the value of ν at the lowest-magnitude earthquakes will also tend to be low, and vice versa. Often ν is estimated from historical data, but the b value is assigned on the basis of regional data or a belief, say, that

"0.9 is the correct plate-margin b value." Even in this case, if uncertainties in v and b are represented, then the values can be correlated.

Values of v and b can readily be combined; for example, three equally weighted values of v can be combined with three equally weighted values of b to obtain a set of nine equally weighted pairs of values. This was done in the analysis described above: the USGS analysis used historical seismicity from three different periods to estimate the background rate, as follows:

Magnitude Range	Mean Magnitude	Period	Number of Earthquakes
$\mathbf{M} > 4$	4.5	1950–1996	200
$\mathbf{M} > 5$	5.5	1930–1949	40
$\mathbf{M} > 6$	6.5	1850–1929	15

For any magnitude range, the mean magnitude $\overline{m}$ for $b = 0.9$ will be approximately $\overline{m} = m_{min} + 1/\beta = m_{min} + 0.48$ (obtained by inverting equation 33), which is indicated above. Weighting the mean magnitude values by the number of earthquakes in each period range gives an overall mean magnitude of about 4.8, which is conveniently close to magnitude 5, the lower bound of the hazard analysis. This justifies treating the rate at $m_{min} = 5.0$ as being uncorrelated with b values. If the overall mean magnitude were substantially different from m_{min}, then it would be possible to compute values of v at the overall mean magnitude, determine pairs of v-β values and weights while assuming no correlation, and translate the $v_{\overline{m}}$ values into $v_{m_{min}}$ for hazard analysis.

In the spirit of demonstrating the effects caused by incorrect assumptions, an additional analysis was performed by using the distance to each area source point, rather than generating rupture distances for each event and computing the distance to each rupture. This mimics the results that would be obtained by ignoring the distance definition in each ground motion equation. Figure 49 compares the mean 1,000-year UHS for the point-source distance analysis and the previous (rupture-distance) analysis. Across the period spectrum, the point-source distance analysis underestimates the correctly computed UHS by 10% or so in ground motion. This illustrates the last point presented in Section 4.2. The error will depend on the magnitudes of earthquakes that dominate the hazard: the higher the dominant magnitudes, the larger the error will be. The lesson is that seismicity must be represented

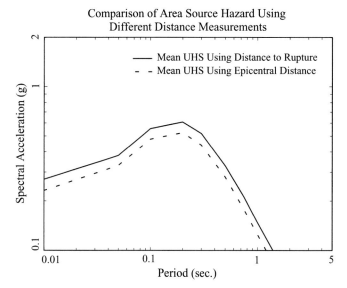

Figure 49. Uniform hazard spectra for a 10^{-3} hazard, using rupture distance and epicentral distance.

in the hazard calculations with the same definitions of magnitude (e.g., **M**) and distance (e.g., the shortest distance to a seismogenic rupture on the fault) that the ground motion equations require.

5.5 *Logic Trees*

As discussed in Section 2, the PSHA integrates over U_R to calculate annual frequencies of exceedance. As for U_K, the standard way to depict it in seismic source and ground motion assumptions is through a logic tree, as illustrated in Figure 50. Each node represents an uncertain assumption, model, or parameter, and the branches extending from each node are discrete alternatives representing that U_K uncertainty. The order of nodes is important: independent nodes (representing assumptions, models, or parameters that do not depend on others) are placed to the left. Dependent nodes are placed to the right, "downstream" from the independent nodes.[4]

---

[4] It is possible to "flip the tree," placing dependent nodes on the left, but this is rarely necessary.

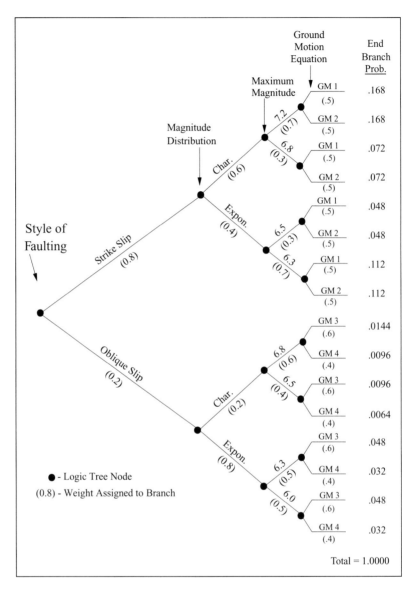

Figure 50. Sample logic tree for one fault.

136

In Figure 50, branches representing the uncertain magnitude distribution, maximum magnitude, and ground motion equation all depend on the style of faulting. The maximum magnitudes for strike-slip faulting are larger than those for oblique faulting. Also, the magnitude distribution and ground motion equations depend on the style of faulting. Each branch has a weight representing the extent of subjective credibility that that branch, conditional on all previous branches, represents the correct interpretation.

Documenting U_K uncertainties with a logic tree has huge benefits. First and foremost, the logic tree organizes one's thinking with respect to the uncertain inputs. It forces the consideration of what depends on what, and it helps one to think conditionally when assigning probabilities. Second, it helps in communicating assignments to others. It is then possible to point to the logic tree and say, "I assigned a probability of 0.7 to $m_{max} = 7.2$, but only given the following conditions." This is enormously helpful when multiple earth science teams are providing inputs into a PSHA and are exchanging ideas and interpretations. It is also extremely helpful to reviewers, who are thereby aided in following the logic of the U_K evaluations.

One danger of a logic tree is that it can appear to trivialize the probability assessments. Looking at Figure 50, someone might observe, "Strike-slip faulting is assigned a credibility of 0.8." This obscures the effort that has gone into that evaluation. Earth scientists may have spent two years digging fault trenches, running a seismic network, reviewing global positioning system (GPS) data, and conducting multiple workshops with a dozen experts to come up with that number. There is no substitute for good documentation of these efforts.

A logic tree is used in the following way. Each end branch represents a complete set of assumptions, and the analyst conducts a PSHA and derives a seismic hazard curve for each end branch. Each seismic hazard curve is assigned a weight equal to the product of the probabilities on the branches leading to its corresponding end branch (the rightmost column of Figure 50). Thus there is a family of hazard curves with weights that sum to unity. From this family, the analyst can calculate the mean and fractiles of annual frequency of exceedance, as illustrated in Figures 41, 43, and 44.

5.6 Effect of Local Site Conditions

Near-surface geologic conditions underlying a site will affect ground motions, and a defensible PSHA must account for these conditions. The term "local site conditions" is often taken to mean "soil conditions," but it can also encompass effects such as near-surface weathering and fracturing of rock or topographic effects that influence the character of seismic waves. In general, any local geologic conditions that differ from the assumptions inherent in the ground motion equations used in the PSHA must be handled as local site conditions. Further background on determining the effect of local site conditions is in EPRI (1993) and Kramer (1996).

There are two ways in which local site conditions can be incorporated into a PSHA. First and most directly, site-specific ground motion equations can be developed that predict ground motion amplitudes at the specific site as a function of m and r. These can be derived either empirically (with data from the specific site and similar sites) or analytically by first estimating rock motions for a range of m and r, then estimating the local site motion given these inputs. If nonlinearity of soil response is important, then it must be included in the calculations. This analytical method is useful when there are specific site data on shear-wave velocities and other geologic properties versus depth.

Second, a PSHA for a baseline condition (e.g., hard rock) can be performed first, then these results can be translated into the site-specific condition. It is easiest to think of translating hard rock UHS into soil UHS, but the same issues arise when any generic baseline hazard is translated into a site-specific result. In these cases, account for uncertainty in the soil response explicitly. This uncertainty (both the U_K and U_R type) will come from deviations of actual soil characteristics (e.g., shear-wave velocity, stiffness degradation, and damping degradation) versus depth from what is assumed; modeling details (characterization of the soil profile into homogeneous layers); and differences in details of the ground motion given the rock UHS (both given an m and r, and for different m and r values). For a rock UHS at any return period rp, the soil amplitudes corresponding to that UHS can be estimated as

$$a^s_{rp} = a_{rp} \overline{AF}_{rp} \exp[0.5 K_H \, \sigma^2_\delta/(1 - K_{AF})^2] \qquad (69)$$

where a^s_{rp} is soil amplitude (at one natural frequency) for return period rp, a_{rp} is the corresponding rock amplitude (at the same frequency), $\overline{AF}_{rp}$ is the *mean* soil amplification factor (soil amplitude/rock amplitude) for rock motions with amplitude a_{rp} input into the soil column, K_H is the (negative) log-log slope of the rock hazard curve, K_{AF}

is the (negative) log-log slope of soil amplification versus rock amplitude, and σ_δ is the logarithmic standard deviation of soil amplification. The latter two variables are assessed at the level of rock input motion a_{rp}. The derivation of equation 69 is included in McGuire, Silva, and Costantino (2002).

Equation 69 shows the importance of uncertainty in site-specific response. Using just the first two terms on the right side of equation 69 would be equivalent to taking the rock UHS and multiplying by a *mean* soil amplification factor, and this will underestimate the soil UHS at the same return period. The exponential factor in equation 69 will equal 1 if σ_δ is 0, but a more typical value for σ_δ is 0.2. Understanding the effects of terms K_H and K_{AF} in equation 69 is straightforward. If the hazard curve is steep (i.e., K_H is high), then rock motions below a_{rp} are very frequent, and the uncertainty in soil response means that a rock motion below a_{rp} combined with a high soil response will give a high value of a_{rp}^s, leading to a higher UHS for soil for that rp. (This is similar to the example of converting intensity to magnitude, as shown in Table 4). As K_{AF} approaches unity, the soil amplitude will be constant for all levels of input rock motion, so very frequent, low amplitudes of rock motion will cause high levels of soil motion, thus increasing a_{rp}^s.

To illustrate the effect of the exponential part of equation 69 that accounts for soil amplification uncertainty, typical values of the exponential factor are calculated by using the soil amplification results reported in McGuire, Silva, and Costantino (2002) for the Meloland site profile in California (Figure 51). Soil amplification was calculated for a range of rock motions at a test site corresponding to 10^{-3}, 10^{-4}, and 10^{-5} annual frequencies of exceedance, and this range is shown in Figure 51. Slopes K_{AF} for each natural frequency are shown in Table 11. It is also assumed in Table 11 that $K_H = 2.1$ and $\sigma_\delta = 0.2$, which are typical values.

Table 11. Sample factors for calculating soil UHS.

	PGA	10 Hz	3 Hz	1 Hz
K_{AF}	0.47	0.72	0.75	0.19
K_H	2.1	2.1	2.1	2.1
σ_δ	0.2	0.2	0.2	0.2
Factor	1.16	1.71	1.96	1.07

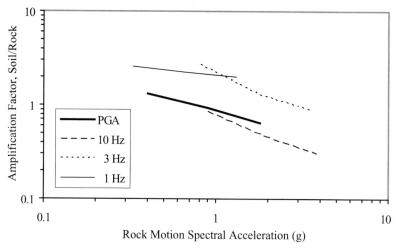

Figure 51. Sample amplification factors as a function of input motion amplitude for the Meloland site profile (from McGuire et al. 2002).

Table 11 shows that the "correction factor," the exponential term in equation 69 that corrects the mean soil amplification, can be close to 2.0, and perhaps higher for other soils or rock hazard curve slopes. The important message is that mean amplification factors alone cannot be used to translate rock hazard results into site-specific hazard results.

To calculate the mean amplification and its uncertainty, the range of input motions must be represented in the site-specific model. This means using multiple rock motions consistent with the rock UHS, representing the range of magnitudes and distances dominating that motion. The PSHA deaggregation is useful in determining these magnitudes and distances (examples are Figures 33, 36, 39, 45, and 46). Uncertainties in soil properties must also be included. All these uncertainties will contribute to σ_δ.

Whether site-specific response is estimated directly or through a rock PSHA, an important question is how much site-specific detail is necessary. The answer lies, once again, in the use of the PSHA. In drawing a seismic hazard map for a seismic building code or estimating total losses for a large number of facilities, it may be acceptable to use general descriptions of site geologic properties to translate baseline hazard results into site-specific results. Some ground motion equations, such as equation 52, allow direct estimation of site response on the basis of shear wave velocity in the upper 30 meters. On the other hand, to design a major facility for which there are site borings and laboratory tests of material behavior under dynamic loads, it is necessary to use that information to derive a site-specific result that can be defended. Unlike other inputs into a PSHA, site conditions can be determined with a high degree of confidence, if sufficient resources are available.

5.7 *Observations*

This example of PSHA has illustrated several important concepts that are sometimes ignored in applications. First, if single hypotheses for seismicity and ground motion equations will be used, be sure that the models and parameters chosen are mean values and can be justified. Otherwise, considering a range of models will give substantially different results. There is no guarantee that using single, mean-valued models and parameters will lead to the accurate calculation of the mean hazard; sets of alternative models and distributions are necessary to do that. If "conservative" models and parameters are selected throughout the analysis, then it is impossible to tell *what* the results correspond to. If ultimately only one ground motion equation is used in the PSHA, then it is always wise to consider multiple ground motion models in selecting and justifying the single equation. Developing ground motion equations always leaves room for multiple interpretations, even in California, which has the most abundant collection of strong-motion records in the world. Ignoring these multiple interpretations will subject the analysis to justified criticism.

A more fundamental conclusion is that it is necessary to explore the details of the hazard to understand what drives the calculated frequencies of exceedance. Sensitivity studies and deaggregation of hazard are the pathways to achieving this understanding and to identifying additional or alternative assumptions that might be considered. Deaggregating the hazard will reveal what magnitudes, distances, and hidden assumptions are crucial and will guide new interpretations that may drive the final hazard calculations. When multiple experts are involved in interpreting seismicity and ground motion, a good communication mechanism must be developed to transmit the sensitivity and deaggregation so the participants can understand the implications of their choices. This way, they can spend additional time making interpretations about the models and parameters that matter.

As mentioned at the beginning of this section, a good PSHA consists of a complete, documented probabilistic analysis that examines alternatives, sensitivities, and uncertainties. When performed properly, a good PSHA will be valid for a number of years and will not be discredited by new theories or data that result from the occurrence of a single earthquake. For this to be so, the PSHA must consider a broad range of assessments that will either encompass future interpretations or have such high credibility that new tectonic or ground motion theories affecting the site will earn only low credibility, at least initially. Of course, even for this rule there are exceptions: the discovery of a major active blind-thrust fault under a site will certainly affect the seismic hazard, as it should. This does not, however, justify assuming that such a fault lies beneath all sites; that would be "punishing the masses for the sins of the few."

This discussion has deliberately not presented "best, final" seismic hazard results for Berkeley that include faults and area sources. To do so would require justifying and documenting the basis for alternative input assumptions and their assigned weights, which has not been done in this exploratory example. Rather, the emphasis has been on the *process* of examining alternatives and sensitivities by using deaggregation and sensitivity studies as guides to show what is important and what is not, so scientists and engineers gain confidence that they are concentrating on the right parts of the problem. Without going through that process, the PSHA results will have little credibility.

Finally, a full PSHA where U_K uncertainties are quantified often shows large U_K uncertainties in calculated annual frequencies and in the ground motion for a specific return period. It is important to understand that these large uncertainties are not the fault of the PSHA; rather, they reflect the state of knowledge about earthquake occurrences and the associated ground motions. A full PSHA only quantifies these uncertainties for decision-making—it does not create them. Alternative methods that ignore these uncertainties will lead to less-informed decisions.

Reasonable trade-offs, be they with respect to operating regulations, below-standard performance, or system malfunction, cannot be made without a quantitative method of evaluating the seismic risk at a site.

Allin Cornell, 1968

6 ESTIMATING SEISMIC RISK

6.1 Introduction

Seismic risk entails a set of events (earthquakes), the associated consequences (damage or loss, in the broadest sense), and the associated probabilities of occurrence (or exceedance) over a defined time period. This concept is consistent with the definition of "risk" in the general risk analysis literature. The damage or loss can be to an individual structure, to a business, to a community, or to the entire infrastructure of a nation. Damage or loss can be measured in monetary terms (the cost of repairing damage, loss of revenue), casualties (injuries and deaths), or loss of function (manufacturing capacity). An example of the latter is a manufacturing facility that loses 50% of its capacity during an earthquake and cannot promptly return to full operation.

Evaluating seismic risk is one logical way to guide decisions about seismic safety. On an absolute basis, it is possible to determine whether seismic retrofitting is warranted or earthquake insurance is cost effective. The Faultline Brewery in Berkeley, California can serve as an example. If the brewery will not collapse during anticipated earthquakes and therefore loss of life is not a consideration, then the owner can balance the cost of plant damage, loss of revenue, and loss of market share against the cost of a seismic retrofit amortized over the plant's lifetime and can compare all these costs with the

143

cost of an earthquake insurance policy that covers facility damage and loss of revenue. If, on the other hand, the brewery might collapse during an extreme earthquake, with associated casualties, then the owner can estimate the annual probability of these losses and decide whether it is acceptable. Whatever damage or loss is being estimated, the probability of occurrence of the loss is a key factor in choosing an appropriate plan of action (or choosing inaction).

On a relative basis, the owner can use seismic risk to put priorities on seismic rehabilitation. This allows the owner to evaluate different types of structures, different earthquake vulnerabilities, and different seismic hazards on a consistent basis. Since the Faultline Brewery has two separate production facilities in Berkeley consisting of a URM building and a concrete moment-frame building, the owner can compare the seismic risk of these two buildings. This allows the owner to invest resources in the most efficient way, for seismic protection.

It must be kept in mind that direct earthquake damage to structures is usually a small part of the total economic loss from an earthquake. Economic losses linked to human casualties (both deaths and injuries) may be large, and loss of revenue and market share for a business may be significant (the latter are examples of "secondary losses"). A company may suffer losses even if its facilities survive intact, because suppliers may be affected or transportation and communications may be disrupted. Local and regional governments may be affected beyond just the costs of emergency services: sales tax revenues may decline because of loss of business, triggered by structural failures (these might be called "tertiary losses"). However wide and varied these losses are, their root cause is damage to structures (including soil structures) and to lifelines. This is why the study of seismic risk is so important.

Evaluating seismic risk is only one way of establishing a basis for making decisions about possible earthquakes. Another method appropriate for design decisions is to calibrate seismic design levels via seismic hazard results, choosing a seismic hazard level that gives ground motions consistent with the average design ground motion over many sites from the previous (perhaps deterministic) seismic code. When the seismic hazard results are used, design levels can be raised where hazard is high and reduced where hazard is low. This process makes use of the broad engineering experience base gained from designing many buildings and evaluating how they performed during earthquakes.

The key building block for estimating seismic risk is to estimate damage to structures and to lifelines as a function of ground motion. Ground shaking is the classic intermediate step between earthquake occurrence and damage, because it allows the use of results from one earthquake (e.g., empirical observations of damage) to estimate damage for future events. It would be straightforward, for example, to plot damage to single-family residences from the 1994 Northridge earthquake as a function of fault distance. But how would those data be used to estimate damage for another magnitude at a different location? This is why ground shaking plays such a key role, and in fact why PSHA (for ground motion) is so important.

Sections 6.2 and 6.3 describe two ways to estimate seismically induced damage on the basis of ground motion levels:

- Using empirical or judgmental estimates of damage, based on the MMI
- Using nonlinear models of structural response, based on spectral acceleration

Each of these methods has advantages and applications, and deciding which to use depends on the application and the analyst's preference. Quantitative results from both methods for single-family residences are compared in Section 6.4.

Probability-based damage estimates ("seismic risk") are described for two types of structures in Section 6.5. These estimates come from combining probabilistic seismic hazard results with damage descriptions illustrated by the above two methods. Section 6.6 examines secondary losses caused by seismic shaking: damage to the contents of buildings, casualties, loss of revenue, and business interruption. Section 6.7 summarizes some observations about estimating seismic risk, and Section 6.8 offers some final thoughts about conducting probabilistic seismic hazard and risk analyses.

6.2 Empirical Methods of Damage Estimation

Seismic risk based on empirical observations of the relationship between damage and ground motion have traditionally relied on an intensity scale such as MMI to represent the ground motion. The reason is simple: in the early years, before strong-motion instruments were widespread, intensity was the only postearthquake measure of ground shaking universally available with which to calibrate a damage scale.

Two of the widely used MMI-based methods were developed by the Applied Technology Council (ATC 1985) and by Steinbrugge (1982).

Apart from the usual problems with using MMI to calibrate anything quantitative, each of these methods has some recognized limitations that should be understood. The ATC (1985) study was an effort to derive a consensus from a group of engineers whose level of experience in studying earthquake damage was varied. Problems with variability estimates imply that the ATC's documented uncertainty measures (standard deviations) may be too small. The Steinbrugge method was based on a lifetime of experience by Karl Steinbrugge. The results are generally reported as a probable maximum loss (PML), which is defined as the "loss"—really, damage as a percentage of replacement value—that will not be exceeded by 9 out of 10 structures; uncertainty estimates are not reported. It must be acknowledged that these limitations were observed years after both studies were published; at the time, they were landmark studies.

The damage to a structure is usually normalized by the total replacement cost, leading to a damage ratio (the cost of repairing the structure divided by replacement cost). Figure 52 compares damage ratios for single-family, wood-frame residences predicted by the ATC (1985) and Steinbrugge (1982) studies with data from the 1994 Northridge earthquake (Toro 1997). It is difficult to obtain a clean, consistent set of data with which to evaluate damage estimates. The estimates and data differ because of several factors:

- The Steinbrugge curve is for a PML estimated to be the 90% confidence level of damage, not the mean or median.
- The ATC (1985) curve is an estimate of the mean damage factor, derived from subjective opinion.
- The Northridge data are summaries of losses paid by insurance companies after deductibles (which averaged 8%) were applied. These losses were reported by the insurers to the California Department of Insurance (Al-Faris and Tan 1996).

The introduction of deductibles on policies significantly reduces the large number of small losses paid by an insurer (which is why insurers use deductibles). Complicating the Northridge data is the qualitative observation that, under heavy political pressure, insurers paid many claims quickly and generously—in some cases not applying deductibles. Many primary insurance companies had reinsurance coverage, so the additional costs were passed on to the reinsurer. Another reason for high insurance losses from the Northridge earthquake was the increased cost of reconstruction and materials because of high demand after the event (such increases are called "demand

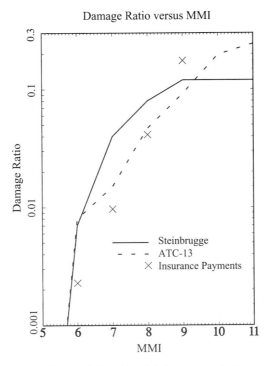

Figure 52. Residential damage ratio from the Northridge earthquake, as indicated by insurance payments (Toro 1997) and as predicted by Steinbrugge (1982) and ATC (1985).

surge"). This might have raised repair costs by 30% or more. All these considerations complicate the estimates of seismic risk for communities, emergency planners, and insurers alike.

In any case, translating seismic hazard into seismic risk is conceptually straightforward. Once the damage function (damage ratio versus intensity) has been chosen, the annual probability of damage $P[damage > d]$ is calculated as

$$P[damage > d] \simeq \sum_{mmi} P[damage > d \mid mmi]\gamma'[mmi] \quad (70)$$

where $\gamma'[mmi]$, the frequency of occurrence of *mmi*, is obtained from the seismic hazard analysis. $P[damage > d|mmi]$ requires a distribution of damage ratio given mmi, meaning a mean value (as illustrated in Figure 52), a standard deviation, and the assumption of a distribution shape.[5] Note that, in this section, MMI represents a random intensity value, and mmi represents a specific intensity value.

The approximation in equation 70 comes from using the frequency $\gamma'[mmi]$ (as derived from the seismic hazard analysis) rather than the probability $P[mmi]$. The frequency is a very close (and slightly conservative) estimator of the probability for cases of usual interest where $\gamma[mmi] < 0.1$. Probabilities (typically, annual probabilities) are used to quantify seismic risk, rather than frequencies, because this is traditional in both earthquake engineering and in risk analysis in general.

Some subtleties in applying equation 70 are important. The ground motion equation in the seismic hazard analysis is usually of the type $E[MMI] = f(m, r)$ and should be derived from MMI observations (not from isoseismals). With this method, mmi = VIII translates into 8.0 on the arabic scale, and $\gamma'[mmi = VIII]$ should be calculated from the hazard analysis as $\gamma[mmi > 7.5] - \gamma[mmi > 8.5]$, not $\gamma[mmi > 8] - \gamma[mmi > 9]$. Thus, $mmi = 7.6$ would be "a low VIII," and $mmi = 8.4$ would be "a high VIII." Designations of the type "mmi = VII–VIII" are usually reserved for assigning the maximum intensity caused by an earthquake, at or near the epicenter; the assignment of VII–VIII would translate into $mmi = 7.5$ on the arabic scale.

In the seismic hazard analysis, scatter in MMI values about the mean value $E[MMI] = f(m, r)$ represents U_R. However, the MMI assignments themselves are an average over observations that a seismologist or engineer makes over a community or small region. Consistency must be maintained in the MMI assignments used for the ground motion equation and in the MMI assignments used for damage estimation. Misunderstanding this point has been the source of needless argument and consequent frustration among seismic risk analysts. If MMI values are assessed as a single value per postal code (zip code, for example), then variability will be observed in MMI values at a given distance from the fault rupture during an earthquake, because of a discontinuous fault rupture process, the focusing of energy toward some azimuths, and heterogeneities in the earth. This variability will define the uncertainty (U_R) in the ground motion equation. In addition, there will be uncertainty (also U_R) in the

---

[5] If it is assumed that a two-parameter distribution is used

damage given *mmi*, because different buildings (of the same general construction type) are constructed differently and therefore respond differently, and the soil conditions and ground motion will vary in unpredictable ways across the zip code. This uncertainty goes into assessing $P[damage > d|mmi]$ in equation 70. If MMI values were assessed on a block-by-block (or a building-by-building) basis, then the first uncertainty (U_R) would increase, and the second (also U_R) would decrease. Conversely, if a larger geographic unit (e.g., a city) were used to assign MMI values, then the first variability would decrease, and the second would increase. As long as the MMI value is assigned in a consistent way to derive uncertainty for the two functions (the ground motion equation and damage relationship), the risk assessment will be consistent.

Of course, one method may be more *accurate* than another, but that is not a matter of consistency in assigning variability. If entire cities are used in assessing MMI values, then the analyst loses the information that some locations within a city may be close to the causative fault and some may be far from it, and this will result in inaccurate loss assessments for those locations. If MMI values are assigned on a block-by-block basis after an earthquake, then there will be many data points for that event (just as there would if statistics were collected on individual building damage). But MMI values cannot be assigned with precision—how can it be determined that the ground motion has "cracked chimneys in some instances" for *mmi* = VI if only one chimney can be seen? So there is some advantage in assessing MMI values on a postal code level: it achieves consistency with past MMI studies and integrates observations at approximately the same distance.

Equation 70 requires a probability distribution on damage when MMI values are given. This means that a distribution shape and measure of dispersion are required, in addition to a mean or median damage. Empirical distributions are hard to come by, for the reasons mentioned in the discussion of Figure 52 and because the best damage data after an earthquake are often proprietary to insurance companies who pay the losses. The beta distribution is useful, because it takes on values over only a limited range (0–100% damage, for example) and because it can represent a variety of shapes. The density function is defined with parameters *t* and *r* as

$$f_x(x) = \frac{1}{\beta} x^{r-1} (1-x)^{t-r-1} \qquad (71)$$

149

where

$$\beta = \frac{\Gamma(r)\Gamma(t-r)}{\Gamma(t)} \qquad (72)$$

and where Γ is the gamma function. A simplification for β is available when t and r are integers. The mean and variance are related to parameters t and r by

$$m_x = r/t \qquad (73)$$

$$\sigma_x^2 = \frac{r(t-r)}{t^2(t-1)} \qquad (74)$$

Parameters t and r (or equivalently the mean and variance) control the shape of the distribution. Often, the analyst can estimate m_x but must make a judgment about σ_x^2. Figure 53 shows five beta distributions, when $t = 4$ for five values of r corresponding to mean damage ratios of $m_x = 0.167, 0.333, 0.5, 0.667$, and 0.833. Appendix E illustrates beta distributions for other values of t. Low values of t give broad distributions (in fact, $t = 2$ and $r = 1$ give a uniform distribution), and high values of t (greater than 8) give narrow distributions. Thus $t = 3–6$ may result in reasonable building damage distributions.

Another distribution used to represent building damage is the lognormal, because it is positively skewed and, for low mean damage with high dispersion, it gives a high probability of near-zero damage. One minor complication with the lognormal is that it is defined from zero to infinity and must be truncated (and renormalized) at 100% or some other upper-bound level of damage (and perhaps at the lower end, if insurance deductibles are considered).

A formulation of the damage distribution that deserves more attention is to break the distribution of damage into two parts:

$$P[damage > d \,|\, mmi] = P[damage >$$
$$0 \,|\, mmi]\, P[damage > d \,|\, damage > 0 \text{ and } mmi] \qquad (75)$$

This formulation is useful whether the MMI or any other measure is used to represent ground motion. It recognizes that there is a spike of probability at zero damage, representing the buildings that have no observable damage. In addition, there is a continuous part of the dis-

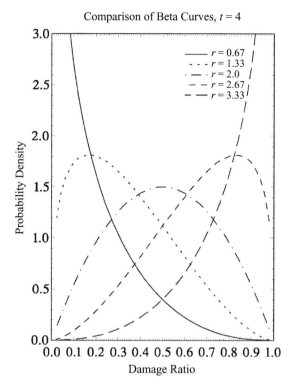

Figure 53. Damage distributions, using
beta distributions with $t = 4$.

tribution representing all structures with damage > 0. For MMI, empirical distributions can be derived from data: the fraction of structures with no damage becomes $1 - P[damage > 0 \mid mmi]$, and the collection of damaged structures defines $P[damage > d \mid damage > 0$ *and mmi*]. This formulation is especially useful in analyzing insurance data on losses paid after an earthquake, where claims below a policy deductible have been excluded from the data set. Of course, then $P[damage > 0 \mid mmi]$ becomes $P[damage > deductible \mid mmi]$. It is also easy to see how a continuous distribution could be transformed into a mixed distribution. For example, in Figure 53, the distribution with $t = 4$ and $r = 0.67$ ($m_x = 0.167$) could be represented with a spike of probability at zero damage with probability 0.5 and a continuous distribution of damage with $m_x = 0.33$ and probability 0.5. This still results in a mean damage of 0.167, and the mixed distribution might be judged to be more accurate, particularly at low damage levels.

More generally for a continuous ground motion variable a, $P[damage > 0|a]$ can be computed if data are plentiful by apportioning a into bins and deriving $P[damage > 0|a]$ statistically. This is the procedure for MMI, which (by design) groups sites by similar ground motion levels. Often, however, data are sparse. In this case, a more sophisticated procedure, a logistic regression, is needed. One form that has been usefully applied is as follows:

$$P[damage > 0|a] = d_0 + \frac{1}{1 + \exp[-(d_1 + d_2 a)]} \qquad (76)$$

where a is the logarithm of peak acceleration or SA, and d_0, d_1, and d_2 are coefficients. The coefficients can be estimated via the maximum-likelihood method, where the likelihood function is

$$l = \prod_i (P[damage > 0|a_i])^{Y_i} \times (1 - P[damage > 0|a_i])^{(1-Y_i)} \qquad (77)$$

where Y_i is 0 if no damage occurs for property i (which experiences ground motion a_i) and 1 if damage does occur. In applications, the log-likelihood function is maximized:

$$\ln l = \sum Y_i \ln P[damage > 0|a_i] + (1 - Y_i)(1 - P[damage > 0|a_i])$$

$$(78)$$

With a set of "damage" and "no damage" observations from an earthquake, and with the corresponding values of a_i, it is possible to solve for the coefficients d_0, d_1, and d_2 that maximize the log-likelihood function. This can be accomplished with commercial spreadsheet programs that use nonlinear solvers.

One set of insurance data from the Northridge earthquake gave $d_0 = 0$, $d_1 = 0.266$, and $d_2 = 2.06$ for $a = \ln$ (PGA) in g. Equation 76 is plotted in Figure 54, with a summary of observations of the fraction of earthquake insurance policies with paid losses above a 10% deductible, plotted at the center of PGA ranges. Equation 76 provides a continuous function for the probability of damage (exceeding the deductible, in this case), and provides realistic estimates.

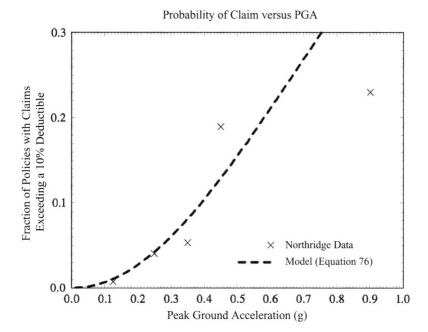

Figure 54. The fraction of policies with claims exceeding a 10% deductible versus PGA in the Northridge earthquake.

A certain complication to estimating damage ratios is important for high damage values. When the damage ratio exceeds a certain amount, often estimated at 0.5, the structure will be declared a total loss and will be razed for reconstruction. Hence the damage ratio distribution should, in some applications, be reconstructed so that all probability for damage ratios between 0.5 and 1 is represented as a spike at 1 (or perhaps at 1.1, if the cost of demolition is 10% of the total reconstruction cost). The application of this concept depends on the particular problem being modeled.

6.3 Analytical Methods of Damage Estimation

A building usually has different characteristics in the two orthogonal horizontal directions, subject to a three-dimensional nonstationary motion. Other structures (bridges, dams, tanks, towers, and so on) have similar complexities. To estimate damage, these structures are often represented with simple SDOF models that neglect nonstructural

153

elements and consider earthquake shaking in each plane of motion separately. The most direct method for seismic risk analysis would be to run the nonlinear model by using a family of recorded strong motions, compute some measure of structural response (e.g., maximum interstory drift) that can be related to damage, regress the structural response on earthquake magnitude and distance, and then perform a direct seismic risk analysis. This risk analysis would use equation 4, except that the structural response would be used for characteristic C.

The problem with this direct approach is that engineers would have to derive a new damage equation and rerun the seismic risk analysis for each structure they wish to study. It makes more sense to analyze nonlinear structural response and relate it to a measure of ground shaking (e.g., the elastic response spectrum) so that, for example, published seismic hazard maps can be used to compute seismic risk at one site.

Analytical methods of damage estimation begin by recognizing that a structure behaves in a nonlinear fashion during strong ground shaking. For a simple representation of a structure, this nonlinearity can be quantified with a force-deformation curve, showing the lateral force required to cause a range of displacements. An equivalent, convenient representation is the acceleration-displacement diagram illustrated in Figure 55. This shows the spectral accelerations associated with a range of spectral displacements for the structural model, and it illustrates that, beyond the yield acceleration SA_y and yield displacement SD_y, the structure can experience large increases in displacement for small increases in acceleration.

Below are examples of yield and ultimate accelerations and displacements for wood-frame structures designed to four code levels, as reported by Kircher et al. (1997):

Design Level	Period T (sec.)	SA_y (g)	SD_y (cm)	SA_u (g)	SD_u (cm)
High code	0.35	0.4	1.22	1.2	29.3
Moderate code	0.35	0.3	0.91	0.9	16.4
Low code	0.35	0.2	0.61	0.6	11.0
Precode	0.35	0.2	0.61	0.6	11.0

Of course, during an earthquake a structure will experience vibratory ground motion and will oscillate, going beyond the yield point several or perhaps many times in each direction. The *maximum* dis-

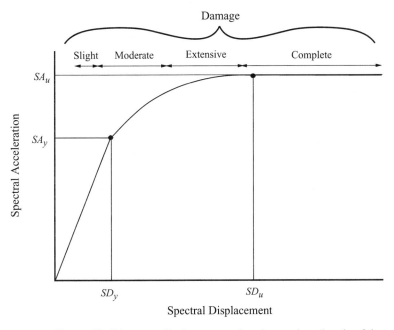

Figure 55. *SA* versus displacement, showing various levels of damage.

placement during this shaking is often thought to correlate best with damage, and ranges of damage (described below) are indicated in Figure 55. Thus damage is estimated through the maximum displacement of the nonlinear model of the structure.

Below are overviews of two methods for estimating nonlinear displacement. A detailed treatment of these methods (or any other analytical method) is beyond the scope of this monograph. See Miranda and Akkar (2002) and ATC (2002) for more detailed comparisons of these methods.

6.3.1 Capacity Spectrum Method This method, described in ATC (1996), recognizes that when the structure is shaken past its yield point, as shown in Figure 55, its effective damping will increase (because it will lose energy through hysteretic damping), and its effective period will increase. Both of these increases are with respect to linear response. The structure will thus respond to a given ground motion as if it were a more heavily damped, longer-period structure.

155

The key to this method is to reduce the 5% damped elastic spectrum of the ground motion to a lower spectrum (representing higher damping) that is consistent with the structure's response. Once that consistency is achieved, usually through iteration, the structural response can be estimated.

To estimate the structural response to a given ground motion, a maximum displacement and acceleration are determined on the capacity curve (Figure 55) that is consistent with the ground motion "demand" at the higher damping and longer period that the structure experiences. The ground motion "demand diagram" quantifies the spectral displacements and accelerations of higher damping levels (Figure 56) for the given ground motion. The estimated displacement of the structure is where the capacity curve crosses the demand diagram, for a consistent damping and period. Rules are available to estimate the demand diagram from the elastic response for a given damping, and the point where the capacity curve crosses the demand

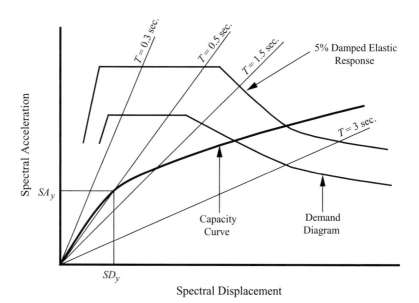

Figure 56. Capacity curve, elastic response curve, and demand diagram. The maximum structural response is estimated to be the point where the capacity curve crosses the demand spectrum.

156

diagram is determined by iteration. This gives the displacement of the structure for a given ground motion, from which damage can be estimated (Figure 55). Further details on the capacity spectrum method are in BSSC (1997).

6.3.2 Displacement coefficient method This method, described in BSSC (1997), is another method of estimating nonlinear structural response that estimates the maximum displacement by using ductility μ. For a range of nonlinear structural models, researchers have studied the relationship among μ, structural period T, and R_y, which is the ratio of elastic *SA* to yield *SA*. "R_y-μ-T" diagrams show the relationships among these variables. One such diagram, presented in Figure 57 (Krawinkler and Nassar 1992), shows a relationship for a bilinear system with a stiffness after yield that is 2% of the elastic stiffness. This relationship allows the development of inelastic demand diagrams from elastic A-D diagrams, as illustrated in Figure 58 (Krawinkler and Nassar 1992), for a broad-banded motion anchored to 0.5 g.

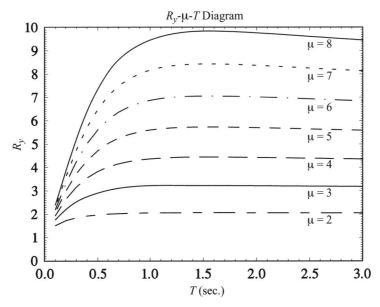

Figure 57. R_y-μ-T relationship for 2% of elastic stiffness after yield, using the Krawinkler and Nassar (1992) model.

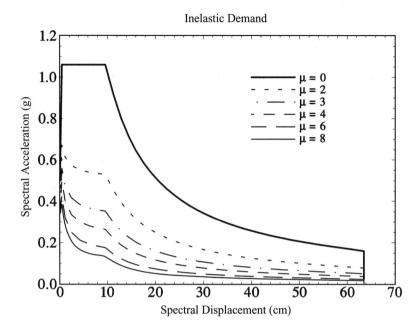

Figure 58. Inelastic demand A-D diagram for broad-banded ground motion, using the Krawinkler and Nassar (1992) R_y-μ-T relationship.

The procedure for estimating nonlinear response for a given input motion then proceeds as follows. Once the elastic SA of the input motion and the yield SA of the structure are known, first calculate R_y as the ratio of the two, next determine μ from an R_y-μ-T relationship such as the one in Figure 57, and then calculate the maximum inelastic displacement as μ times SD_y. For structures with $T > 0.6$ sec., which are in the velocity- or displacement-controlled region of the ground motion spectrum, this procedure gives inelastic displacements that follow the "equal displacement rule" (Veletsos and Newmark 1960, Chopra 2001), whereby inelastic displacements are independent of yield strength and approximately equal the deformation of the elastic system with the same period.

Once the inelastic displacement is known, it is possible to calculate the damage from a relationship such as the one in Figure 55.

6.3.3 Calculation of Damage Once response has been estimated for a given structural capacity and inelastic demand, damage must still be estimated. This can be done in a number of ways. As an illustration, FEMA's "HAZUS" methodology (FEMA 2001) uses four damage states, defined as follows, for light wood-frame structures (designated "W1"):

1. Slight damage: Small plaster or gypsum-board cracks at corners of door and window openings and wall-ceiling intersections, small cracks in masonry chimneys and masonry veneer.
2. Moderate damage: Large plaster or gypsum-board cracks at corners of door and window openings; small diagonal cracks across shear wall panels exhibited by small cracks in stucco and gypsum wall panels; large cracks in brick chimneys; toppling of tall masonry chimneys.
3. Extensive damage: Large diagonal cracks across shear wall panels or large cracks at plywood joints; permanent lateral movement of floors and roof; toppling of most brick chimneys; cracks in foundations; splitting of wood sill plates and/or slippage of structure over foundations; partial collapse of "room-over-garage" or other "soft-story" configurations; small foundation cracks.
4. Complete damage: Structure may have large permanent lateral displacement, may collapse, or be in imminent danger of collapse due to cripple wall failure or the failure of the lateral load resisting system; some structures may slip and fall off the foundations; large foundation cracks. Approximately 3% of the total area of W1 buildings with complete damage is expected to be collapsed.

    Note: small cracks are assumed to be visible cracks with a maximum width of less than 3mm. Cracks wider than 3mm are referred to as large cracks.

For each damage state ds and for a given spectral displacement sd, the methodology calculates the probability of equaling or exceeding ds from the lognormal distribution

$$P[ds|sd] = \Phi\left[\frac{1}{\beta_{ds}}\ln\left(\frac{sd}{\hat{sd}_{ds}}\right)\right] \qquad (79)$$

where Φ is the Gaussian complementary cumulative function, β_{ds} is the standard deviation of the natural log of sd for damage state ds, and $\hat{sd}_{ds}$ is the median spectral displacement at which the structure reaches the threshold of damage state ds. Under a set of assumptions about story height, modal height, and interstory drift corresponding to each damage state ds, the HAZUS methodology gives the following values for $\hat{sd}_{ds}$ and the logarithmic standard deviation β_{ds} for structural system damage to wood-frame dwellings:

Design Level	Slight Damage	Moderate Damage	Extensive Damage	Complete Damage
High code	1.27, 0.80	3.84, 0.81	12.8, 0.85	32.0, 0.97
Moderate code	1.27, 0.84	3.18, 0.86	9.80, 0.89	24.0, 1.04
Low code	1.27, 0.93	3.18, 0.98	9.80, 1.02	24.0, 0.99
Precode	1.02, 1.01	2.54, 1.05	7.85, 1.07	19.2, 1.06

Thus, with sd calculated from the demand and capacity curves, $P[ds|sd]$ can be determined, and the probability of damage *equaling* any particular damage state ds can be derived as

$$P[ds = i|sd] = P[ds|sd] - P[ds + 1|sd] \qquad (80)$$

Expressed verbally, the probability of any damage state given sd is the probability of equaling or exceeding that damage state, minus the probability of equaling or exceeding the next-higher damage state.

Note from the above summary of β_{ds} values that $\beta_{ds} = 0.8$–1.07, meaning that the standard deviation of displacement for each damage state is close to, or exceeds, the mean. This is typical of structures: there is large scatter in the displacement that will cause any level of damage. This (once again) points to the importance of probability methods in earthquake damage estimation.

Of course, damage states are defined qualitatively above. For a quantitative analysis of damage, those descriptions must be translated into a percentage of the structure's value. The translation used by HAZUS for damage as a percentage of building replacement cost is as follows:

Damage State	Structural and Nonstructural Systems	Contents
Slight	2%	1%
Moderate	10%	5%
Extensive	50%	25%
Complete	100%	50%

With this translation of damage state into a percentage of re-placement cost, the probabilities of experiencing the damage states for a given spectral demand can be used to calculate an expected damage as a percentage of replacement cost.

6.4 Comparisons of Damage Estimates

Comparing the damage estimates among methods requires several assumptions to make the comparison valid, and to the extent that the assumptions are approximate, so will be the comparison. That being said, it is useful to pursue such comparisons to better understand the methods available.

Table 12 compares mean damage estimates from several empirical and analytical methods, for three sets of magnitudes and distances:

$$\mathbf{M} = 7.7, r = 10 \text{ km}$$
$$\mathbf{M} = 7.7, r = 24 \text{ km}$$
$$\mathbf{M} = 7.7, r = 50 \text{ km}$$

These sets were chosen because they correspond to MMI levels IX, VIII, and VII on soil, respectively. For the empirical damage estimates, the MMI values were used. For the analytical estimates, the sets of magnitude and distance were converted to peak acceleration by using an average of three ground motion equations, as indicated in Table 12.

Table 12. Comparison of methods for determining expected damage to single-family residences.

Method	$\mathbf{M} = 7.7$, $r = 10$ km	$\mathbf{M} = 7.7$, $r = 24$ km	$\mathbf{M} = 7.7$, $r = 50$ km
Empirical, MMI:	IX	VIII	VII
ATC-13 (1985) class 1	9.2%	4.7%	1.5%
Steinbrugge (1982) wood frame	12%	8.5%	2.5%
Analytical, PGA[a]:	0.43 g	0.26 g	0.14 g
Capacity spectrum, high code	7.3%	3.0%	0.8%
Capacity spectrum, low code	12.0%	5.3%	1.6%
Displacement coefficient, high code	9.8%	2.9%	2.0%
Displacement coefficient, low code	13.0%	6.5%	2.8%

[a] Average of Abrahamson and Silva (1997), deep soil; Boore, Joyner, and Fumal (1997), firm soil; and Sadigh et al. (1997), soil.

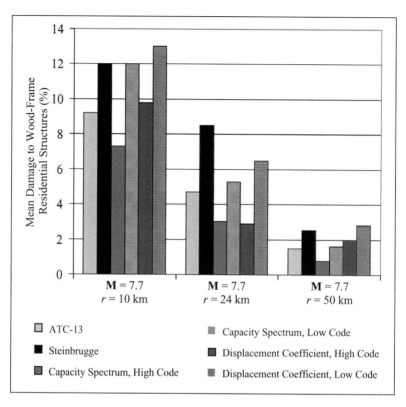

Figure 59. Comparison of mean damage estimates to wood-frame residential structures for **M** = 7.7 at *r* = 10, 24, and 50 km.

Although there are differences among the estimates, there still is general agreement for each set of magnitude and distance. This is illustrated in Figure 59, which plots the data from Table 12. For instance, for **M** = 7.7 and *r* = 10 km, about 8–10% damage would be expected for well-designed wood-frame residences, and about 12–13% damage would be expected for less-well-designed residences.

Table 12 and Figure 59 show comparisons for specific sets of events. This follows the recommendation in Section 4 about Figure 10. To estimate damage from MMI values, predict MMI directly and make damage estimates from it; this same guideline applies for PGA. In particular, for damage purposes, do not estimate PGA as a function of MMI values. As stated in Section 4, do not cross from one side of Figure 10 to the other but rather follow either the right side or the left side.

6.5 Integrating Seismic Hazard to Seismic Risk

6.5.1 Direct Integration With damage estimates available as a function of ground-shaking level, calculating seismic risk by using probabilistic estimates of damage (Section 2.4) is straightforward. In continuous form, this calculation is

$$P[damage > d] \cong \int_a P[damage > d \,|\, a] \gamma'(a) da \qquad (81)$$

which is just a re-expression of equations 8 and 70 with ground motion amplitude a; $P[damage > d]$ is an annual probability, and $\gamma'(a)$ is the annual frequency of occurrence of amplitude a. Note that the probability on the right side of this equation requires a *distribution* of damage, not just a mean value. This emphasizes the importance of developing accurate and defensible damage distributions, as discussed in Section 6.2.

Under certain conditions, equation 81 can be rewritten to calculate the probability of failure of a facility. These conditions are that the ground motion amplitude a is continuous and that the definition of structural response is discrete; some examples are as follows:

- A component of the building, or the building itself, is either "safe" or "failed."
- A certain damage state has either occurred or not occurred.
- An earth dam is either functional or nonfunctional.

This method has been used with success in the nuclear power industry and elsewhere to determine failure probabilities, particularly when system failure can be defined as a set of component failures.

Both the hazard and structural fragility (see below) must be expressed by using a ground motion amplitude a, which can be peak acceleration, SA at a defined period, or any other parameter used in the facility's seismic design or evaluation. Then the failure probability is

$$P_F \cong \int_0^\infty \gamma(a) \frac{dP_{F|a}}{da} \qquad (82)$$

where $\gamma(a)$ is the hazard curve (the annual frequency of exceeding amplitude a) and $P_{F|a}$ is the probability of failure (the "fragility") given ground motion amplitude a. Equation 82 is equivalent to equa-

163

tion 81; in equation 81, damage is expressed as a complementary cumulative function and amplitude as a density, whereas in equation 82 these are reversed. $P_{F|a}$ captures uncertainties both in the response of the structure (given amplitude a) and in the capacity of the structure or component to remain safe under ground motion amplitude a. For further discussion, see equations 5a and 5b in Kennedy and Short (1994). As discussed elsewhere for the calculation of seismic risk, the approximation in equation 82 comes from using the hazard curve, defined as a *frequency*, to calculate the annual *probability* of failure. For typical annual probabilities of failure (< 0.1 per year), this is a very good approximation.

The integrand in equation 82 is represented in Figure 60. Expressed verbally, equation 82 says that the probability of failure is the probability that the component capacity is a, multiplied by the annual frequency that a is exceeded, integrated over all values of a. If the component capacity distribution is moved to the right (thus increasing its strength), then P_F goes down. If it is moved to the left, then P_F goes up.

Several parameters define the capacity distribution. The central value is the median capacity, designated as $\hat{c}$. The variability of capacity is often assumed to be lognormal, with a logarithmic standard deviation $\sigma_{\ln\ CAPACITY} = \beta_c$. The design value for the structure, component, or equipment is designated the point of high confidence of low probability of failure (HCLPF). Because of conservative design, material properties, and analytical procedures, the occurrence of a ground motion at the design value will typically imply a low probability of failure (1% has been used in the nuclear power industry). An important effect is related to the slope of the hazard curve. Figure 61 illustrates two hazard curves with different slopes, and these are quantified with parameter K_H. K_H is the negative slope of the hazard curve on a log-log scale; steeper curves have higher K_H values. Typical K_H values for midplate regions (e.g., the central and eastern United States) range from 1.5 to 6. At active plate margins, K_H tends to be higher (i.e., the hazard curves are steeper) because facilities are designed to a standard that is closer to the maximum ground motion generated by faults, and the hazard curve falls off faster with higher ground motions. For a specific site, K_H tends to be lower for low-frequency spectral accelerations and higher for high-frequency spectral accelerations.

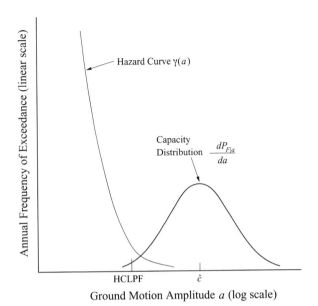

Figure 60. Curves for failure calculation.

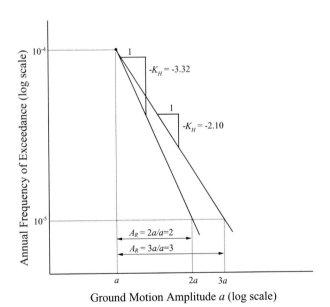

Figure 61. Hazard curve with different K_H slopes.

165

The other parameter related to K_H that is sometimes used to describe the hazard curve slope is A_R, and the two are related by

$$A_R = 10^{\frac{1}{K_H}} \quad \text{or} \quad K_H = \frac{1}{\log_{10} A_R} \tag{83}$$

A_R is the increase in ground motion corresponding to a factor-of-ten decrease in annual frequency. As Figure 61 illustrates, $K_H = 3.32$ corresponds to $A_R = 2.0$, and $K_H = 2.10$ corresponds to $A_R = 3.0$.

In Figure 62, two hazard curves $\gamma_1(a)$ and $\gamma_2(a)$ with different slopes are compared with a capacity curve. If the curves are the same at some annual probability (e.g., 10^{-4}) for a low-amplitude ground motion, then the curve with the shallower slope (lower K_H, higher A_R) will cause a larger P_F. This is because, at all a values of interest, $\gamma_2(a) > \gamma_1(a)$.

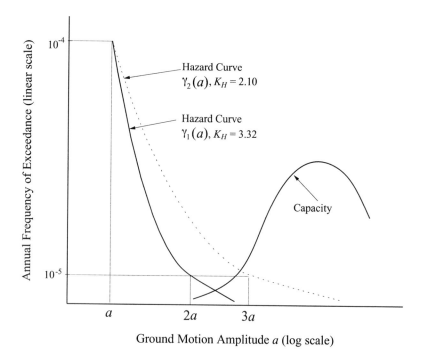

Figure 62. Hazard curves with different slopes, compared with a capacity curve.

6.5.2 Risk Equation With some realistic assumptions about the shape of the hazard curve and the fragility curve, a simple closed-form expression can be derived for P_F. This derivation has been performed previously (e.g., Sewell, Toro, and McGuire 1991; Sewell, Toro, and McGuire 1996; Kennedy and Short 1994) and is included in Appendix F for completeness.

Under the assumptions that the seismic hazard curve is linear in log-log space and that the structure or component capacity is lognormally distributed, both of which are widely applicable assumptions, the probability of failure can be calculated as

$$P_F = \gamma(a^*)(a^*/\hat{c})^{K_H} \exp\left[\frac{1}{2}(K_H \beta_c)^2\right] \qquad (84)$$

or

$$P_F = \gamma(a^*) f_s^{-K_H} \exp\left[-x_p K_H \beta_c + \frac{1}{2}(K_H \beta_c)^2\right] \qquad (85)$$

which are two forms of the "risk equation."

Here, $\gamma(a^*)$ is the annual frequency of exceedance (e.g., 10^{-4}) at the reference design amplitude a^*, f_s is a factor of safety (i.e., HCLPF/a^*), K_H is the slope of the hazard curve in log-log space, β_c is $\sigma_{\ln CAPACITY}$, and x_p is 2.326 when the design point in terms of capacity (the HCLPF) corresponds to a 1% probability of failure (x_p is the number of standard deviations corresponding to the HCLPF, for a normal distribution). These are amazingly simple expressions for the integration of ground motion hazard and fragility. It is possible to determine the effect of the hazard curve slope, factor of safety, median capacity, and capacity uncertainty for the probability of failure from these equations.

It is important to understand the general applicability of equations 84 and 85. Traditionally, these equations have been used to estimate risk for structures and components that have a no-yes definition of failure (they are either "safe" or "failed"). A more general application is in estimating the risks associated with seismic performance levels. For this application, equations 84 and 85 apply with $\beta_c = \beta_{ds}$.

An example is the Faultline Brewery, with its URM building and concrete moment-frame building. On the basis of the HAZUS methodology (FEMA 2001), the equivalent PGA fragilities for these

Table 13. Equivalent PGA fragilities from HAZUS
for lifeline-related structures.

Damage State	URM, Lowrise, Low-Code Design		Concrete Moment Frame, Lowrise, Moderate-Code Design	
	Median ($\hat{c}$)	β_{ds}	Median ($\hat{c}$)	β_{ds}
Slight	0.14	0.64	0.16	0.64
Moderate	0.20	0.64	0.23	0.64
Extensive	0.32	0.64	0.41	0.64
Complete	0.46	0.64	0.77	0.64

two building types and four damage states are shown in Table 13.
These fragilities were derived, strictly, for structures comprising lifeline facilities, and they are adopted for this example with the whim-
sical reasoning that brewery production facilities will constitute a
lifeline to a substantial segment of the earthquake engineering and
earth science professions.

The estimates of capacity in Table 13 are based on a soil spectrum
from a large-magnitude ($\mathbf{M} \simeq 7$) earthquake in the western United States
at a short distance from a fault (this is a typical dominant magnitude and
distance for the Hayward Fault; see Figure 36). No corrections are made
for other magnitudes or distances, although they could be made by using
the factors cited in the HAZUS 99-SR2 technical manual (FEMA 2001).

For Berkeley, the PGA seismic hazard results described in Section 5 are adopted for faults and area sources. The total seismic hazard curves for PGA are shown (only as an illustration) in Figure 63.
For this example, the PGA amplitudes for soft rock are adjusted upward by a factor of 1.2 to estimate PGA on stiff soil; this is an approximate factor recommended by HAZUS to account for the response of different soil types.

To apply equation 84 in calculating the seismic risk for existing
utilities, the analyst must choose acceleration a^* at which to determine the hazard γ. A good rule of thumb is to use the point at the
median minus 1σ capacity; i.e., at $\hat{c} \exp(-\beta_c)$. For "extensive" damage, this is a PGA of 0.17 g for URM buildings and 0.22 g for con-
crete moment-frame buildings, from Table 13. For "complete" dam-

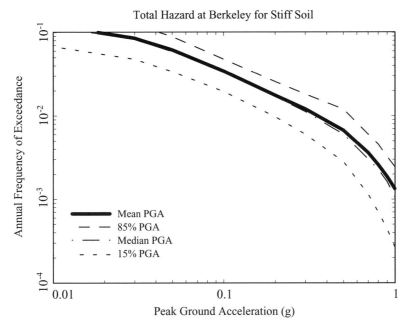

Figure 63. Mean and fractile PGA hazard curves for Berkeley, as used in an example of seismic risk.

age, the respective PGA values are 0.22 g and 0.41 g. It is appropriate to determine the slope K_H as the secant slope between the hazard at amplitudes a^* and $\hat{c}$, as this is generally the amplitude range that contributes the most to the probability of failure. Table 14 shows the parameters and the resulting estimate of seismic risk for the "extensive" and "complete" damage states using equation 84.

Several caveats are important for this example. First, a real application would use a site-specific seismic hazard analysis conducted for the actual soil conditions at the site, preferably with uncertainties characterized. Also, a structure-specific capacity function would be developed on the basis of a review of the actual facilities and their estimated seismic performance. For example, the existence of a large hops bin adjacent to the building (Figure 64) would warrant a fragility analysis to determine how failure would affect the adjacent structure. The use here of sample seismic hazard curves and of generic structural capacity estimates is meant to illustrate that, once these functions are derived on a consistent basis, the calculation of seis-

Table 14. Calculation of seismic risk for "extensive" and "complete" damage.

Damage Parameters	URM		Concrete Moment Frame	
	Extensive	Complete	Extensive	Complete
a^*	0.17	0.24	0.22	0.41
K_H	0.92	1.17	1.09	1.82
$\gamma(a^*)$	0.024	0.018	0.018	0.012
$\hat{c}$	0.32	0.46	0.41	0.77
β_{ds}	0.64	0.64	0.64	0.64
P_F (mean)	0.016	0.011	0.012	0.0074
Total P_F (mean)	0.027		0.019	
Total P_F (85%)	0.047		0.033	
Total P_F (15%)	0.013		0.0095	

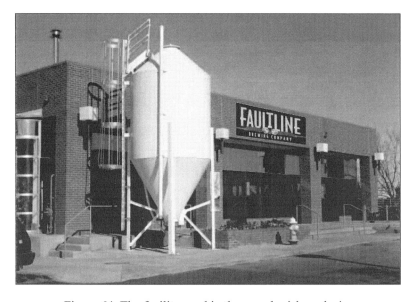

Figure 64. The facility used in the sample risk analysis.

mic risk is straightforward. Finally, the 15% and 85% P_F values in Table 14 are only approximations: they include U_K in the seismic hazard curve but not in the damage function. A more defensible estimate of the 15% and 85% P_F values would require a designation of the U_K uncertainty in the damage function, and an integration of hazard curve U_K and damage function U_K, to calculate the total U_K in P_F.

This illustrative example clearly affords insight into seismic risk calculations. The calculations confirm that the URM structure is about 50% more likely to sustain extensive or complete damage than the concrete moment-frame structure. From the mean numbers, the annual probabilities are 2.7% and 1.9%, respectively, which might lead the owner to retrofit one or both structures. When the uncertainties in the hazard are taken into account, the 85% P_F values are 4.7% and 3.3%, respectively, which would imply a 29%–38% probability of extensive or complete damage over a 10-year period (using a binomial distribution), which is a high enough likelihood that seismic retrofitting might be warranted. As an *approximation*, for the latter numbers, estimate that there is an annual probability of 3.3% that both structures would sustain extensive or complete damage, and a 1.4% annual probability (4.7% minus 3.3%) that only the URM structure would be damaged. An accurate calculation of the joint probability of the two structures' being damaged must be made with a seismic risk calculation that accounts for the proximity of the structures, the correlation in site conditions and ground motion amplitudes at the two sites, and any correlation in building capacity (for example, the two structures may have been designed to the same building code).

Suppose that the URM structure were in a somewhat less seismic region where the annual frequency for any ground motion amplitude is lower by a factor of 2 than in Berkeley. From equations 84 and 85, it is clear that P_F is directly proportional to $\gamma(a^*)$. For this less seismic region, the mean P_F for the URM structure would be 0.0135 (one half of 0.027) versus 0.019 for the concrete moment-frame structure in Berkeley. Then it might make more sense to retrofit the concrete frame structure in Berkeley than the URM structure in the less seismic region. The seismic risk calculation allows the integration of different seismic hazards with different building capacities, to evaluate structures on a consistent basis.

6.6 Other Losses

As mentioned in Section 6.1, damage to a structure will probably be only a small part of the total loss inflicted by an earthquake, but structural damage is the key because it is the root cause of many other losses. Therefore, in concept at least, other losses can be estimated after structural damage has been determined. In practice, this is difficult, because other losses must be estimated empirically and because hard data on catastrophic losses are difficult to obtain, in large part because catastrophic losses are, thankfully, rare.

6.6.1 Contents Loss of a building's contents may exceed the loss from structural damage. An extreme but possible example is a warehouse valued at $1 million that collapses, destroying $100 million worth of computer chips. Another example, prevalent in the 1994 Northridge earthquake, is a building that sustains no structural damage but whose fire sprinkler heads are damaged during shaking, resulting in significant loss of contents from water damage. To estimate loss of contents, first determine their value, then estimate a loss function (loss of contents versus ground motion or versus structural damage). One very crude approximation is that the contents loss function (as a percentage of value) is half of the damage function (as a percentage of value) for the structure; for example, if the expected structural damage is 8% of value for a given ground motion, then the expected contents loss is 4% of value. This approximation should be used only for preliminary estimates of contents loss, until more accurate loss functions can be developed.

6.6.2 Casualties Fatal and nonfatal injuries to people vary over a wide range, for a number of reasons. The time of day of the earthquake determines the location of the exposed population, and this affects the number of casualties caused by structural failures. The number and proximity of available hospitals determines the number of serious injuries that prove fatal. The age demographics of the affected population strongly influence the number of casualties.

The HAZUS study (FEMA 2001) categorized casualties into four severity levels, as shown in Table 15. More detailed casualty descriptions have been proposed, including the Abbreviated Injury Severity Scale (Peek-Asa et al. 2000) and a classification scheme for structural damage and injuries (Shoaf et al. 2001). More detailed schemes allow finer precision in identifying losses, at the expense of fewer data in each category with which to make empirically based predictions.

Table 15. HAZUS injury classification scale (from FEMA 2001).

Injury Severity Level	Description
1	Injuries requiring basic medical aid that could be administered by paraprofessionals. These types of injuries would require bandages or observation. Some examples are a sprain, a severe cut requiring stitches, a minor burn (first degree or second degree on a small part of the body), or a bump on the head without loss of consciousness. Injuries of lesser severity that could be self treated are not estimated by HAZUS.
2	Injuries requiring a greater degree of medical care and use of medical technology such as x-rays or surgery but not expected to progress to a life threatening status. Some examples are third degree burns or second degree burns over large parts of the body, a bump on the head that causes loss of consciousness, fractured bone, dehydration, or exposure.
3	Injuries that pose an immediate life threatening condition if not treated adequately and expeditiously. Some examples are uncontrolled bleeding, punctured organ, other internal injuries, spinal column injuries, or crush syndrome.
4	Instantaneously killed or mortal injury.

For risk estimates, predictions of casualties must ultimately be based on structural damage or ground motion. Table 16 shows casualty rates from HAZUS (FEMA 2001) for the four casualty severity levels in Table 15, as a function of structural damage. Interestingly, Peek-Asa et al. (2000) found that, for the 1994 Northridge earthquake, ground motion levels (MMI or PGA) were better predictors of casualty rates than building damage was. The reasons for this finding are that thorough documentation of damage was limited at sites where injuries occurred, there was a limited amount of "significant" structural damage in the moderate Northridge earthquake (except for a few notable structural collapses), and many injuries had causes other than structural damage or collapse. Experience from the 1987 Whittier Narrows, 1989 Loma Prieta, and 1994 Northridge earthquakes in California indicates that minor injuries result primarily from

Table 16. Casualty rates for most structures as a percentage of occupants (FEMA 2001).[a]

Structural Damage	Casualty Severity Level			
	1. Nonfatal, No Hospitalization	2. Nonfatal, Hospitalization	3. Life-Threatening, Immediate Assistance	4. Immediately Fatal
Slight	0.05%	0%	0	0
Moderate	0.2%	0.025–0.030%	0	0
Extensive	1%	0.1%	0.001%	0.001%
Complete, no collapse	5%	1%	0.01%	0.01%
Complete, collapse	40%	20%	5%	10%

[a] URM structures typically have higher casualty rates. Some structures (e.g., wood-frame structures) have lower casualty rates for collapse.

being struck by objects and from falling, although in some cases these injuries require hospitalization. The MMI allows a very crude prediction of casualty rates based on the population that is subjected to various intensity levels. Table 17 (Peek-Asa et al. 2000) summarizes these casualty rates. It is important to recognize that the type of construction, severity of injury, and other factors are not taken into account.

The total number of reported nonfatal injuries from earthquakes has been found to be 3 to 4 times the number of fatalities (Alexander 1996), although the ratio varies greatly from earthquake to earthquake. An average ratio from 3:1 to 4:1 allows preliminary estimates to be made. This ratio is probably representative of serious and moderate injuries (those requiring treatment at a hospital), because minor injuries can be very numerous. For example, Shoaf et al. (2001) found that *all* injuries from the 1994 Northridge earthquake (including those that were not treated) numbered in the hundreds of thousands, whereas there were only 33 fatalities. Peek-Asa et al. (1998) found that a predominant number of casualties in that earthquake involved older people: people over age 65 accounted for 31.2% of the fatalities and 75.8% of the hospitalized injuries. This suggests that older people move less quickly to evacuate damaged buildings and to avoid falling objects, and they are more vulnerable to traumatic injuries. Both these studies reviewed data from only the Northridge earthquake, and further verification requires additional data.

Table 17. Casualty rate as a function of MMI from the
1994 Northridge earthquake (Peek-Asa et al. 2000).

MMI Level	Casualty Rate[a] per 100,000 Population
<VI	0.03
VI	0.16
VII	2.1
VIII	5.1
IX	44

[a] Fatalities and injuries requiring hospitalization

6.6.3 Business Interruption One of the most difficult post-earthquake losses to quantify is loss of business. This loss can take many forms, depending on the circumstance. For manufacturing or retail facilities, damage to structures and contents can mean closure (either temporary or permanent), leading to loss of revenue. For lifelines, damage to facilities can mean less ability to deliver resources and services (such as electricity, water, natural gas, and telephone service), also leading to loss of revenue. An example occurred during the 1989 Loma Prieta earthquake, which caused one span of the San Francisco-Oakland Bay Bridge to collapse. Damage to the structure was one cause of loss, but the loss of revenue from bridge tolls was a significant additional cause of loss.

The best models for business interruption are conditioned on the amount of structural damage, because that influences the length of time necessary to repair the structure. These estimates should be in the form of a distribution and should depend on the extent of structural damage. If damage to contents is a factor in resuming business, then this should be included. Any loss of revenue during the period of repairs should also be estimated. More time for repairs might be needed if the demand for structural repairs exceeds the supply of qualified contractors. Estimates of the time needed for repair will be highly uncertain for a large earthquake in a major metropolitan area in many parts of the world, because of the lack of experience and prior data.

Estimating the loss from business interruption is one area in which a logic tree (Section 5.5) is extremely useful. The nodes of the logic tree can be ordered in a logical sequence, such as the following:

1. Structural damage
2. Loss of contents or inventory
3. Time to repair the structure
4. Time to replace contents or inventory
5. Associated losses:
    (a) Reduced production of goods or performance of services
    (b) Replacement or retraining of personnel
    (c) Temporary reduction of demand for goods and services
    (d) Temporary or permanent reduction of market share

Estimates of losses for node 5, above, are facilitated by making these estimates conditional on the first four nodes. Even if structural damage and loss of contents or inventory are minimal, there may be some estimated loss because local utility services are affected (such as lack of water, power, or natural gas) or even because employees' means of commuting are disrupted. Data from past earthquakes can be used here, if they are detailed enough to itemize the losses by cause.

6.6.4 Insurance To the extent that structures and businesses are insured against earthquakes, calculated losses will pass to the insurer, thus reducing the owner's loss and increasing the insurer's loss. Accurately calculating the insurance loss requires the modeling of the effects of insurance policy conditions, including deductibles, on the amount of loss that is reimbursed. A key requirement is to calculate the entire *distribution* of loss, rather than just the mean loss. The expected loss after the deductible amount (the loss that the insurer will incur) is *not* just the mean loss before the deductible, minus the deductible. As an example, if for one ground motion level the mean loss to a class of buildings before the deductible is 10% of the value, and the deductible on insurance policies for those buildings is 10%, then the expected loss by the insurer is *not* zero. The reason is that some buildings will sustain 5% loss, and some will sustain 15% loss; the insurer will make loss payments for all buildings that sustain more than 10% loss. This is an example of why estimating the *distribution* of damage (illustrated in Section 6.2 for structural damage, and described above for other losses) is so important.

6.7 *Summary of Seismic Risk*

There are several ways to convert seismic hazard into seismic risk. Methods based on empirical observations of the MMI values and postearthquake damage are well grounded in empirical data, but they require direct estimates of the MMI values to make use of the correlations with damage. Methods based on spectral ordinates and nonlinear structural response avoid this conversion, but they must be carefully calibrated to observations.

The distinction between *accuracy* and *precision* is important here, as it is in many areas of earthquake engineering. A method may be more precise (i.e., it may produce better-defined results) because it allows more factors to be taken into account, such as the nonlinear behavior of structures, code conformity issues, and duration of shaking. This does not mean that such a method is more accurate (i.e., that it produces results that are closer to the truth); the estimated effects may be so approximately represented that an empirically based method, such as one based on the MMI, may be just as accurate. However, MMI-based methods may have been based on data from decades ago and may therefore be inaccurate for a specific, modern structure. Detailed analytical methods of damage estimation will become better calibrated in the future and are valid tools for accurately estimating seismic damage today.

The alternatives—namely, avoiding action under the guise of collecting more data, or assuming the worst conceivable event under the mantle of being conservative—are the refuges of those unwilling to make difficult decisions in an uncertain world.

6.8 Final Thoughts

Probabilistic seismic hazard and risk analyses can take into account unknowns in all the technical fields that affect decisions about earthquake risk mitigation. These unknowns include where, when, and how large earthquakes will be; what ground motions they will generate; and what effects they will have on people and structures. With these analyses, informed decisions can be made about what level of resources to expend to mitigate seismic risk and how best to achieve that mitigation.

It should be clear that many assumptions and interpretations are made during a thorough seismic hazard or risk study. This is not surprising, because many technical fields are involved, from geology and seismology to geotechnical and earthquake engineering. A seismic risk study integrates the information from these fields by using a common thread of mean values and uncertainties, to reach results that are unbiased by uninformed intuition or preconceived notions of how large or small the risk is.

If there is a single bit of advice that runs throughout this monograph, it is this: the analyst must be aware of the ultimate use of a probabilistic hazard or risk study before undertaking it. What might be a critical assumption or model for one application might be irrelevant for another. For example, modeling the annual frequencies and ground motions of small earthquakes might be critical in estimating average annual losses for a URM structure, but it might be unimportant in the design of a nuclear power plant. A thorough seismic hazard or risk study takes substantial energy and resources, and the analyst must concentrate on the issues that are most influential for the problem at hand. A corollary to this rule is that no single probabilistic seismic hazard or risk analysis is valid for all problems. A national seismic hazard map developed for a building code for typical structures is not applicable for the seismic design of power plants and dams.

In the twentieth century, North America and Europe were spared destructive earthquakes (with the notable exception of the 1908 Messina earthquake) that could have caused tens or hundreds of thousands of deaths, although such events occurred in South America and Asia. With continuing global population growth and the proliferation of structures to house this population and provide workspace, such earthquakes can be expected to inflict severe damage and loss of life. It would be easy to propose that each new structure be twice as strong seismically and to require retrofits for existing structures, thereby reducing the seismic risk. Yet resources for seismic strengthening compete with resources for other justifiable social, health, and welfare goals. And who is to say that "twice as strong" is strong enough?

In the end, decisions about seismic risk mitigation must feel right, in light of professional experience. Probabilistic seismic hazard and risk analyses inform professional judgment in a rational way. If one professional's judgment differs from that of a colleague who has studied the same problem, then their analyses let them break the problem down into its components, see where they differ, and argue about those differences. This is the real value of these analyses.

The ultimate goal should be to make rational, informed decisions to reduce seismic risk to acceptable levels, even in the face of uncertainties in earthquake characteristics and effects. If this can be achieved, then analysts will have used their "knowledge of earthquakes and their peculiar mode of action" to take "proper precautions against injury," as the Seismological Society of America counseled almost a century ago.

REFERENCES

Abrahamson, N.A. and W. J. Silva, 1997. Empirical response spectral attenuation relations for shallow crustal earthquakes. *Seis. Res. Ltrs.* 68 (1): 94–127.

Abrahamson, N.A. and R.R. Youngs, 1992. A stable algorithm for regression analyses using the random effects model. *Bull. Seis. Soc. Am.* 82 (1): 505–510.

Alexander, D., 1996. The health effects of earthquakes in the mid-1990's. *Disaster*. 30 (3): 231–247.

Al-Faris, K.B. and B. Tan, 1996. Northridge earthquake insurance loss report. August. California Department of Insurance, Sacramento, CA.

Anderson, J.G. and J.N. Brune, 1999. Probabilistic seismic hazard analysis without the ergodic assumption. *Seis. Res. Ltrs.* 70 (1): 19–28.

ATC, 1985. Earthquake damage evaluation data for California. Report ATC-13. Applied Technology Council, Redwood City, CA.

ATC, 1996. Seismic evaluation and retrofit of concrete buildings. Report ATC-40. Applied Technology Council, Redwood City, CA.

ATC, 2002. Summary of evaluation of current nonlinear static procedures—SDOF studios. Report ATC-55. Applied Technology Council, Redwood City, CA.

Atkinson, G.M. and I. Beresnev, 1997. Don't call it stress drop. *Seis. Res. Ltrs*. 68 (1): 3–4.

Atkinson, G.M. and D.M. Boore, 1995. Ground motion relations for eastern North America. *Bull. Seis. Soc. Am.* 85(1): 17-30.

Atkinson, G.M and W.J. Silva, 2000. Stochastic modeling of California ground motions. *Bull. Seis. Soc. Am.* 90 (2): 255–274.

Bazzurro, P. and C.A. Cornell, 2002. "Vector-valued probabilistic seismic hazard analysis (VPSHA)." July. *Proc. 7th Nat. Conf. on Earthquake Eng.*, Boston, MA.

Benjamin, J.R. and C.A. Cornell, 1970. *Probability, Statistics, and Decision for Civil Engineers.* New York, NY: McGraw-Hill.

Bolt, B., 1999. *Earthquakes.* Fourth edition. New York, NY: W.H. Freeman.

Bommer, J.J. and A. Martinez-Pereira, 1999. The effective duration of earthquake strong motion. *J. Earthquake Eng.* 3 (2): 127–172.

Bommer, J.J., S.G. Scott, and S.K. Sarma, 2000. Hazard-consistent earthquake scenarios. *Soil Dynamics and Earthquake Eng.* 19: 219–231.

Bonilla, M.G., R.K. Mark, and J.J. Lienkaemper, 1984. Statistical relations among earthquake magnitude, surface rupture length, and surface fault displacement. *Bull. Seis. Soc. Am.* 74 (6): 2379–2411.

Boore, D.M., 1983. Stochastic simulation of high-frequency ground motions based on seismological models of the radiated spectra. *Bull. Seis. Soc. Am.* 73 (6): 1865–1894.

Boore, D.M., 1996. SMSIM-Fortran programs for simulating ground motions from earthquakes. Version 1.0. USGS Open-File Reports. 96-80A (text) and 96-80B (programs). Available at www.geol.vt.edu/iasphand/CD_volume/8513Boore/8513.html.

Boore, D.M., 2003. Simulation of ground motion using the stochastic method. *Pure and Applied Geophys.* Birkhauser Verlag, 160: 635-676.

Boore, D.M. and W.B. Joyner, 1982. The empirical prediction of ground motion. *Bull. Soc. Seis. Am.* 72 (6): S43–S60.

Boore, D.M., W.B. Joyner, and T.E. Fumal, 1997. Equations for estimating horizontal response spectra and peak acceleration from western North American earthquakes: a summary of recent work. *Seis. Res. Ltrs.* 68 (1): 128–153.

Brillinger, D.R. and H.K. Preisler, 1985. Further analysis of the Joyner-Boore attenuation data. *Bull. Seis. Soc. Am.* 75 (2): 611–614.

Brune, J.N., 1970. Tectonic stress and the spectra of seismic shear waves from earthquakes. *J. Geophys. Res.* 75: 4997–5009.

Brune, J.N., 1971. Correction. *J. Geophys. Res.* 76: 5002.

Brune, J.N., 1999. Precarious rocks along the Mojave section of the San Andreas Fault, California: constraints on ground motion great earthquakes. *Seis. Res. Ltrs.* 70 (1): 29–33.

BSSC, 1997. NEHRP guidelines for the seismic rehabilitation of buildings. Building Seismic Safety Council, Reports. FEMA 273 (Guidelines) and FEMA 274 (Commentary). Federal Emergency Management Agency, Washington, DC.

Campbell, K.W., 1997. Empirical near-source attenuation relationships for horizontal and vertical components of peak ground acceleration, peak ground velocity, and pseudo-absolute acceleration response spectra. *Seis. Res. Ltrs.* 68 (1): 154–179.

Cartwright, D.E. and M.S. Longuet-Higgins, 1956. The statistical distribution of the maxima of a random function. *Proc. Roy. Soc. London Ser.* A237: 212–223.

Chopra, A.K., 2001. *Dynamics of Structures: Theory and Applications to Earthquake Engineering.* Second edition. Englewood Cliffs, NJ: Prentice-Hall.

Cornell, C.A., 1968. Engineering seismic risk analysis. *Bull. Seis. Soc. Am.* 58 (5): 1583–1606.

Cornell, C.A. and S.R. Winterstein, 1988. Temporal and magnitude dependence in earthquake recurrence models. *Bull. Seis. Soc. Am.* 28 (4): 1522–1537.

EPRI, 1986. Seismic hazard methodology for the central and eastern United States. July. Report NP-4726, 1, Methodology, Section 4. Electric Power Research Institute, Palo Alto, CA.

EPRI, 1993. Guidelines for determining design basis ground motions. November. Report TR-102293, 5 volumes. Electric Power Research Institute, Palo Alto, CA.

FEMA, 2001. Earthquake loss estimation methodology, HAZUS99. Service Release 2 (SR2), Technical Manual. Federal Emergency Management Agency, Washington, DC. Available at www.fema.gov/hazus/dl_sr2.htm.

Griscom, M. and W.J. Arabasz, 1979. A local magnitude (M_L) in the Wasatch Front and Utah Region: Wood-Anderson calibration, coda-duration estimates of M_L, and M_L versus m_b. In W.J. Arabasz,

R.B. Smith, and W.D. Richins, eds. *Earthquake Studies in Utah 1850 to 1978*. Salt Lake City, Utah: University of Utah.

Grunthal, G., 1998. European Macroseismic Scale 1998. Conseil de L'Europe, Cahiers du Centre European de Geodynamique et de Seismologie, Luxembourg, 15.

Gutenberg, B., 1945a. Amplitudes of P, PP, and S and magnitudes of shallow earthquakes. *Bull. Seis. Soc. Am.* 35: 57–69.

Gutenberg, B., 1945b. Amplitudes of surface waves and magnitudes of shallow earthquakes. *Bull. Seis. Soc. Am.* 35: 3–12.

Gutenberg, B. and C.F. Richter, 1942. Earthquake magnitude, intensity, energy, and acceleration. *Bull. Seis. Soc. Am.* 32 (3): 163–191.

Gutenberg, B. and C.F. Richter, 1956. Earthquake magnitude, intensity, energy, and acceleration (second paper). *Bull. Seis. Soc. Am.* 46 (1): 105–145.

Hanks, T.C. and W.H. Bakun, 2002. A bilinear source-scaling model for **M**-log A observations of continental earthquakes. *Bull. Seis. Soc. Am.* 92 (5): 1841–1846.

Hanks, T.C. and D.M. Boore, 1984. Moment-magnitude relations in theory and practice. *J. Geophys. Res.* 89: 6229–6235.

Hanks, T.C. and C.A. Cornell, 1999. Probabilistic seismic hazard analysis: a beginner's guide. Submitted to *Earthquake Spectra*. Available from T.C. Hanks at thanks@usgs.gov.

Hanks, T.C. and A.C. Johnston, 1992. Common features of the excitation and propagation of strong ground motion for North American earthquakes. *Bull. Seis. Soc. Am.* 82 (1): 1–23.

Hanks, T.C. and H. Kanamori, 1979. A moment magnitude scale. *J. Geophys. Res.* 84: 2348–2350.

Hanks, T.C. and R.K. McGuire, 1981. The character of high-frequency strong ground motions. *Bull. Seis. Soc. Am.* 71 (6): 2071–2095.

Hanks, T.C., J.A. Hileman, and W. Thatcher, 1975. Seismic moments of the larger earthquakes of the Southern California region. *Bull. Geol. Soc. Am.* 86: 1131–1139.

Idriss, I.M., 1993. Procedures for selecting earthquake ground motions at rock sites. NIST GCR 93-625. National Institute of Standards and Technology, Gaithersburg, MD.

Johnston, A.C., 1996. Moment magnitude assessment of stable continental earthquakes, Part 1: instrumental seismicity. *Geophys. J. Intl.* 124; 381-414.

Johnston, A.C., 1994. The stable continental region earthquake database. The earthquakes of stable continental regions, Volume 1: assessment of large earthquake potential. December. Report TR-102261-V1. Electric Power Research Institute, Palo Alto, CA.

Joyner, W.B. and D.M. Boore, 1981. Peak horizontal acceleration and velocity from strong-motion records including records from the 1979 Imperial Valley, California, earthquake. *Bull. Seis. Soc. Am.* 71 (6): 2011–2038.

Kanamori, H., 1983. Magnitude scale and quantification of earthquakes. *Tectonophysics.* 93: 185–199.

Kennedy, R.P. and S.A. Short, 1994. Basis for seismic provisions of DOE-STD-1020. April. UCRL-CR-111478. Prepared for U.S. Department of Energy, Washington, DC.

Kircher, C.A., A.A. Nassar, O. Kuster, and W.T. Holmes, 1997. Development of building damage functions for earthquake loss estimation. *Earthquake Spectra.* 13 (4): 663–682.

Khater, M., C. Scawthorn, and J.J. Johnson, 2003. Loss estimation. In W.F. Chen and C. Scawthorn, eds. *Earthquake Engineering Handbook.* Boca Raton, FL: CRC Press.

Kramer, S.L., 1996. *Geotechnical Earthquake Engineering.* Englewood Cliffs, NJ: Prentice-Hall.

Krawinkler, H. and A.A. Nassar, 1992. Seismic design based on ductility and cumulative damage demands and capacities. In P. Fajfar and H. Krawinkler, eds. *Nonlinear Seismic Analysis and Design of Reinforced-Concrete Buildings.* NY: Elsevier Applied Science.

Lomnitz-Adler, J. and C. Lomnitz, 1979. A modified form of the Gutenberg-Richter magnitude-frequency relation. *Bull. Seis. Soc. Am.* 69 (4): 1209–1214.

McGuire, R.K. and W.J. Arabasz, 1990. An introduction to probabilistic seismic hazard analysis. In S.H. Ward, ed. *Geotechnical and Environmental Geophysics, Volume 1: Review and Tutorial.* Tulsa, OK: Society of Exploration Geophysics.

McGuire, R.K., W.J. Silva, and C.J. Costantino, 2002. Technical basis for revision of regulatory guidance on design ground motions: development of hazard- and risk-consistent seismic spectra for two sites. April. Report NUREG/CR-6769. U.S. Nuclear Regulatory Commission, Washington, DC.

Merz, H. A. and C.A. Cornell, 1973. Seismic risk based on a quadratic magnitude-frequency low. *Bull. Seis. Soc. Am.* 69 (4): 1209–1214.

Miranda, E. and S.D. Akkar, 2002. "Evaluation of approximate methods to estimate target displacements in nonlinear static procedures." October. *Proc. 5th US-Japan Workshop on Performance-Based Design of Reinforced-Concrete Structures.* Toba, Japan.

Nuttli, O.W., 1974. A magnitude-recurrence relation for central Mississippi Valley earthquakes. *Bull. Seis. Soc. Am.* 64 (4): 1189–1207.

Nuttli, O.W. and R.B. Herrmann, 1978. Credible earthquakes for the central United States. Miscellaneous Paper S-73-1, Report 12. U.S. Army Engineers Waterways Experiment Station. Vicksburg, MS.

Nuttli, O.W. and J.E. Zollweg, 1974. The relation between felt area and magnitude for central United States earthquake. *Bull. Geol. Soc. Am.* 64 (1): 73–85.

Nuttli, O.W., G.A. Bollinger, and D.W. Griffiths, 1979. On the relation between Modified Mercalli intensity and body-wave magnitude. *Bull. Seis. Soc. Am.* 69 (3): 893–909.

Ou, G.B. and R.B. Herrmann, 1990. A statistical model for ground motion produced by earthquakes at local and regional distances. *Bull. Seis. Soc. Am.* 80 (6): 1397–1417.

Owens, D.B., 1980. A table of normal integrals. *Comm. Statist.-Simula. Computa.* B9 (4): 389–419.

Peek-Asa, C., J.F. Kraus, L.B. Bourque, D. Vimalachandra, J. Yu, and J. Abrams, 1998. Fatal and hospitalized injuries resulting from the 1994 Northridge earthquake. *Int. J. Epidemiol.* 27: 459–465.

Peek-Asa, C., M.R. Ramirez, K. Shoaf, H. Seligson, and J.F. Kraus, 2000. A GIS mapping of earthquake-related deaths and hospital admissions from the 1994 Northridge, California earthquake. *Ann. Epidemiol.* 10: 5–13.

PG&E, 1988. Final report of the Diablo Canyon seismic program. July. Docket Nos. 50-275 and 50-323. Pacific Gas and Electric Company, San Francisco, CA.

Real, C.R. and T.L. Teng, 1973. Local Richter magnitude and total signal duration in Southern California. *Bull. Seis. Soc. Am.* 63 (5) 1809–1827.

Risk Engineering, Inc., 2002. Technical basis for revision of regulatory guidance on design ground motions: development of hazard- and risk-consistent seismic spectra for two sites. April. NUREG/CR-6769. U.S. Nuclear Regulatory Commission, Washington, DC.

Reiter, Leon, 1990. *Earthquake Hazard Analysis*. New York, NY: Columbia University Press.

Richter, C.F., 1935. An instrumental earthquake magnitude scale. *Bull. Seis. Soc. Am.* 25 (1): 1–32.

Richter, C.F., 1958. *Elementary Seismology*. San Francisco, CA: W.H. Freeman.

Sadigh, K., C.-Y. Chang, J.A. Egan, F. Makdisi, and R.R. Youngs, 1997. Attenuation relationships for shallow crustal earthquakes based on California strong-motion data. *Seis. Res. Ltrs.* 68 (1): 180–189.

Schwartz, D.P. and K. J. Coppersmith, 1984. Fault behavior and characteristic earthquakes: examples from the Wasatch and San Andreas faults. *J. Geophys. Res.* 89: 5681–5698.

Seeber, L. and J.G. Armbruster, 1991. The NCEER-91 earthquake catalog: improved intensity-based magnitudes and recurrence relations for U.S. earthquakes east of New Madrid. August. NCEER-91-0021. Buffalo, NY.

Sewell, R.T., G.R. Toro, and R.K. McGuire, 1991. Impact of ground motion characterization on conservatism and variability in seismic risk estimates. May. NUREG/CR-6467. U.S. Nuclear Regulatory Commission, Washington, DC.

Sewell, R.T., G.R. Toro, and R.K. McGuire, 1996. Impact of ground motion characterization on conservatism and variability in seismic risk estimates. July. NUREG/CR-6467. U.S. Nuclear Regulatory Commission, Washington, DC.

Shoaf, K.I., H. Seligson, C. Peek-Asa, and M. Mahue-Giangreco, 2001. "Enhancement of casualty models for post-earthquake response and mitigation." August. *Proc. US-Japan Joint Workshop and 3rd Grantee's Mtg.: US-Japan Coop. Res. in Urban Earthquake Disaster Mitigation*. Seattle, WA.

Sieberg, A., 1923. *Erdbebenkunde*. 102–104. Jena, Germany.

Silva, W.J. and K. Lee, 1987. WES RASCAL code for synthesizing earthquake ground motions. State-of-the-art for assessing earthquake hazards in the U.S. Report 24, Miscellaneous Paper S-73-1. U.S. Army Engineers Waterways Experiment Station. Vicksburg, MS.

Somerville, P.G., N.F. Smith, R.W. Graves, and N.A. Abrahamson, 1997. Modification of empirical strong ground motion attenuation relations to include the amplitude and duration effects of rupture directivity. *Seis. Res. Ltrs*. 68: 199–222.

Sponheur, W., 1960. Methoden zur Herdtiefenbesttimmung in der Makroseismik. *Freiburger Forsch*, H, C88.

Steinbrugge, K.V., 1982. *Earthquakes, Volcanoes, and Tsunamis: an Anatomy of Hazard*. New York, NY: Skandia America Group.

Stewart, J.P., S.J. Chiou, J.D. Bray, R.W. Graves, P.G. Somerville, and N.A. Abrahamson, 2001. Ground motion evaluation procedures for performance-based design. September. Publication PEER 2001/09. Pacific Earthquake Engineering Research Center, Berkeley, CA.

Street, R.L. and F.T. Turcotte, 1977. A study of northeastern North American spectral moments, magnitudes, and intensities. *Bull. Seis. Soc. Am*. 67 (3): 599–614.

Thatcher, W. and T.C. Hanks, 1973. Source parameters of Southern California earthquakes. *J. Geophys. Res*. 78: 8547–8576.

Thenhaus, P.C. and K.W. Campbell, 2003. Seismic hazard analysis. In W.F. Chen and C. Scawthorn, eds. *Earthquake Engineering Handbook*. Boca Raton, FL: CRC Press.

Toro, G.R., 1997. Spectral-ordinate based loss models for earthquakes. September. Report to USGS, Grant 1434-HQ-96-GR-02717. Risk Engineering, Inc., Boulder, CO.

Toro, G.R. and R.K. McGuire, 1987. An investigation into earthquake ground motion characteristics in eastern North America. *Bull. Seis. Soc. Am.* 77 (2): 468–489.

USGS, 2001. Development of the USGS seismic maps. NEHRP recommended provisions for seismic regulations for new buildings and other structures, 2000 edition, commentary, Appendix B. FEMA Document 369. Building Seismic Safety Council, Washington, DC.

Vanmarcke, E.H., 1976. Structural response to earthquakes. In C. Lomnitz and E. Rosenblueth, eds. *Seismic Risk and Engineering Decisions.* Amsterdam, The Netherlands: Elsevier Publishing Co.

Veletsos, A.S. and N.M. Newmark, 1960. "Effects of inelastic behavior on the response of simple systems to earthquake motions." *Proc. 2nd World Conf. on Earthquake Eng.* 2: 895–912. Tokyo, Japan.

Weichert, D.H., 1980. Estimation of the earthquake recurrence parameters for unequal observation periods for different magnitudes. *Bull. Seis. Soc. Am.* 70 (4): 1337–1346.

Wells, D.L. and K.J. Coppersmith, 1994. New empirical relationships among magnitude, rupture length, rupture width, rupture area, and surface displacement. *Bull. Seis. Soc. Am.* 84 (4): 974–1002.

WGCEP, 1999. Earthquake probabilities in the San Francisco Bay Region: 2000 to 2030—a summary of findings. USGS Open-File Report 99–517. Working Group on California Earthquake Probabilities. USGS, Washington, DC.

Wood, H.O. and F. Neumann, 1931. Modified Mercalli intensity scale of 1931. *Bull. Seis. Soc. Am.* 21 (4): 277–283.

Yeats, R.S., K. Sieh, and C.R. Allen, 1997. *The Geology of Earthquakes.* New York, NY: Oxford University Press.

Youngs, R.R., N.A. Abrahamson, F.I. Makdisi, and K. Sadigh, 1995. Magnitude-dependent variance of peak ground acceleration. *Bull. Seis. Soc. Am.* 85 (4): 1161–1176.

Estimation of recurrence parameters in the Gutenberg-Richter relation should always employ a maximum likelihood method.

Dieter Weichert, 1980

APPENDIX A

DERIVATION OF β AND RATE FOR THE EXPONENTIAL MAGNITUDE DISTRIBUTION FOR DATA WITH UNEQUAL PERIODS OF COMPLETENESS

Weichert (1980) first published this derivation of β and seismic activity rate, and his paper includes a computer program. Suppose there are, as historical data, observations of earthquakes in discrete magnitude intervals, with the ith interval containing z_i earthquakes during a period of completeness of t_i years. The ith interval is represented by central magnitude m_i, the magnitude interval is Δm, and the total number of events is z. These observations represent one realization of what is a multinomial distribution:

$$P[z_1 \text{ events of } m_1 \text{ during } t_1, z_2 \text{ events}$$
$$\text{of } m_2 \text{ during } t_2, \ldots | \beta] = \frac{z!}{\prod_i z_i!} \prod_i p_i^{z_i} \quad \text{(A1)}$$

where p_i is the probability that, given all the magnitude intervals and their periods of completeness, a randomly selected earthquake will fall into the ith magnitude interval and time window. To evaluate this, it can be observed first that equation 20 allows the calculation of the ratio

$$\frac{P[m \ within \ \Delta m \ of \ m_i]}{P[m \ within \ \Delta m \ of \ m_j]} = \frac{e^{-\beta m_i}}{e^{-\beta m_j}} \qquad (A2)$$

It follows that

$$P[m \ within \ \Delta m \ of \ m_i] = \frac{e^{-\beta m_i}}{\sum_j e^{-\beta m_j}} \qquad (A3)$$

To account for the different periods of completeness, the exponentials in equation A3 are multiplied by the appropriate completeness periods to obtain

$$p_i = \frac{t_i e^{-\beta m_i}}{\sum_j t_j e^{-\beta m_j}} \qquad (A4)$$

Given the earthquake observations, the likelihood for β, $l(\beta)$, equals the quantity in equation A1. The next step is to substitute p_i from equation A4 into equation A1, take the logarithm of $l(\beta)$, take the derivative of $\ln l(\beta)$ with respect to β, and equate this to 0. This leads to the following condition for a maximum-likelihood value of β:

$$\frac{\sum_i t_i m_i e^{-\beta m_i}}{\sum_i t_i e^{-\beta m_i}} = \frac{\sum_i m_i z_i}{z} = \overline{m} \qquad (A5)$$

where $\overline{m}$ is the average magnitude of the data (in interval representation). Equation A5 must be solved recursively, but the solution is easily programmed.

The maximum-likelihood rate of activity $\nu_{m_{\min}}$ can be determined in a manner similar to β:

$$l(\nu_{m_{\min}}) = P[z_1 \ events \ of \ m_1 \ during \ t_1, \ldots | \nu_{m_{\min}}] \qquad (A6)$$

The solution is illustrated for the common assumption that earthquakes occur in interval m_i as a Poisson process under random selection with the rate

$$\nu_i = \nu_{m_{min}} P[m \text{ within } \Delta m \text{ of } m_i] = \nu_{m_{min}} \frac{e^{-\beta m_i}}{\sum_i e^{-\beta m_j}} \qquad (\text{A7})$$

The second equality above follows from equation A3. Then the likelihood function for $\nu_{m_{min}}$ is

$$l(\nu_{m_{min}}) = \pi_i \frac{(\nu_i t_i)^{z_i} e^{-\nu_i t_i}}{z!} \qquad (\text{A8})$$

Solving for the maximum-likelihood value in the usual way gives

$$\nu_{m_{min}} = z \frac{\sum_i e^{-\beta m_i}}{\sum_i t_i e^{-\beta m_i}} \qquad (\text{A9})$$

When all $t_i = t$, this gives $\nu_{m_{min}} = z/t$, which is the same as equation 37.

The general distribution of earthquakes can be represented rather simply.

Charles Richter, 1958

APPENDIX B

ALTERNATIVE MAGNITUDE DISTRIBUTIONS

Several exponential-type distributions have been proposed that differ from the standard truncated exponential distribution (equations 22 through 25).

One alternative distribution is the "nonlinear truncated exponential magnitude distribution," in which the probability density function is made nonlinear by subtracting a constant from the exponential term:

$$f_M(m) = \beta k' \left[e^{-\beta(m - m_{min})} - e^{-\beta(m_{max} - m_{min})} \right]$$
$$m_{min} \le m \le m_{max} \tag{B1}$$

where

$$k' = \left[1 - (1 + \beta m_{max} - \beta m_{min}) e^{-\beta(m_{max} - m_{min})} \right]^{-1} \tag{B2}$$

The corresponding complementary cumulative function is

$$G_M(m) = 1 - k' - k' e^{-\beta(m - m_{min})} + k'(m - m_{min})\beta e^{-\beta(m_{max} - m_{min})}$$
$$m_{min} \le m \le m_{max} \tag{B3}$$

When m_{min} and m_{max} are fixed, this distribution has one parameter (β), as does the truncated exponential distribution. The complementary cumulative form of this distribution is more nonlinear than the corresponding form of the truncated exponential distribution.

The "quadratic magnitude distribution" uses two parameters to fit the distribution to observed statistics. In complementary cumulative form, this distribution is

$$G_M(m) = 1 - k'' - k'' e^{-\beta_1(m - m_{min}) - \beta_2(m^2 - m^2_{min})}$$

$$m_{min} \leq m \leq m_{max} \tag{B4}$$

where

$$k'' = \left[1 - e^{-\beta_1(m_{max} - m_{min}) - \beta_2(m^2_{max} - m^2_{min})}\right]^{-1} \tag{B5}$$

The corresponding density function is

$$f_M(m) = k''(\beta_1 + 2m\beta_2) e^{-\beta_1(m - m_{min}) - \beta_2(m^2 - m^2_{min})}$$

$$m_{min} \leq m \leq m_{max} \tag{B6}$$

Both parameters β_1 and β_2 can be fitted so that the quadratic exponential distribution can be either more or less nonlinear than the complementary cumulative form of the truncated exponential distribution. Merz and Cornell (1973) investigated this distribution.

A distribution with three parameters is the "double exponential distribution":

$$G_M(m) = k_1 \exp\{-k_2 \exp[-k_3(m - m_{min})]\}$$

$$m_{min} \leq m \tag{B7}$$

$$f_M(m) = k_1 k_2 k_3 \{\exp - k_2 \exp[-k_3(m - m_{min})] - k_3(m - m_{min})\}$$

$$m_{min} \leq m \tag{B8}$$

In this case, no upper-bound magnitude is assumed, and k_1, k_2, and k_3 are fitted to available data. Lomnitz-Alder and Lomnitz (1979) proposed using this type of distribution.

All these alternative distributions can be converted to cumulative numbers of earthquakes by using (as in equation 26)

$$n(m) = \nu_{m\,min} G_M(m) \tag{B9}$$

The number of events in a magnitude interval Δm centered on m can be obtained (as in equation 27) as

$$n_f(m) = n(m - \Delta m/2) - n(m + \Delta m/2) \qquad (B10)$$

which, to close approximation for a reasonably small Δm, will be

$$n_f(m) \simeq \nu_{m_{min}} f_M(m) \Delta m \qquad (B11)$$

Data can be summarized in cumulative or frequency form, and parameters of the distributions (including $\nu_{m_{min}}$) can be estimated, at least conceptually, by the methods discussed in Section 3.3. In practice, techniques such as nonlinear regression analysis may be required.

We are not yet in position to correlate destructive effects with instrumental data so as to establish an adequate measure of intensity.

Harry O. Wood and Frank Neumann, 1931

APPENDIX C

MMI SCALE OF 1931

The following scale has been adapted from the Seiberg (1923) Mercalli-Cancani scale, which was modified and condensed by Wood and Neumann (1931).

I. Not felt—or, except rarely under especially favorable circumstances. Under certain conditions, at and outside the boundary of the area in which a great shock is felt:

> Sometimes birds, animals, reported uneasy or disturbed.
> Sometimes dizziness or nausea is experienced.
> Sometimes trees, structures, liquids, bodies of water, may sway—doors may swing, very slowly.

II. Felt indoors by few, especially on upper floors, or by sensitive or nervous persons.

> Also, as in grade I, but often more noticeably:
> Sometimes hanging objects may swing, especially when delicately suspended.
> Sometimes trees, structures, liquids, bodies of water, may sway, doors may swing, very slowly.
> Sometimes birds, animals, reported uneasy or disturbed.
> Sometimes dizziness or nausea is experienced.

III. Felt indoors by several, motion usually rapid vibration.
      Sometimes not recognized to be an earthquake at first.
      Duration estimated in some cases.
      Vibration like that due to passing of light, or lightly loaded
          trucks, or heavy trucks some distance away.
      Hanging objects may sway slightly.
      Movements may be appreciable on upper levels of tall
          structures.
      Rocked standing motorcars slightly.

IV.   Felt indoors by many, outdoors by few.
      Awakened few, especially light sleepers.
      Frightened no one, unless apprehensive from previous ex-
          perience.
      Vibration like that due to passing of heavy, or heavily
          loaded trucks.
      Sensation like heavy body striking building, or falling of
          heavy objects inside.
      Rattling of dishes, windows, doors; glassware and crock-
          ery clink and clash.
      Creaking of walls, frame, especially in the upper range of
          this grade.
      Hanging objects swung, in numerous instances.
      Disturbed liquids in open vessels slightly.
      Rocked standing motorcars noticeably.

V.   Felt indoors by practically all, outdoors by many or most: out-
      doors direction estimated.
      Awakened many, or most.
      Frightened few—slight excitement, a few ran outdoors.
      Buildings trembled throughout.
      Broke dishes, glassware, to some extent.
      Cracked windows—in some cases, but not generally.
      Overturned vases, small or unstable objects, in many in-
          stances, with occasional fall.
      Hanging objects, doors, swing generally or considerably.
      Knocked pictures against walls, or swung them out of place.
      Opened—or closed—doors, shutters, abruptly.
      Pendulum clocks stopped, started, or ran fast or slow.
      Moved small objects, furnishings, the latter to slight extent.

Spilled liquids in small amounts from well-filled open containers.

Trees, bushes shaken slightly.

VI. Felt by all, indoors and outdoors.

Frightened many, excitement general, some alarm, many ran outdoors.

Awakened all.

Persons made to move unsteadily.

Trees, bushes shaken slightly to moderately.

Liquid set in strong motion.

Small bells rang—church, chapel, school, etc.

Damage slight in poorly built buildings.

Fall of plaster in small amount.

Cracked plaster somewhat, especially fine cracks, chimneys in some instances.

Broke dishes, glassware, in considerable quantity, also some windows.

Fall of knickknacks, books, pictures.

Overturned furniture in many instances.

Moved furnishings of moderately heavy kind.

VII. Frightened all—general alarm, all ran outdoors.

Some, or many, found it difficult to stand.

Noticed by persons driving motorcars.

Trees and bushes shaken moderately to strongly.

Waves on ponds, lakes, and running water.

Water turbid from mud stirred up.

Incaving to some extent of sand or gravel stream banks.

Rang large church bells, etc.

Suspended objects made to quiver.

Damage negligible in buildings of good design and construction, slight to moderate in well-built ordinary buildings, considerable in poorly built or badly designed buildings, adobe houses, old walls (especially where laid up without mortar), spires, etc.

Cracked chimneys to considerable extent, walls to some extent.

Fall of plaster in considerable to large amount, also some stucco.

Broke numerous windows, furniture to some extent.

Shook down loosened brickwork and tiles.

Broke weak chimneys at the roofline (sometimes damaging roofs).

Fall of cornices from towers and high buildings.

Dislodged bricks and stones.

Overturned heavy furniture, with damage from breaking.

Damage considerable to concrete irrigation ditches.

VIII. Fright general—alarm approaches panic.

Disturbed persons driving motorcars.

Trees shaken strongly—branches, trunks, broken off, especially palm trees.

Ejected sand and mud in small amounts.

Changes: temporary, permanent; in flow of springs and wells; dry wells renewed flow; in temperature of spring and well waters.

Damage slight to structures (brick) built especially to withstand earthquakes.

Considerable in ordinary substantial buildings, partial collapse; racked, tumbled down, wooden houses in some cases; threw out panel walls in frame structures, broke off decaying piling.

Fall of walls.

Cracked, broke, solid stone walls seriously.

Twisting, fall, of chimneys, columns, monuments, also factory stacks, towers.

Moved conspicuously, overturned, very heavy furniture.

IX. Panic general.

Cracked ground conspicuously.

Damage considerable in (masonry) structures built especially to withstand earthquakes.

Threw out of plumb some wood-frame houses built especially to withstand earthquakes.

Great in substantial (masonry) buildings, some collapse in large part; or wholly shifted frame buildings off foundations, racked frames;

Serious to reservoirs; underground pipes sometimes broken.

X. Cracked ground, especially when loose and wet, up to widths of several inches; fissures up to a yard in width ran parallel to canal and stream banks.

> Landslides considerable from river banks and steep coasts.
> Shifted sand and mud horizontally on beaches and flat land.
> Changed level of water in wells.
> Threw water on banks of canals, lakes, rivers, etc.
> Damage serious to dams, dikes, embankments.
> Damage severe to well-built wooden structures and bridges, some destroyed.
> Developed dangerous cracks in excellent brick walls.
> Destroyed most masonry and frame structures, also their foundations.
> Bent railroad rails slightly.
> Tore apart, or crushed endwise, pipelines buried in earth.
> Open cracks and broad wavy folds in cement pavements and asphalt road surfaces.

XI. Disturbances in ground many and widespread, varying with ground material.

> Broad fissures, earth slumps, and land slips in soft, wet ground.
> Ejected water in large amount charged with sand and mud.
> Caused sea waves (tidal waves) of significant magnitude.
> Damage severe to wood-frame structures, especially near shock centers.
> Great to dams, dikes, embankments, often for long distances.
> Few, if any (masonry), structures remained standing.
> Destroyed large well-built bridges by the wrecking of supporting piers, or pillars.
> Affected yielding wooden bridges less.
> Bent railroad rails greatly, and thrust them endwise.
> Put pipelines buried in earth completely out of service.

XII. Damage total—practically all works of construction damaged greatly or destroyed.

> Disturbances in ground great and varied, numerous shearing cracks.
> Landslides, falls of rock of significant character, slumping of river banks, etc., numerous and extensive.

Wrenched loose, tore off, large rock masses.

Fault slips in firm rock, with notable horizontal and vertical offset displacements.

Water channels, surface and underground, disturbed and modified greatly.

Dammed lakes, produced waterfalls, deflected rivers, etc.

Waves seen on ground surfaces (actually seen, probably, in some cases).

Distorted lines of sight and level.

Threw objects upward into the air.

Random vibration theory offers an elegant and efficient way of predicting peak motions from a knowledge of the spectra of radiated energy.

Dave Boore and Bill Joyner, 1984

APPENDIX D

STOCHASTIC METHODS OF ESTIMATING GROUND MOTION

Stochastic methods of estimating ground motion use a set of assumptions about the earthquake source spectrum and about the effects of path and site conditions. The ground motion is then transformed into spectral response by using the transfer function of a linear SDOF oscillator. These assumptions are described below. Further background on the origins of the stochastic method in ground motion prediction is in Hanks and McGuire (1981), Boore (1983), and Boore (2003); the latter includes a useful list of references and comparisons of assumptions.

Source Spectrum At locations far from the source (far enough that the earthquake energy appears to come from a point) a "single-corner, omega-squared" model of source energy is usually used to estimate the Fourier amplitude (FA) of acceleration $a'(f)$ that is due to shear waves in a whole space:

$$a'(f) = c_1 \frac{f^2}{1 + (f/f_c)^2} \frac{M_o}{r} \qquad \text{(D1)}$$

where f is frequency,

$$c_1 = \pi \, r_{\theta\phi}/\rho v_s^3 \tag{D2}$$

f_c is the corner frequency of the source, M_o is seismic moment, $r_{\theta\phi}$ is the effect of radiation pattern, ρ is density of the crust, v_s is shear wave velocity, and r is distance to the point source. The dependence of the acceleration $a(f)$ on r^{-1} just reflects the geometrical attenuation of energy on a spherical wave front as distance increases. In application, $r_{\theta\phi}$ is set equal to 0.55, which is the average of the shear wave radiation pattern over a sphere. Equation D1 is called the "source spectrum" (although it estimates the spectrum of acceleration at a distance r from the source), because it represents all the effects on the spectrum caused by the earthquake source.

Equation D1 produces constant acceleration energy above the corner frequency f_c. An alternative source model that has been proposed (Atkinson and Silva 2000) involves two corner frequencies of the source, with varying energy across the frequency band. This source spectrum can be incorporated into the stochastic model by substituting it for equation D1.

The source spectrum can be scaled by the independent parameters magnitude and stress drop by using the following relation:

$$\log M_o = 1.5 \, \mathbf{M} + 16.05 \tag{D3}$$

which is from Hanks and Kanamori (1979) and

$$f_c = \beta[\Delta\sigma/(8.44 M_o)]^{1/3} \tag{D4}$$

which is from Brune (1970) and Brune (1971), where $\mathbf{M}$ is moment magnitude and $\Delta\sigma$ is stress drop. Note that equation D3 is a definition, not a physical or statistical relationship. These relations make it possible to estimate the spectrum of whole-space ground acceleration at a distance r as a function of magnitude $\mathbf{M}$, stress drop $\Delta\sigma$, and physical properties of the earth.

Path and Site Effects The effects of path and site conditions are treated by adding the following factors to estimate motion on the surface of a homogeneous half-space at distance r from the source

$$a(f) = a'(f)c_2 p(f)c(f)e^{-\pi f r/[q(f)\beta]} \tag{D5}$$

where

c_2 accounts for the free-surface effect (a factor of 2) times the division of energy between two horizontal components ($1/\sqrt{2}$). This equals $\sqrt{2}$.

$p(f)$ is a high-frequency filter caused by near-surface rock or soil properties.

$c(f)$ is amplification (or deamplification) of the ground motion caused by soil, near-surface rock, and crustal amplifications.

$q(f) = q_o f^{\eta}$ is a frequency-dependent quality factor that accounts for anelastic attenuation within the source-to-site travel path.

A commonly used high-frequency filter is

$$p(f) = \exp(-\pi\kappa f) \qquad\qquad \text{(D6)}$$

where

$$\kappa = h/(v_s q_s) \qquad\qquad \text{(D7)}$$

In equation D6, the term κ (kappa) is commonly taken to be distance-independent, although a distance dependence may be incorporated. The depth h is the depth to which the site properties (average shear wave velocity v_s and quality factor q_s) govern the fundamental site response.

The distance term r^{-1} in equation D1 is often modified in intraplate regions to be $0.1r^{-1/2}$ for $r > 100$ km, to account for the slower attenuation of surface waves—and their larger contribution to strong ground motion than shear waves—at distances beyond 100 km. This accounts for mantle-refracted waves that may play an important role in increasing ground motions at $r \sim 120$ km over what simple shear- or surface-wave attenuation would predict (Ou and Herrmann 1990).

Responses of SDOF Oscillators With the FA of ground acceleration predicted at the ground surface from equation D5, the final step is to estimate the responses of SDOF linear oscillators. This is done by first estimating the RMS response, then estimating the peak response with a "peak factor," which is just the ratio of peak to RMS response. Subsequent equations follow convention and use circular frequency $\omega = 2\pi f$.

The one-sided power spectral density function $g_a(\omega)$ is calculated from the locally averaged FA $a(\omega)$ by using

$$g_a(\omega) = \overline{|a(\omega)|}^2 / \pi s \qquad \text{(D8)}$$

where s is the duration of shaking. Duration s is commonly taken as the inverse of the source corner frequency f_c for plate margin regions, but it is increased in intraplate regions to account for scattering and surface wave arrivals. One proposed equation for estimating the increase in duration for eastern North America (Toro and McGuire 1987) is

$$s = \begin{cases} 1/f_c & \text{for } r \le 100 \text{ km} \\ 1/f_c + 0.1(r-100) & \text{for } 100 < r \le 200 \text{ km} \\ 1/f_c + 0.05r & \text{for } r > 200 \text{ km} \end{cases} \qquad \text{(D9)}$$

The spectral density function of oscillator acceleration response $g_x(\omega)$ is calculated from $g_a(\omega)$ by

$$g_x(\omega) = g_a(\omega)\,|h_x(\omega)|^2 \qquad \text{(D10)}$$

where $h_x(\omega)$ is the transfer function of the SDOF linear oscillator. For ω_n^2 times the oscillator displacement (which gives pseudoabsolute acceleration, the response quantity usually plotted by earthquake engineers), the transfer function is

$$h_x(\omega) = \frac{\omega_n^2}{-\omega_n^2 + 2i\xi\omega_n\omega + \omega^2} \qquad \text{(D11)}$$

where ξ is the fraction of critical damping. For the RMS and peak factor, it is convenient to represent the moments of the spectral density function $g_x(\omega)$ with the notation

$$\lambda_k = 2\int_0^\infty \omega^k g_x(\omega)\,d\omega \qquad \text{(D12)}$$

With this last equation, it is possible to estimate the RMS response and the central frequency f_{cent} with (Vanmarcke 1976)

$$\sigma_x = (\lambda_0)^{1/2} \tag{D13}$$

$$f_{cent} = \frac{1}{2\pi}\left(\frac{\lambda_2}{\lambda_0}\right)^{1/2} \tag{D14}$$

For a lightly damped oscillator with natural frequency f_n less than the maximum frequency in the ground motion, which represents many applications, these two quantities can be represented as

$$\sigma_x \cong [g_x(2\pi f_n)/4\xi f_n)]^{1/2} \tag{D15}$$

$$f_{cent} \cong f_n \tag{D16}$$

Once σ_x is estimated, an estimate of the mean peak factor (the ratio of peak to RMS response of the oscillator) (Cartwright and Longuet-Higgins 1956) is

$$p_f = \sqrt{2\ln n} + 0.577/\sqrt{2\ln n} \tag{D17}$$

where n is the number of half-cycles of vibration, which is determined by

$$n = \max(2f_{cent}s, 1.33) \tag{D18}$$

Equation D16 assumes stationary response and does not account for the correlation of motion from peak to peak. For earthquake applications, these factors are accounted for by modifying the peak factor to (Toro and McGuire 1987)

$$p_f = \left(\sqrt{2\ln n} + 0.577/\sqrt{2\ln n}\right)\left[1 - \exp(-2\xi\omega_n s)\right]^{1/2} \tag{D19}$$

where the number of half-cycles n is

$$n = \max[2f_{cent}s(1.63\delta^{0.45} - 0.38), 1.33] \tag{D20}$$

and δ is Vanmarcke's (1976) bandwidth measure:

$$\delta = [1 - \lambda_1^2/(\lambda_0\lambda_2)]^{1/2} \tag{D21}$$

This derivation of oscillator response applies to a wide range of frequencies, dampings, and durations, and it is pretty abstract. It is worthwhile to simplify the equations and look at some important dependencies. For a lightly damped oscillator that achieves stationary response (i.e., $s \gg 1/f_n$), the mean square acceleration is (Vanmarcke 1976)

$$\sigma_a^2 \cong \frac{a^2(\omega_n)}{\pi s} \omega_n \left(\frac{\pi}{4\xi} - 1 \right) + \frac{1}{\pi s} \int_0^{\omega_n} a^2(\omega) d\omega$$

(D22)

Two important cases are worth considering. First, for oscillators whose natural frequency is well within the range of frequencies generated by the earthquake, the first term in equation D22 will dominate the response—that is, the response will be driven by ground motion energy at and near the natural frequency of the oscillator, and response will depend on damping ξ. Figure D1 illustrates this case on both a logarithmic and linear scale for amplitude and frequency. In this case, the second term of equation D22 can be ignored.

In the second important case (Figure D2), the natural frequency of the oscillator is above the range of frequencies that dominate the ground motion. In this case, the second term in equation D22 dominates—that is, the oscillator is driven by energy in the motion that is below f_n, and the response is of a rigid body, independent of damping.

In a third case, not handled by equation D22, f_n is below the dominant frequency range of the motion. In this case, the full derivation of oscillator response (equation D13) must be used. This case is important in calculating the response at low frequencies ($f < 1$ Hz) to small-magnitude earthquakes (e.g., $\mathbf{M} < 5$).

The effects of surficial layers on ground motion are taken into account with $c(f)$ in equation D5, and these are usually important except for very hard rock. Figure D3 illustrates calculated smoothed mean ratios of FA at the surface versus FA at the source for typical California rock and soil conditions. At high frequencies, surficial layers amplify ground motion energy by a factor of 3.75 (for rock) to 4.1 (for soil) because of impedance contrasts between properties at the surface and at depth. The calculation of surface amplification is amplitude-dependent, particularly for soils. The mean ratio should be used to obtain mean ground motions and also when stochastic methods in inversions are used to estimate source properties such as stress drop.

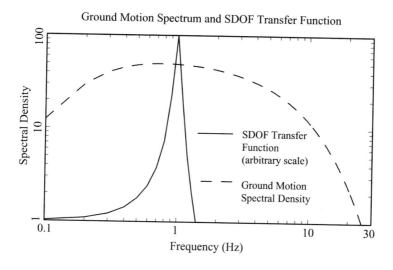

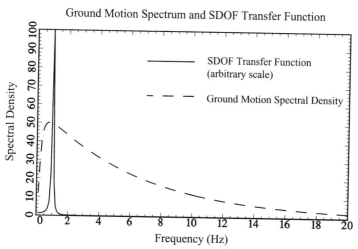

Figure D1. Ground motion spectral density and SDOF oscillator transfer function for a 1-Hz, 5% damped oscillator. The upper graph shows logarithmic scales for frequency and amplitude, and the lower graph shows linear scales.

209

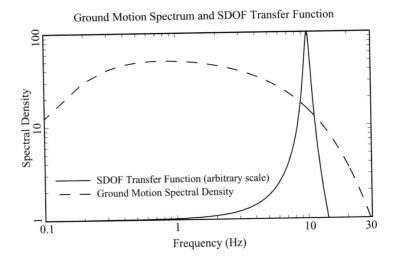

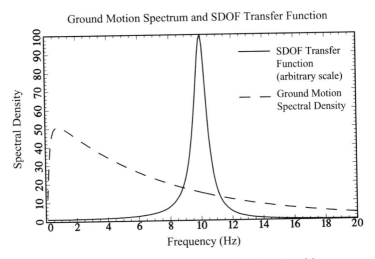

Figure D2. Ground motion spectral density (in arbitrary units) and SDOF oscillator transfer function for a 10-Hz, 5% damped oscillator. The upper graph shows logarithmic scales for frequency and amplitude, and the lower graph shows linear scales.

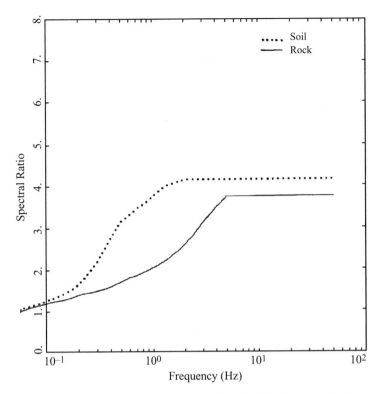

Figure D3. Mean Fourier spectral ratio of surface motion/
source motion for typical California soft rock and soil (W.J.
Silva, personal communication).

Even with considerable and reliable data, the parameters involved in the earthquake damage problem are complex and are subject to considerable dispersion from their mean.

John Blume, 1978

APPENDIX E

BETA DISTRIBUTION PLOTS

Figures E1 through E5 illustrate beta distributions (equation 71) for t = 2, 3, 4, 6, and 8, respectively. In each plot, the values of r have been chosen to give mean damage ratios of 0.167, 0.333, 0.5, 0.667, and 0.833. These plots supplement the discussion of the beta distribution in Section 6.2, where the plot for t = 4 was presented (Figure 53).

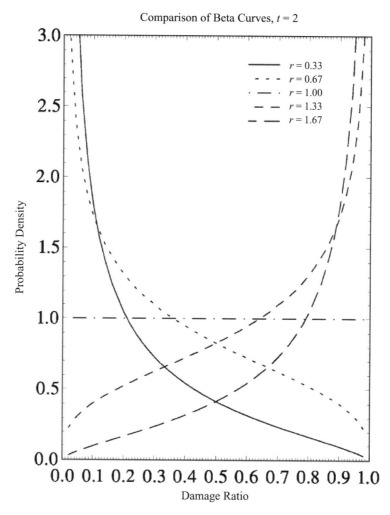

Figure E1. Loss distribution from beta distribution with $t = 2$.

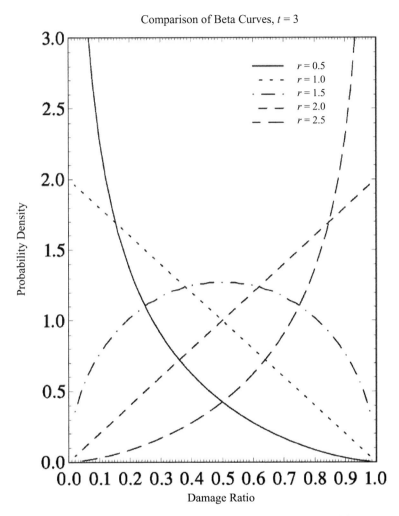

Figure E2. Loss distribution from beta distribution with $t = 3$.

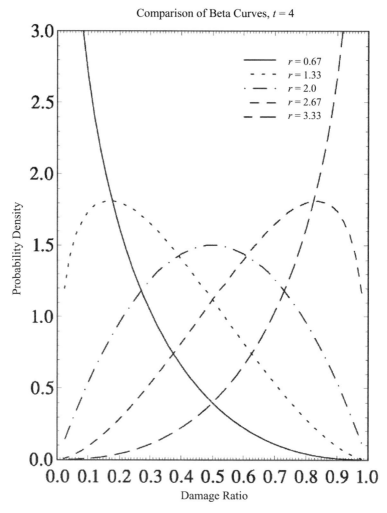

Figure E3. Loss distribution from beta distribution with $t = 4$.

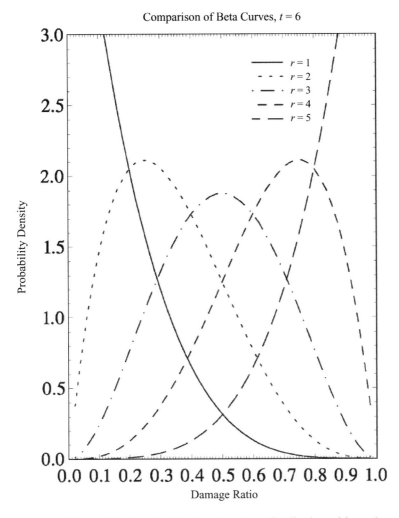

Figure E4. Loss distribution from beta distribution with $t = 6$.

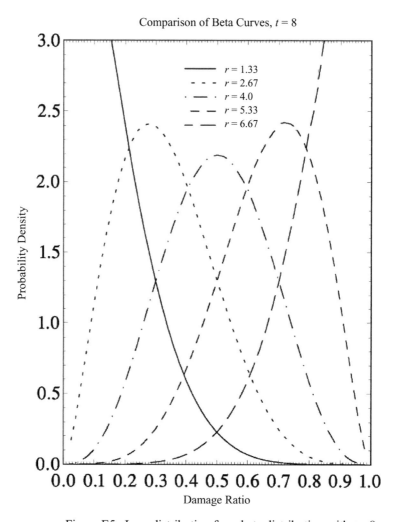

Figure E5. Loss distribution from beta distribution with $t = 8$.

In many instances, particularly for critical facilities,
studies indicating probability of losses are desirable.

K. Aki, 1988

APPENDIX F

DERIVATION OF RISK EQUATION

This appendix derives the risk equation, which is discussed in Section 6.5 and presented as equations 84 and 85. The risk equation was first developed during discussions between G.R. Toro and C.A. Cornell in 1990, and it was published in Sewell, Toro, and McGuire (1991) and Sewell, Toro, and McGuire (1996).

First, it is assumed that the hazard curve $\gamma(a)$ is linear on a log-log scale, that is

$$\gamma(a) = ka^{-K_H} \qquad \text{(F1)}$$

Actual hazard curves tend to get steeper at higher amplitudes, but over the important range of amplitudes for P_F calculations they can be approximated as linear on a log-log scale.

Second, it is assumed that component fragilities are lognormally distributed. This means that

$$P_{F|a} = \int_0^a \frac{1}{y\sqrt{2\pi}\beta_c} \exp\left[-\frac{(\ln y - \overline{\ln y})^2}{2\beta_c^2}\right] dy \qquad \text{(F2)}$$

where $\overline{\ln y} = \ln \hat{c}$ (i.e., the logarithm of the median capacity) and $\sigma_{\ln CAPACITY} = \beta_c$.

Substituting equations F2 and F1 into equation 82 gives

$$P_F = \int_0^\infty ka^{-K_H} \frac{1}{a\sqrt{2\pi}\beta_c} \exp\left[-\frac{(\ln a - \overline{\ln y})^2}{2\beta_c^2}\right] da \quad (F3)$$

Transforming the integration variable a to variable $x = \ln a$ gives

$$P_F = \frac{k}{\sqrt{2\pi}\beta_c} \int_{-\infty}^\infty \exp(-K_H x) \exp\left[-\frac{(x - \overline{\ln y})^2}{2\beta_c^2}\right] dx \quad (F4)$$

The integrand above is in the form

$$\exp(cx) Z(x) \quad (F5)$$

where c is a constant and $Z(x)$ is the normal density function. The definite integral equation F4 can be solved by expansion or by published methods of integrating functions of a normal probability distribution (e.g., Owens 1980), yielding

$$P_F = k\hat{c}^{-K_H} \exp\left[\frac{1}{2}(K_H\beta_c)^2\right] \quad (F6)$$

Expressing the hazard γ at a ground motion level a^* corresponding to a chosen design level, such as a UHS, by using equation F1 gives

$$\gamma(a^*) = k(a^*)^{-K_H} \quad (F7)$$

Solving for k and substituting into equation F6 gives

$$P_F = \gamma(a^*)(a^*/\hat{c})^{K_H} \exp\left[\frac{1}{2}(K_H\beta_c)^2\right] \quad (F8)$$

which is equation 84. This allows P_F to be expressed by using the seismic hazard γ and its slope K_H at a convenient value a^* and by using parameters of the capacity curve ($\hat{c}$ and β_c).

Often, the design HCLPF is designated as the design ground motion a^* times a factor of safety f_s:

$$\text{HCLPF} = a^* \cdot f_s \qquad \text{(F9)}$$

and the HCLPF itself can be represented by using $\hat{c}$ and β_c:

$$\text{HCLPF} = \hat{c} \exp\left(-x_p \beta_c\right) \qquad \text{(F10)}$$

where x_p is the number of standard deviations corresponding to the "low probability" in the HCLPF, which is $x_p = 2.326$ for a 1% probability of failure.

When the last two equations are used to express $\hat{c}$, and substitutions are made into equation F8, the result is

$$P_F = \gamma(a^*) f_s^{-K_H} \exp\left[-x_p K_H \beta_c + \frac{1}{2}(K_H \beta_c)^2\right] \qquad \text{(F11)}$$

which is equation 85. These two expressions for P_F are amazingly simple expressions for the integration of ground motion and fragility. Equations F8 and F11 can be used to determine the effect of the hazard curve slope, factor of safety, median capacity, and capacity uncertainty on the probability of failure.

221